Mental
Retardation
An Educational Viewpoint

OLIVER P. KOLSTOE

University of Northern Colorado
Greeley, Colorado

HOLT, RINEHART AND WINSTON, INC.
New York / Chicago / San Francisco / Atlanta
Dallas / Montreal / Toronto / London / Sydney

This book is dedicated to students
who made the whole project possible and enjoyable

Library of Congress Catalog Card Number: 71–182030
ISBN: 0–03–086669–3
Printed in the United States of America
4   5   038   9   8   7   6   5   4   3   2

PREFACE

During the past 15 years I have been engaged in a project based on the conviction that the large majority of the people who demonstrate the condition we call mental retardation should be considered a natural resource whose talents and abilities, when properly nurtured, can add a dimension of great worth to our world. The project has been to prepare a trilogy of books which deal with related aspects of educational nurture, each of which can stand alone, but each of which can complement the others.

The books have actually been written in reverse order: *A High School Work Study Program for the Mentally Subnormal Student,* written with Roger Marshall Frey, was prepared first because my own research dealt with that area. The second book, *Teaching Educable Mentally Retarded Children,* dealt primarily with the preschool, primary, elementary, prevocational, and vocational levels because no contemporary text was available. This book, which presents the conceptual framework, the learning characteristics, and the educational antecedents for our present programs, could not have been written before the other two simply because I was not yet ready to apply the theoretical formulations of Jean Piaget, George Miller, Eugene Galanter, and Karl Pribram to the condition of mental retardation. Research on the learning characteristics of the retarded did not become voluminous until well into the 1960s and much of that needed to be summarized and evaluated before it provided a meaningful picture. Indeed, many of the studies which provided missing pieces in the research puzzles were identified and executed by students and colleagues who were aware of my efforts, frustrations, and need for additional bits of information.

Although writing is a lonely enterprise, no one's work is exclusively his own. Each productive effort stands upon the shoulders of many people who have worked hard and thought seriously about the meaning of their findings. To them I can only express my gratitude in general. To Professors A. M. Winchester and Alonzo Hannaford I am specifically indebted for help, criticism, and information. As to the project itself, I am happy to be relieved of the tyranny of the commitment, but I shall miss the excitement of the work.

Greeley, Colorado   OLIVER P. KOLSTOE
November 1971

CONTENTS

CHAPTER 1

The Condition
of Mental
Retardation

Students of the history of mental retardation (Kagan 1967, Farber 1968) have called attention to changes in public treatment of fools and idiots as reflected in the literary commentaries of popular, contemporary writers. The books of Homer, Chaucer, Shakespeare, Dostoyevsky, Molière, Mary Shelley, Faulkner, and Steinbeck provide characterizations of the retarded which reflect the manner in which this unusual condition was handled by the people of the day. The documentation is a story of progress which identifies practices that start with extermination and proceed through asylum and ridicule to our present educational efforts.

Although the literary commentaries are probably accurate pictures of historical practices, they provide scant information about what mental retardation was thought to be. Yet if we expect to provide educational programs for the retarded which will be of maximum benefit to them, it is necessary that we systematically examine what is known about the condition. At the most basic level, it is important to accept or develop some definition of the condition which is clearly defensible. Although there are many reasons why we need a definition, the most compelling one is that it provides a common conceptual basis for the rest of the discussion. Thus even though the definition used is not completely acceptable, at least it provides a framework which is

1

understood by all. Next we need to indicate how the condition can be discovered, for this also is a crucial aspect of an effective educational program. To be treated, the retarded must be found. Then if we wish to attend to the basic rather than the superficial dimensions, we need to examine the root causes of the condition, for prevention must start there, not with symptoms. Finally, we need to evaluate educational practices of the past to determine which practices, if any, may have a contemporary value. Our purpose then as professional educators is to find out what mental retardation is, how it may be detected, what its causes are, what has been done for retardates in the past, and what should be done in the future.

Probably the first official reference to the condition was in the Twelve Tablets of Rome in 449 B.C. According to Lindman and McIntyre (1961), the tablets directed:

> If a person is a fool, let his person and goods be under the protection of his family or his parental relatives. . . .

It is clear that under Roman law fools and idiots were not considered capable of managing their own property or affairs. Equally important was the mandate that the management of both the person and his possessions was a family matter and, in lieu of parents, a responsibility of relatives. The implication that fools and idiots are considered inadequate to the tasks of self-management is evident. Yet whether a person is a fool because he cannot manage his affairs or whether a person cannot manage his affairs because he is a fool is unclear. The cause and effect sequence probably remained confused until at least 1300 years later. The *de praerogative regis* (prerogatives of the King) issued between 1255 and 1290 A.D. defined an idiot as one who "hath no understanding from his nativity." This first, though primitive, definition of mental retardation had as an operational term the word "understanding." Yet "understanding" was not precisely defined, being left to the judgment of whatever officials were concerned or interested.

Some 200 years elapsed before Sir Anthony Fitzherbert added some precision by stating that an idiot was:

> Such a person who cannot account or number, nor can tell who was his father or mother, nor how old he is, etc., so as it may appear he

had not understanding of reason what shall be his profit or his loss (Guttmacher and Weihofen, 1952).

The manner of determining an individual's "understanding" suggested by Fitzherbert was apparently unchallenged at least until the development of tests of intelligence in the middle 1900s. Thus, it appears that intellectual incompetence or lack of understanding has been the definitive characteristic of mental retardation throughout recorded history. In the words of Lord Coke,

> An idiot, or natural fool, is one who from his nativity, by perpetual infirmity, is *non compos mentis* (person with unsound mind). (Norsworthy 1906; translation by author).

This definition has resulted in two lines of concern about the retarded, their effect on society and society's effect upon them. Kolstoe and Frey (1965) have pointed out that political philosophy has played an important part in determining the attitude of society toward the presence of the mentally retarded. Extermination of the incompetent was a method designed to assure a strong populace. Ridicule of the infirm contributed to the development of a class system. Asylum provided a humane method of separating the unwanted from society. Education was the medium for capitalizing on each person's latent talents. Each treatment was fundamentally concerned with the political aspirations of the day and the real or imagined effect the retarded have on the realization of societal goals.

The Philosophical Background

Concern for the individual who is mentally retarded, according to Kagan (1967), has been influenced by two schools of philosophy: one originating with Aristotle, the other with Plato. Both of these venerable Greeks were concerned with the nature of the world and the ultimate nature of the human condition.

Plato believed that the perfect form exists only in the prior world in which we dwelled before we were born and that the physical world is imperfect. He, therefore, speculated that since we cannot remember that prior world our only guide to what is good is conscience. His belief was that only conscience provided the way man could achieve perfection. The subsequent contributions of St. Augustine sustained Plato's belief, but personalized perfection in the life style of Christ, and saw faith as the vehicle through which the search for perfection should proceed. Implicit in this reliance on conscience and faith was the notion that man's behavior was modifiable. John Locke carried the concept of modifiability a step further when he postulated that a man was born with a blank mind to be written on by experience. It required no great logical jump to recognize that education could be a significant force in shaping man's behavior.

In contradistinction with Platonic philosophy, Aristotle's speculation of a world where form and substance were inseparable led to a different notion of man's modifiability. St. Thomas Aquinas provided the religious link by declaring that matter and form were designed by God·and created to fulfill His purposes. For Aristotle, reason was the ability which differentiated man from lower animals. Aristotle's influence caused humanism to become synonymous with reason and the quest for purpose guided by reason. Education as a necessary tool in developing reason was a logical extension of this speculative trend.

Mental retardation viewed in Aristotelian perspective has quite different consequences than when seen from the Platonic position. If, as Aristotle believed, reason is the characteristic that separates man from the beasts, man without reason is a brute, incapable even of seeking perfection. Mental retardation, therefore, emerges as the opposite of good—in essence, a "bad" condition. It is small wonder that Wallin (1955) describes the denouncing and scourging of the retarded during the middle ages as "a vain attempt to exorcise the demons." At the same time it is more than a little ironic that the humanistic view of man had its beginnings in the philosophy of Aristotle. However, his belief in the power of reason had as a basic assumption an intact intellect. Those without adequate intelligence were really not even human, but subhuman.

Platonic philosophy as extended by St. Augustine held that whatever was, was created by God for some purpose. Thus, mental retardation was not bad but good because it was part of God's doing. The logical imperative of this position was to work constructively in order to fulfill God's purpose. Furthermore, faith was possible in all humans. Reason was not a requirement of the human condition, so all people, the mentally retarded as well as the intellectually intact, were welcome in God's world.

From both Platonic and Aristotelian thought, education emerges as central to human purpose. As an instrument for bettering human living, education was supported not only in European society, but even more strongly in colonial America. The Protestant doctrine which held that each man must interpret God's purposes with his native reason and his abiding faith provided one motive for the support of universal education; the Bible needed to be read to be understood. The need for wise leadership in the developing colonies also demanded literacy. With the political revolution and the subsequent industrial revolution, an informed and enlightened citizenry became mandatory.

Philosophically, however, the need for modifying the human condition made strange bedfellows of the competing notions of modification through reason and modification through faith. A reconciliation was not possible. Instead, a new philosophical line of thought developed: pragmatism.

The emergence from the age of reason into the age of scientific inquiry was heralded by Charles Darwin's documentation of selective evolution. In 1859, his *Origin of the Species* demonstrated that animals and plants adapt to environmental stress through the survival of the fittest principle. Thus, Darwin forwarded the doctrine that the world is characterized by change: it is not predetermined and immutable. By extension, what is real today may not even exist tomorrow. The corresponding rise of experimentation as a technique for discovery and change found its educational voice in the pragmatic philosophy of John Dewey.

Rather than speculating on the nature of form and substance, pragmatism starts with the premise that whatever exists is real but not necessarily permanent. No *a priori* speculations on what is perfect or what is imperfect, whether the world was created or evolved, or what is good or bad need be made. Pragmatism simply accepts what is and bids us discover what we can about it.

While the recognition of fools and idiots certainly was evident as early as the Twelve Tablets of Rome, suspension of a judgment as to whether the condition is bad or good probably should be credited to Itard. Prior to the early 1800s, followers of Aristotle believed that mental retardation was a subhuman or "bad" condition. The Platonists identified the retarded as "innocents"—unfortunate, yet children of God. Itard, however, believed that all persons were conceived in perfection, but that their final condition resulted from their interaction with an imperfect world. His attempts to teach the young "savage" boy Victor were the first recorded instances in which mental retardation was regarded as a condition which could be tampered with in order to find out about it. His continuing experiments in sense training during the five years he worked with Victor were conducted with an optimism that he could somehow turn this base metal "savage" into the golden human being he was at conception.

Seguin some fifty years later was likewise a tamperer. His lack of perfect progress he attributed to neurological pathology in his retarded patients. His conclusions were a significant forward step in speculating on what mental retardation is. In Seguin's words, there are "defects in the central or peripheral nervous system which prevent sense impulses from reaching the brain or being imprinted on it." As was the case with the definition of Sir Anthony Fitzherbert in the 1500s, mental retardation was seen in the 1800s as a condition of intellectual inadequacy. Norsworthy (1906) quotes Esquirol in the early 1800s:

> Idiocy is not a disease but a condition in which intellectual facilities are never manifested.

Esquirol's comment takes on added significance because it calls attention to two aspects of mental retardation; first, it refers to medical terminology (apparently for the first time) and second, to the permanence of the condition while reemphasizing the chief characteristic of the condition as intellectual inadequacy. Identifying mental retardation as proper to the medical sphere was a significant step away from judging the goodness or badness of the condition, for it opened the way for inquiring into the nature of the condition as in any other medical condition.

The Nature of Intelligence

Systematic examination of the nature of intellectual inadequacy started with Binet and Simon in Paris in the 1890s. Charged by the officials of Paris with determining "those children who can profit from education" in the Paris school system, these two investigators first attempted to find characteristics which were related to intellectual adequacy. The scientific techniques of Wundt at Leipzig and Sir Francis Galton were put to use in correlational studies of children judged to be bright and dull. Various anthropometric characteristics such as height, weight, a cephalic index, handwriting analysis, reaction time, and many others were used to no avail. The bright and the dull did not differ systematically in physical characteristics. In a burst of genius, Binet and Simon switched their inquiries from what the bright and dull looked like, to what they could do. They presented children of a given age with tasks which required the exercise of "judgment" for successful completion. These tasks were then arranged in an order of difficulty according to the age at which roughly half of the children in each age group could solve them successfully. A preliminary scale was developed in 1904 with an improved version appearing a year later in 1905.

The importance of this mental scale can scarcely be overestimated, but it was not until eleven years later that the Binet scale achieved the kind of refinement that resulted in a useful tool for finding out what mental retardation is. This occurred with the Stanford University revision of the Binet scale by Louis Terman and his colleagues.

Meanwhile attempts to understand the condition more fully were proceeding both in the United States and Europe. J. Shaw Bolton in 1912, according to Berry and Gordon (1931), distinguished between two types of mental retardation:

> Primary Amentia . . . that form of mental deficiency attributable to causes operative on the fertilized ovum and resulting in an insufficiency of neuroblasts and neurons.
>
> Secondary Amentia . . . those cases where the causative factor is to be sought at, or after, birth.

While no causative agent was identified, the nature of the condition was clearly believed by Bolton to be an insufficiency of neuroblasts and neurons regardless of the time at which the damage may have occurred. This reference to the underlying physiological condition provides reinforcement to the notion of mental retardation as an intellectual problem. A new dimension was added as a result of the enactment of the English Mental Deficiency Act of 1913. This act defined mental deficiency as:

> A condition of arrest or incomplete development of the mind, existing before the age of eighteen years, whether arising from inherent causes or induced by disease or injury. (Clarke and Clarke 1958)

The act then went on to classify types of deficiency:

> Idiots, that is to say, persons in whose case there exists mental defectiveness of such a degree that they are unable to guard themselves against common physical dangers.
> Imbeciles, that is to say, persons in whose case there exists mental defectiveness which, though not amounting to idiocy, is yet so pronounced that they are incapable of managing themselves or their affairs, or in the case of children, of being taught to do so.
> Feebleminded persons, that is to say, persons in whose case there exists mental defectiveness which, though not amounting to imbecility, is yet so pronounced that they require care, supervision, and control for their own protection or for the protection of others, or in the case of children, that they appear to be permanently incapable by reason of defectiveness of receiving proper benefit from the instruction in ordinary schools.
> Moral defectives, that is to say, persons in whose case there exists mental defectiveness coupled with strongly vicious or criminal propensities and who require care, supervision, and control for the protection of others.

The Mental Deficiency Act of 1913 was remarkable because the descriptions of mental retardation recognized degrees of severity. Equally important, however, the act described the social functioning of the retarded; first in personal terms of avoiding dangers or the degree to which they could protect themselves. Then the act added a category which was termed "Moral Defectives" whose chief characteristic involved a threat to others. For the first time mental retardation was considered in the light of social consequences or in modern parlance, adaptive behavior. In addition this is the first time that behavior control rather than intellectual inadequacy assumed dominance. Thus, a dualism emerged from the Act which pitted acceptable social behavior as the primary concern against the concern for intellectual competence.

Thanks to a philosophical commitment to pragmatism, serious workers in the field of mental retardation in the early 1900s were able to suspend judgment on the question of the goodness or badness of the condition. The fortuitous arrival of the Stanford revision of the Binet Test of Intelligence in 1916 and again in 1937 provided a tool which enabled serious study of the condition.

This line of inquiry focused upon the intellectual differences between retarded, average, and bright people. One of the earliest investigations was that of Maude Merrill in 1924. Using the children in the standardization population for the Stanford–Binet, Merrill identified children who made low scores, average scores, and high scores and compared item performance to see if any specific intellectual tasks would distinguish the three groups. She reported that the mentally retarded confined their successes to those items which were concrete in character while the average and bright did better on those tasks which called for the ability to abstract.

Several factors cast doubt on these results. First, the test was used to identify the three groups, then an analysis of the test protocols was used to describe the intellectual differences. This procedure is a classical example of failing to use an outside criterion for performance determination. That is analogous to identifying skillful, average, and poor archers by having them shoot arrows at a target and then describing the poor archers as having poor eye–hand coordination, a condition involved in the task of archery itself. Legitimately, a conclusion of poor eye–hand coordination could be made only in relation to some outside task such as putting pegs in holes in a pegboard.

Second, the test itself emerged as an operational definition of intellectual functions. While the test was clearly the most comprehensive tool for identifying thought processes developed at that time, it could scarcely be credited with probing all of the facets of intelligence. Thus, the intellectual functions which were left out of the test were not available for study. In essence, not all of the possible differences between the retarded and intellectually nonretarded could be identified simply because the tools available were inadequate.

Third, comparing children of unequal IQs but equal mental ages also forces the chronological ages to differ. The retarded children will be several years older than bright children. Experience in living, therefore, favors the retarded. If intellectual ability is affected by interaction with the environment, then the mentally retarded are clearly at some advantage even though what the advantage may be is uncertain.

Fourth, the notion that equal mental ages represent the same level of mental maturity is not warranted. Mental age is computed by adding the credit for each item passed. Two children can earn the same credit, but successfully pass quite different test items. Thus, equal mental ages may represent widely disparate individual intellectual skills.

Wallin and Rappert summarized the research on the intellectual differences between retarded and nonretarded individuals up to 1950 by saying:

> Many observations or experimental studies have been made on the differences in mental traits between normal and mentally deficient children. The main question at issue has been whether the differences between the defectives and the normals (and numerous differences exist) are qualitative or quantitative in nature. . . . It is not true, for example, that there is a qualitative memory difference. . . . While they do not possess as much logical memory as normal children do, they do possess some, and what logical memory they do have is akin to the logical memory possessed by normal children of the same intelligence level. The difference is one of degree rather than kind or quality.

The notion of quantitative intellectual differences has been a pervading theme in the field. Mentally retarded persons are presumed to have the same intellectual characteristics as the nonretarded but to a lesser degree. This is reflected not only in tests, but also in such terms as mental deficiency and retardation.

An additional theme evident from the first writings on fools and idiots has been that of social incompetence. This was well articulated in the 1929 report of the English Joint Mental Deficiency committee of the Board of Education and Board of Control which wrote:

> The only really satisfactory criterion of mental deficiency is the social one, and if a person is suffering from a degree of incomplete mental development which renders him incapable of independent social adaptation and which necessitates external care, supervision, and control, then such a person is a mental defective.

Doll (1941) carried the notion of social incompetence a step further by defining mental deficiency in the following manner:

> The mentally deficient person is (1) socially incompetent; that is, socially inadequate and occupationally incompetent and unable to manage his own affairs; (2) mentally subnormal; (3) retarded intellectually from birth or early age; (4) retarded at maturity; (5) mentally deficient as a result of constitutional origin through heredity or disease; and (6) essentially incurable.

In 1950 Doll further clarified the concept by stating:

> If social adequacy is the essential criterion of mental deficiency, the mental criterion must be validated against it . . . moreover, the mental criterion serves to *explain* rather than to replace the social criterion.

This emphasis on social inadequacy is a detour from the task of finding out what mental retardation is. It focuses on the consequences rather than the nature of the condition. To follow this path, logically, mental retardation depends on social inadequacy. By inference, a person who is below average in intellectual functions would not be considered retarded unless he exhibited social incompetence.

Such a relationship is rejected by Sarason (1955) who states:

> Mental retardation refers to individuals who, for temporary or long standing reasons, function intellectually below the average of their peer groups but whose social adequacy is not in question.

He then defines mental deficiency as referring to:

> Individuals who are socially inadequate as a result of an intellectual deficit which is a reflection of an impairment in the central nervous system which is essentially incurable.

In rejecting the social adequacy criterion Sarason raises the question again of quantitative versus qualitative intellectual functions. In his considerations, he differentiates between the mentally retarded and the mentally deficient. His statement suggests that retardation is a quantitative difference subject to improvement and that mental deficiency is a qualitative difference not readily ameliorable. In any case, he clearly differentiates between the deficient and the retarded as belonging in discrete groups joined only by low scores on tests which yield an IQ.

The discussion so far can be stated in a series of questions for purposes of clarification:

1. Are all socially inadequate persons mentally retarded? The answer is no. Many persons are socially unable to cope with society because of insanity, neurosis, drug addiction, and a host of other problems, or they simply may not wish to participate. A criterion of social inadequacy is not sufficient for a diagnosis of mental subnormality.

2. Are all persons who make low scores on a test which yields an IQ mentally retarded? The answer is equivocal. Individuals have been identified whose earned IQs have changed from a low of 50 to above 120 during their development from early childhood to adulthood. (Kirk, 1958; Skeels and Skodak, 1966)
3. If a person earns a low IQ but is socially adequate is he mentally retarded? The answer hinges on the criterion of "social adequacy." Because there is no really objective method for determining social adequacy, an equivocal answer must be forthcoming. In a simple environment it may be impossible to distinguish such a person from his peers, yet in a complex environment he may be socially helpless.
4. If a person earns a low score on a test which yields an IQ, is this sufficient evidence of intellectual inadequacy? The answer depends upon whether the test performance is confounded by lack of motivation, emotional problems, sensory inadequacy, or motor incoordination. Even in the absence of these interfering problems, bilingualism and lack of exposure to the culture on which the test is based may also contribute to low scores.
5. Do individual tests which yield an IQ sample all facets of intellectual activity? The answer is quite clearly no. Since different theorists espouse widely differing theories concerning intelligence, no one test could cover all the disparate viewpoints represented by people such as Spearman, Thurstone, Piaget, and Guilford.

In short, an individual has been identified as mentally retarded when he consistently (over a period of several years) earns a low score on a test which yields an IQ, provided the low score is not the product of poor motivation, sensory deficit, emotional problems, motor incoordination, language problems, or based on a culture to which he has not had the same exposure as his peers with whom his performance is compared. Social inadequacy is not a necessary corollary.

Since mental retardation has been identified by tests which purport to measure intellectual adequacy, progress in finding out the nature of mental retardation is closely linked to progress in determining the nature of intellectual differences between the retarded and nonretarded on tasks which call for intellectual ability as reflected by current theories of the structure and function of intellect. To describe mental retardation as intellectual inadequacy first requires a useful definition of intelligence and then an operational definition of inadequacy.

Notions concerning the nature of intelligence have probably been with us since the earliest encounters of man with his fellow man. Plato, for one, recognized individual differences in ability when he suggested in his *Republic* that the quick and able train for leadership roles in the state, leaving those of lesser abilities to do the more mundane tasks required for maintenance. Likewise, Alexander the Great, who was taught by Aristotle, is reported to have conducted a vast talent search among the young in order to find those with great potential for leadership training. The exact criteria were never specified, but the persistent theme of "ability to reason" permeated nearly all of the early reports and has recently been suggested again by Jensen (1969) as a synonym for high ability.

Binet and Simon were more explicit in describing intellectual ability as they searched for an instrument which would identify it. After futile attempts to identify ability by appearance, Binet and Simon settled on the criterion of comparative performance. In essence, they reasoned that bright people could do things and would know things their less gifted peers could not. Thus, achievement in intellectual tasks became the principle which defined ability and the items included in their test reflected this concern for knowing and doing.

Because the original Binet test was highly loaded with tasks which required a verbal response, David Wechsler (1939) believed that it did not tap an important facet of intellectual ability. This belief gave rise to his attempts to develop a test which gave equal weight to performance—tasks of a problem solving nature which required judgment, reasoning, foresight, and planning, but which did not need to be talked about, only performed. Furthermore, he felt that the various intellectual components could be assessed better separately. He therefore developed verbal subtests which probed information, comprehension, memory, likenesses and differences, arithmetic and vocabulary, and performance tests for assembly, block design, ordering pictures, completing pictures, coding, and solving mazes.

Workers in the field of mental retardation compared the performance of retarded youngsters with the nonretarded on nearly all the tests which were developed, attempting to find out whether there were specific areas in which the retarded were systematically inferior or superior. Thus, the analyses of test performance were aimed at finding out whether retardation was exclusively a quantitative intellectual problem or whether the condition was a qualitative one (pattern or factors of intellectual differences) or both. Unfortunately, one of the barriers to securing precise information resided in the tests used; any differences which could be detected were limited to those which were contained in the tests.

Spearman, in England, was one of the first of the 20th century psychometrists to suggest authoritatively that intelligence was not a unitary thing. His highly statistical work suggested that there was a general factor of intelligence in which individuals differed by a quantitatively measurable amount, but that there were also specific factors, such as social judgment, motor ability, and nonverbal abilities which were possessed by people in differing quantities and these specific factors could account for qualitative differences.

Before Spearman's influence could be substantially felt, Thurstone (1938) brought the statistical tool of factor analysis to bear on the testing movement. Factor analysis (in slightly oversimplified form) is a mathematical system for determining relationships between tasks. Even though this is a powerful tool for analyzing relationships, it is limited to the tasks involved and by the mathematical strength of the relationship accepted. Nevertheless, Thurstone probed the common elements of nearly all the tests available at that time, (some 32 different tests) and identified five primary mental abilities: reasoning, memory, space, arithmetic, and word fluency. Researchers in mental retardation again attended to the quantitative–qualitative question and incorporated Thurstone's test of Primary Mental Abilities (PMA) into the search.

Rameseshan (1949) identified the mental ages of 600 children from scores on the PMA. She then grouped the youngsters by chronological age from eleven to seventeen years and compared bright and dull youngsters who had equal mental ages. She reported the dull to be inferior in verbal meaning and reasoning but superior in space with a tendency toward superiority in number, word fluency and memory. Her study suggests that the theory of qualitative differences might be substantiated. However, like Maude Merrill, Rameseshan used the same instrument to identify the youngsters as for the analysis. Thus, since the youngsters were to have equal mental ages (which they did) any superiority in one group would have to be compensated for by inferiority in other factors. Like a teeter-totter, a shift of weight on one end requires a compensating shift on the other, else the balance is upset.

A study by Kolstoe (1952) used 26 bright youngsters (IQ between 121–138) and 26 dull children (IQ between 72–84) who had equal mental ages on the Stanford–Binet test. An analysis of their performances on the PMA showed no real differences to exist. In this study the Stanford–Binet was used as the identifying instrument and PMA performance as the criterion. It is therefore likely that the findings are more acceptable than those of Rameseshan. These findings support the position that mental retardates differ from the nonretarded in quantity of ability but not in quality. However, the mental ages of the youngsters ranged from about ten and a half years to twelve and a half years. Furthermore, the bright youngsters were between eight and a half and nine and a half years old. We shall see that this factor of age emerges as a critical consideration in light of the findings of Jean Piaget.

Guilford (1966) and his colleagues in California extended the factors of Thurstone and proposed a model of the structure of intellect which involved the three dimensions of intellectual processes, content, and products. It was the contention of these investigators that the five processes of memory, cognition, convergent thinking, divergent thinking, and evaluation used the four contents of figures, semantics, symbols, and behavior to produce units, classes, relations, systems, transformations, and implications. The resultant 120 cells ($5\times4\times6$) formed a three-dimensional structure embracing all possible intellectual elements. Their method of deriving the model, however, stemmed primarily from analysis of the tests devised by preceding test developers.

The Approach of Piaget

Piaget and his colleagues have been studying the thought processes of children since the 1930s. Their particular approach has been unique in studying only a very few children, who have been the subject of observation for the greater part of their lives. Thus, Piaget has attended to changes in thinking processes as they have emerged over an extended period of time.

From his observations Piaget has suggested that intellectual growth is characterized by changes in quality and not just in quantity as a child matures. Piaget maintains that there are specific stages in intellectual growth which are identified by certain kinds of intellectual operations peculiar to chronological age. During the first two years of life, children are limited, generally, to sensory-motor development— at first purely reflexive, then encompassing voluntary activity. The voluntary movements are random in the beginning, but become goal-oriented even before a child is a year old. With increased practice, a child soon can coordinate his movements and examine the efficiency of various means as well as ends. Before the age of two, object permanence is an established fact for the child.

The sensory-motor period of development is essentially devoted to perceptual organization. The child is primarily involved in exploring his immediate environment to discover what things are and what he can do with them. Kephart (1960) has underscored the importance of this period of life in asserting that motor exploration is the final arbiter of all future perceptual understandings. Feeling, touching and manipulating things are the medium for establishing what things are like and how they relate to the child and to other things. The most important aspect of early perceptual development is the recognition that signs can represent things. This is the beginning of ordering the world.

It is Piaget's contention that the conceptual period begins at about the age of two years and reaches full development at about the age of eleven. During these years the intellectual ability of the child changes markedly. First, the system of signs developed to help in categorizing and ordering perceptions is replaced by symbols. At a primitive level, for example, a stick becomes a gun or words become things. Later, symbol systems like words or numbers become the media for communications with others as well as self-communication.

At about the age of four, the intuitive stage begins to appear. This stage is marked by increased precision in symbol systems for classifying and ordering things. The ordering is limited to the most salient feature of the item (such as size), and cause and effect relationships are confused with congruence or coincidence. The rain, for instance, is often believed to be caused by thunder and lightning or vice-versa.

The concrete-operational stage of development begins at about age seven. During this stage, intuition gives way to careful attention to the reality of the world. Things, it is discovered, have a physical constancy which can vary in form without changing in nature. A ball of clay, for instance, can be made flat like a pancake or long like a stick, and even though its dimensions change, the amount of clay remains the same. Second, the child discovers that classes can include subclasses which are interrelated. Boys, for example, are people, but not all people are boys. Third, the notion of "greater than" and "less than" is understood as necessary to serial ordering. Thus, knowing that 5 is less than 6 but greater than 4 is fundamental to the fourth operation, reversibility. This last characteristic allows the child to see that $3 + 2 = 2 + 3 = 10 - 5 = 5$.

All of the thought processes which emerge during the concrete-operational stage—form constancy, class inclusion, serial ordering, and reversibility—are necessary for ordering and categorizing things, but they do not lend themselves to doing much else of a higher intellectual nature. They are necessary for knowing what is, but not very usable for speculating on what might be.

Formal thought processes begin to develop at about age eleven. They represent a quality of thinking not hitherto possible—hypothetical or propositional thought. Formal thought is distinguishable from concrete operations in several ways. First, a child can use a symbol system (language or number) to reason about nonpresent things. Words which have no real base in things, for example, *liberty*, can become a basis for quite eloquent argument concerning their application to life and living. Second, the child can check his own logic for its reasonableness. Absurdities, incongruity and sudden shifts of reference are recognized as funny—often hilarious. Third, the child can combine mental operations previously learned to solve problems. This ability is often exhibited in the proposing of alternative solutions to problems, any one of which is a "best" solution depending upon the circumstances. Implicit in this operation is the ability to evaluate—to set criteria for deciding on which alternative best meets the purpose, and to answer the question, "best for what?" This ability to set criteria and then suspend judgment until trial and error solutions have been evaluated is the chief characteristic which differentiates formal thought from the concrete and sensory-motor stages.

The careful work of Piaget has demonstrated that thinking at succeeding stages of development is qualitatively different than at lower levels. If Piaget is correct, then intelligence is not a continuum of abilities which increase as a baby grows to become an adult. Rather, intelligence is represented by the ability of an individual to develop new systems of thinking. At succeeding stages of growth, he is able to use different and more complex systems of data processing.

The investigation of the condition of mental retardation from the point of view of the intellectual development described by Piaget was not even begun until after the early 1960s. Wohlwill (1960), Inhelder (1966—reported by Stephens), and Woodward (1961) have applied the developmental system to populations of mentally retarded children, but their conclusions have been concerned with limited aspects of performance on a comparative basis and not on what mental retardation may mean. Kolstoe in an unpublished work in 1968, used some of the tests developed by Guilford and others (1966) with retarded young adults (ages 16–21) to investigate the adequacy of formal or propositional thought and found none. Similarly, an attempt by Sweeter (1968) to teach educable mentally retarded children to develop hypotheses for science experiments resulted in failure. Likewise, Inhelder, as reported by Stephens (1966), could find no retarded individuals who displayed any ability to use formal thought processes. Farber (1968) has suggested that mentally retarded adults may never achieve the level of formal thought described by Piaget. From the limited evidence available—Inhelder (1966), Sweeter (1968), Clausen (1968), and Kolstoe (1968)—it would appear that Farber's suggestion should be taken seriously.

From the earliest descriptions of the behavior of fools and idiots to the most recent descriptions of the intellectual processes of the retarded, the theme of inability to reason recurs. From Piaget's developmental system, it is now possible to describe reason as the ability to set criteria and evaluate alternative solutions using the medium of a symbol system—to engage in hypothetical or propositional thought. (For a more extended discussion of this point see Voyat, 1969.) The evidence that the retarded do not display the formal thought processes which are evident among average children at about eleven years of age, suggests that mental retardation is not just less of the same intellectual abilities possessed by normal people, but is an absence of the quality of hypothetical thought.

If Piaget is correct in holding that intelligence is not a continuum of abilities which cumulate as a baby grows to become an adult, the implication is that the neurophysiological capability for change is for whatever reason not present in any retarded person. Thus, mental retardation can be identified by noting the quality of thought relative to the age of an individual, but it must be understood at the neurophysiological level. The observation of Esquirol, in the 1800s, that "Idiocy is not a disease but a condition in which intellectual facilities are never manifested" contains more substance than was once thought. The 1912 declaration of Bolton of the ". . . insufficiency of neuroblasts and neurons" in the retarded alludes to the same underlying neurophysiological problem.

Any reference to neurophysiology depends for its validity on our present knowledge of the structure and function of the most complex part of man: his brain. Since it is not possible to observe the brain functions of man at present, we must make inferences from current theory even though this is a tenuous procedure. Hebb (1949), however, has proposed a theory of neurological organization which has withstood the scrutiny of intensive research for over 20 years. In the absence of definitive comparative information on the anatomy and physiology associated with intelligence, Hebb's theory provides a conceptual framework of great utility. A brief review of his theory may be helpful in assessing its relationship to Piaget's work.

Hebb has theorized that an individual interacts with his environment through his sense organs. When a sensory organ is excited by stimuli, the sensation is transmitted through nerve pathways to the brain. The electrochemical transmission causes neural cells in the brain to be activated, essentially to "record" the impulse by electrochemical activity. Repeated sense stimulation transmitted to the same area of the brain causes the cells in a specific area to record the impulse consistently. This consistent response by the cells is called a cell assembly and is essential to perceptual organization. Perceptions are dependent on the consistency of the firing of neural cells. In forming thousands of sensory perceptions the cell assembly is the critical unit for recording and storing information.

The relating of cell assemblies to perform meaningful acts is called phase sequence or intercellular associations. This is accomplished by the successsive firing of cell assemblies in orderly fashion. Habitual behavior like the sequence of movements in walking or other motor acts as well as grammatical construction or counting are illustrative. Phase sequence also performs the service of short-circuiting perceptions; relating like elements of bits of information to form concepts, thus, essentially reducing the numbered specific perceptions needed. This is roughly analogous to building a house. Perceptions are like the nails, bricks, and boards. If a carpenter had to make each nail, brick, or board needed, building the house would be a nearly endless project. Being able to use already formed elements greatly simplifies the task. Furthermore, prefabrication, as illustrated by concepts, can considerably reduce the time and trouble of construction. Thus, using perceptions and concepts simplifies the tasks of behavior.

Well defined perceptions and concepts are the basic content of any kind of higher thought. Thinking—the categorizing, relating, and evaluating of information—is accounted for in Hebb's theory by phase cycle. Phase cycle, sometimes called superordinate associations, essentially is the associating of stimuli with previously established cell assemblies and phase sequences. All of the operations described by Piaget as indigenous to the concrete operational and formal operational levels would be represented in phase cycle. Hebb's theory, however, does not differentiate between concrete and formal operations. It only has been used to explain how these processes are neurologically possible. As such, it lends theoretical validity to Piaget's observations.

Among theorists attending to mental retardation, Benoit (1959) was the first to relate Hebb's theory to retardation when he stated the condition was caused by:

> . . . diminished efficiency of the central nervous system, thus entailing a lessened general capacity for growth in perceptual and conceptual integration. . . .

Benoit's definition included the underlying central nervous system, but it dealt only with perceptual and conceptual integration, not with the processes involved in this integration. Of course, Piaget's discoveries were not generally available in 1959 and, therefore, could not be evaluated for a possible contribution to understanding what mental retardation is. Nonetheless, Benoit's definition points sharply to mental retardation as a condition of intellectual inadequacy and to its underlying neurophysiological base. Social competence is quite clearly a side issue and could be an effect of intellectual inadequacy but not a necessary corollary. Unfortunately, Benoit's definition does not deal with the issue of qualitative or quantitative intellectual differences between the retarded and nonretarded, an issue which must be resolved if the condition is to be satisfactorily defined.

The nature of intelligence once again emerges as a central consideration. If presently available tests which yield an IQ are believed to be measures of all the intellectual functions of human beings, then mental retardation is demonstrated by an earned IQ significantly lower than one's peers. Intelligence, however, is a theoretical construct which has typically been identified by inference. Binet and Simon, as was mentioned previously, believed that children who knew and could do more than their age peers were intelligent. Similarly, analysis of the tasks included in the Stanford revision of the Binet led to the belief that such things as memory, seeing likenesses and differences, understanding words and numbers, judgment, foresight, reasoning, and the like combined to make up intelligence. Later Spearman spoke of general intelligence made up of abstract and concrete factors plus specific factors. Thurstone identified word fluency, reasoning, arithmetic, space, and memory as the primary factors of intelligence. Wechsler developed tests to reveal verbal and performance intelligence. Guilford developed a model of the structure of intellect which included thought processes, content, and the products of the content and processes.

In each attempt to identify intelligence except Guilford's, behaviors were recorded and compared with a representative sample of peers and an inference was made concerning the relative amount of intelligence displayed. In essence, the factors observed were presumed to be present from birth or an early age and to grow in quantity as the child matured. Arguments about "true" versus "manifest" ability centered about differences in cultural exposure, language skills, motivation, the reliabilities of the various tests, and the skill of the examiner. Guilford's model is an exception because it is theoretical and does not have tests developed for all the 120 cells represented in the model or normative data on relative performance even on the tests which have been derived. However, all of the tests mentioned, including Guilford's, assume that intelligence is a continuum of abilities which increases in quantity with age and is demonstrated by the ease and efficiency with which one learns.

The departure of Piaget from the work of previous psychometrists is most notable because he rejects the assumption of intelligence as a quantitative construct. While previous workers described qualitative intellectual differences as an absence or below average demonstration of some factor, Piaget noted new abilities of maturing children. As children grew up, Piaget found they displayed new ways of thinking which were not present in previous stages of development. He also noted that some previously used skills were discarded; for example, contiguity as a major vector in cause and effect relationships.

Piaget has emphasized that each stage in intellectual development is characterized by qualitative changes in thinking. From the early sensory-motor exploration of the environment up to the concrete operational level, the child deals with what is. At the formal operations level, he is able to deal with what might be. It would seem that the mentally retarded do not display this quality of becoming conversant with the possible. They do not inhabit the world of what might be. Furthermore, the research on the concept of the mental age indicates a delay in the retarded in the age at which the thought processes they do have appear. It would seem that the sensory-motor stage for the retarded may extend for a year or two longer than the usual age of two, reported for normal children. Similarly, succeeding stages may require an extra year or two for development. This could account for the observed phenomenon that mentally retarded children can solve problems typically solved by normal children considerably younger in chronological age, and would serve to explain why Kolstoe's 1952 examination found no differences in the thought processes of children whose mental ages were about ten years.

A Proposed Definition

In summary, if intelligence is believed to be revealed by the ability of a person to learn efficiently and is related to his comparative intellectual skills such as memory, then it must be presumed to be a "something" represented in people in different amounts. It is a quantitative concept. On the other hand if Piaget's observations are correct, intellectual growth is revealed by the addition of qualitatively new dimensions of thinking at specific stages of development. In this case it would be reasonable to offer the explanation that intelligence is fundamentally *a neurophysiological capacity to develop more complex thought processes as a function of maturation and environmental interaction.*

As a corollary, the fact that no investigator found the retarded able to demonstrate hypothetical thought would indicate that mental retardation can now be defined as *a condition of intellectual arrest at some level below Piaget's level of formal thought.*

Conceptually, mental retardation would appear from a neurophysiological viewpoint to be a *"diminished efficiency of the central nervous system" which results in a limited capacity for the formation of cell assemblies, intercellular and superordinate associations and a consequent reduced ability for perceptual and conceptual integration.*

There are several distinct advantages to the proposed definition. First, such a definition and conceptualization can accommodate all of the known causes of the condition; medical, genetic, environmental, and dietary, since it is the level of thinking, not the reason or reasons for the intellectual arrest, which is the core of the condition.

Second, the various degrees of mental retardation can be ordered by the kinds of thought processes demonstrated. At the most severe level, thinking would be confined to goal-oriented behavior, object permanence, and sign and symbol systems. At a more moderate level the individual can order by one dimension, use a symbol system for communication, be aware of physical constancy but is limited in cause–effect relationships to congruence or coincidence rather than principle. At a mild level the individual can use the intellectual processes of form constancy, class inclusion, serial ordering by two dimensions, and reversibility. His thinking, however, is limited to what is; it does not extend to what might be.

Third, the definition has the distinct advantage of not dealing with social behavior. By attending only to intellectual complexity, we relegate social behavior to the area of learned behavior. Mental retardation does not carry the connotation of being inherently either good or bad. The condition is an intellectually limiting one but it is no more good or bad than is limited vision or hearing or orthopedic mobility.

Fourth, and most salutary, the definition emphasizes the kinds of thinking which the retarded can do rather than dwelling on what they cannot do. Rather than describe retardation in terms of poor memory, reasoning, and so on, educability, for example, implies the ability to deal with concrete objects using thought processes of form constancy, class inclusion, serial ordering by two dimensions and reversibility. This is a positive rather than a negative description of the condition.

Fifth, from an educational viewpoint, the definition implies an orderly sequence of development of succeedingly more complex thought processes as they apply to the acquisition of skills and content. Thus a curricular guide of a developmental nature which emphasizes positive abilities is provided. Teachers can concentrate on course content consistent with the thought processes of the children so that both methods and materials are relevant to what the children can do. Furthermore the definition calls attention to the need for careful analysis of the intellectual components of adult role behavior so appropriate skills for adult living can be built into the educational program.

On the negative side, the definition brings us face to face with some serious problems. First, present tests which yield an IQ are useful to the degree that they provide information about an individual's intellectual functioning and the kinds of thinking he can do. Since present tests are not designed to provide information of the type identified by Piaget it would appear that new tests based on Piaget's discoveries will need to be developed and standardized.

A second problem involves the lack of predictive strength of Piaget's levels. In order to arrive at a firm diagnosis of mental retardation it is necessary to wait until a person is mature before determining his final level of thinking. The condition cannot be a sure diagnosis until a person has reached chronological adulthood. This situation does have the positive attribute of not allowing the premature labeling of children based solely on IQ; nevertheless, it is a problem.

Third, the relatively precise comparative ordering possible from IQ scores is not possible from an ordering by levels. Furthermore, IQ scores allow not only ordering, but also statistical manipulations of means, medians, modes, standard deviations, and the like. The loss of data amenable to statistical treatment looms as the most serious of the limitations of Piaget's system.

To use Piaget's discoveries and the definition of mental retardation here proposed it will be necessary to develop tests which not only identify the thought processes, but also include comparative data which yield a precise order, have predictive value, and provide data which can be treated statistically, approximating the normal probability distribution.

Since IQ scores are so much more versatile than descriptive intellectual levels, it would seem prudent to use IQs. However, the choice depends primarily on the validity of the label—the degree to which it denotes an unambiguous, exclusive condition. In this area an almost endless list of writers has called attention to the danger of relying on IQ scores for the identification of mental retardation.

As a consequence, professionals face a dilemma. On the one hand, Piaget's level appears to provide the framework in which an accurate, exclusive identification of mental retardation can fit. On the other hand, IQ scores lend themselves to prediction, precise ordering, and statistical treatment. Neither appears to be complete satisfactorily by itself. A possible solution to this problem is that low IQ scores can become an alerting symptom, providing a tentative identification, with the final intellectual level of functioning as the confirming validation. Until such time as test developers are able to provide an instrument which combines the virtues of the Piaget levels and the IQ distribution, the accurate detection of mental retardation must wait until the child grows up.

The compromise, however, may not be all that bad. Sarason and Doris (1969) have pointed out that the original classifications of the feebleminded by Alfred Binet and subsequently by Henry Goddard used mental ages for divisions. The classification of idiot included those persons whose mental ages did not exceed two, imbeciles up to seven and morons up to twelve. The striking congruence with the Piaget levels of sensory-motor up to two years, intuitive up to seven and concrete up to eleven, lends credence to the solution here proposed.

For these reasons, it now seems reasonable to propose that mental retardation be defined as a condition of intellectual arrest at some level below Piaget's level of formal thought. In addition it would seem that subaverage intelligence test performance can function as a thermometer in reverse. When a person has a temperature which is above normal, we are alerted to the need for some kind of medical attention. An elevated temperature does not, however, diagnose the illness. It only alerts us to a problem. Similarly a low earned IQ does not identify mental retardation. It only calls our attention to a problem which needs attention. Since we can be quite certain that the low IQ heralds subsequent difficulties in mastering academic skills, we would be remiss in our duties as professional educators if we did not provide immediate educational steps to try to correct the condition. But we would be equally subject to criticism were we to assign the label of mental retardation to a child before he conclusively demonstrates arrested thought processes.

Present detection instruments give us little choice other than to wait for a final diagnosis until a child becomes an adult. While this is not altogether desirable, it is certainly better than premature labeling. Therefore it seems urgent that we turn our attention to developing psychometric instruments consistent with this definition and the accompanying underlying neurophysiological conceptualization. In the meanwhile, the proposed conceptualization of mental retardation allows us to capitalize on its positive aspects rather than to referring only to its deficits.

References

Benoit, E. Paul, "Toward a New Definition of Mental Retardation." *American Journal of Mental Deficiency*, Vol. 63, No. 4, January 1959, pp. 559–565.

Berry, Richard J. A. and R. G. Gordon, *The Mentally Defective: A Problem in Social Efficiency*. New York: McGraw-Hill, Inc., 1931.

Clarke, Ann M. and A. D. B. Clarke, *Mental Deficiency, The Changing Outlook*. Glencoe, Illinois: The Free Press, 1958.

Clausen, Johs., *Ability Structure and Subgroups in Mental Retardation*. Washington: Spartan Books, 1966.

Doll, Edgar A., "Definition of Mental Deficiency." *Training School Bulletin*, Vol. 47, 1950, p. 92v–92w.

Doll, Edgar A., "The Essentials of An Inclusive Concept of Mental Deficiency." *American Journal of Mental Deficiency*, Vol. 46, No. 1941, pp. 214–19.

Farber, Bernard, *Mental Retardation: Its Social Context and Social Consequences*. Boston: Houghton Mifflin Company, 1968.

Flavell, John H., *The Developmental Psychology of Jean Piaget*. Princeton, New Jersey: D. Van Nostrand Company, Inc., 1963.

Guilford, J. P., "Intelligence: 1965 Model." *American Psychologist*, Vol. 2, No. 1, January 1966, pp. 20–26.

Guttmacher, Manfred and Henry Weihofen, *Psychiatry and the Law*. New York: W. W. Wolton and Company, Inc., 1952.

Hebb, D. O., *The Organization of Behavior*. New York: John Wiley & Sons, Inc., 1949.

Jensen, Arthur R., "How Much Can We Boost I.Q. and Scholastic Achievement?" *Harvard Educational Review*, Vol. 39, No. 2, Winter 1969.

Kagan, Edwin F., Jr., "The Literary and Philosophical Antecedents of the Concept of Adaptive Behavior." Unpublished paper presented at the annual convention of the American Association on Mental Deficiency, Denver, Colorado, May 8, 1967.

Kephart, Newell C., *The Slow Learner in the Classroom*, 2d Ed. Columbus, Ohio: Charles E. Merrill Books, Inc., 1971.

Kirk, Samuel A., *Early Education of the Mentally Retarded*. Urbana, Illinois: University of Illinois Press, 1958.

Kolstoe, Oliver P., "A Comparison of Mental Abilities of Bright and Dull Children of Comparable Mental Ages," *Journal of Educational Psychology*, Vol. 45, No. 3, March 1954, pp. 161–167.

Kolstoe, Oliver P. and Roger M. Frey, *A High School Work Study Program for Mentally Subnormal Students*. Carbondale, Illinois: Southern Illinois University Press, 1965.

Lindman, F. T. and K. M. McIntyre, *The Mentally Disabled and The Law*. Chicago: University of Chicago Press, 1961.

Merrill, Maude A., "On the Relation of Intelligence to Achievement in Cases of Mentally Retarded Children." *Comparative Psychology Monographs,* Vol. 2, September 1924.

Norsworthy, Naomi, *The Psychology of Mentally Deficient Children.* New York: The Science Press, 1906.

Rameseshan, Rukmini Selyan, "An Experimental Study of the Mental Age Concept." Unpublished Masters thesis, State University of Iowa, June 1949.

Sarason, Seymour B. "Mentally Retarded and Mentally Defective Children, Major Psychosocial Problems," in Cruickshank, William W., ed., *Psychology of Exceptional Children and Youth.* New York: Prentice-Hall, 1955, Chap. 9, pp. 440–492.

Sarason, Seymour, *Psychological Problems in Mental Deficiency.* New York: The Science Press, 1906.

Sarason, Seymour and John Doris, *Psychological Problems in Mental Deficiency,* 4th ed. New York: Harper & Row, 1969.

Skeels, Harold and Marie Skodak, "Adult Status of Individuals Who Experience Early Intervention." Unpublished paper presented at the 90th Convention of the American Association on Mental Deficiency, Chicago, May 1966.

Spearman, C., *The Abilities of Man: Their Nature and Measurement.* New York: The Macmillan Company, 1927.

Stephens, Will Beth, "Piaget and Inhelder—Application of Theory and Diagnostic Technique to the Area of Mental Retardation." *Education and Training of the Mentally Retarded,* Vol. 1, No. 2, April 1966, pp. 75–86.

Sweeter, Robert, "Discovery Oriented Instruction in Science Skills for Educable Mentally Retarded Children." Unpublished doctoral dissertation, Colorado State College, 1968.

Thurstone, L. L., *Primary Mental Abilities.* Chicago: University of Chicago Press, 1938.

Voyat, Gilbert, "IQ: God-Given or Man Made." *Saturday Review,* May 17, 1969, pp. 73–75, 86, 87.

Wallin, J. E. Wallace and Harold C. Rippert, "Mental Deficiency." *Encyclopedia of Educational Research,* rev. ed. New York: The Macmillan Company, 1950, pp. 729.

Wechsler, David, *The Measurement of Adult Intelligence.* Baltimore: The Williams and Wilkins Company, 1939.

Wohlwill, J. F., "Developmental Studies of Perception." *Psychological Bulletin,* Vol. 57, No. 4, 1960, pp. 249–288.

Woodword, Mary, "Concepts of Number in the Mentally Subnormal Studied by Piaget's Method." *Journal of Child Psychology and Psychiatry,* Vol. 2, No. 4, 1961, pp. 249–259.

CHAPTER 2

Identifying the Mentally Retarded

When we reject the idea that an individual's level of intelligence is demonstrated by his performance on a test which yields an IQ and instead insist that intelligence is revealed by the ability to develop succeedingly more complex thought processes as a function of the interaction of an individual with his environment, we are left with no completely satisfactory tools for detection. Until better measuring instruments are developed, it is necessary to effect a compromise between what we have and what we need. A low score on a test which yields an IQ can be considered an alerting symptom and can be accepted as a tentative detection. Final determination must wait for the observation of intellectual functioning arrested below the level of formal thought in an individual of chronological adulthood. This confusion of a quantitative measurement of intelligence with a qualitative definition is a bothersome problem, but inaction is too serious a consequence to tolerate. We must try to find children with learning problems as soon as possible and treat them as best we know how. But finding children of low intellectual functioning is the first priority.

The Nature of Measurement

Any measurement involves comparison and is always relative and approximate. If we wish to measure the height of a table, we must first obtain some type of scale against which the table can be compared. In our American measuring system such a scale has been developed and accepted. It consists of a basic unit which we call an inch. Each inch is the same length as any other inch. That is, the distance represented between two inches and three inches is the same as the distance between 56 and 57 inches or 131 and 132 inches. The scale, therefore, is made up of equal units of measurement.

In making a comparison of the height of the table with the measuring scale, it is necessary to start at the bottom or zero and add as many units as necessary to reach the top of the table. In other words, the scale must be a continuum capable of extending from zero to infinity. Therefore, physical measurement involves the following:

1. An equal unit scale or continuum
2. A zero or floor
3. A ceiling or theoretical infinity

Psychological measurement or comparing people on psychological traits such as honesty, personality, or intelligence presents a rather different problem. What, for instance, is zero intelligence? Similarly, what is perfect or infinite intelligence? Since neither exists, it is obvious that physical measurement techniques are not appropriate for measuring psychological traits. To be sure, it is necessary to start with some agreed upon scale which has equal units so that comparisons between people will have universal meaning, but there the similarity stops. Since there is no zero in psychological traits a different point of reference must be found. This reference point has been established as the average or typical performance of a large group of people. Finding such a reference point constitutes a large part of the history of the psychological testing movement.

The History of Intelligence Testing*

When Binet and Simon were asked in 1904 by the commission appointed by the Minister of Public Instruction in France to find a method for identifying children who would be unable to profit from the instruction given in ordinary schools, they had little to go on but

* For a more detailed discussion, the reader is referred to Anastasi (1968).

the work of Sir Francis Galton in England and Wilhelm Wundt in Leipzig. Thus, they attempted to use essentially physical measurement techniques. Both Galton and Wundt believed that tests of sensory discrimination could differentiate between those who were bright and those who were dull. It is small wonder that Binet and Simon should start by comparing height, weight, cephalic index, reaction time, handwriting, and palmistry between groups of children judged by their teachers to be bright and dull. However, it was not until they abandoned physical measurement techniques that they were able to make progress.

Binet and Simon deserve much greater credit than they have received for recognizing (albeit intuitively) that a radically different technique of measurement needed to be employed for the successful comparison of psychological functions than for physical attributes.

The series of thirty tests which they included in their first mental scale were arranged in order of difficulty and presented to some fifty normal children aged three to eleven. No scoring system was presented, apparently because it had not occurred to Binet and Simon in 1905 just what kind of technique they were using. They had made the switch from appearance to performance, but they had not yet established a reference point which allowed meaningful comparison. The items started with simple tests such as following a lighted match with the eyes and distinguishing between food and inedible substances and progressed to identifying the difference between weariness and sadness. Sarason and Doris (1969) point out that on the 1905 test Binet and Simon discovered that idiots did not progress beyond test number six and that normal children at various age levels reached higher performance ceilings: three-year-olds, test nine and five-year-olds, test fourteen. This was at least a primitive recognition of a subsequent mental age scale.

It was not, however, until the 1908 version was developed that Binet and Simon grouped the subtests according to the age at which a majority of the children succeeded in passing. This constituted a further refinement of a mental age scale, since it was the beginning of the establishment of a reference point for typical performance at a given age. It was now possible to say that a given performance was typical of five-year-olds or six-year-olds, etc. The required reference point for comparison was established; crude, but essential to meaningful psychological measurement. When Louis Terman and his colleagues at Stanford University revised and standardized the test, a usable technique for measuring psychological traits was born.

The 1916 Stanford–Binet Test of Intelligence was an extraordinary achievement. The 1911 Binet consisted of 39 problems arranged by age levels from age three to age ten and with 5 additional problems at age twelve, age fifteen, and adult. The total of 54 problems allowed a determination of mental level by providing months credits for each problem correctly solved. If a child solved all the problems through age eight, then passed two tests at age nine, one at age ten and failed all at age twelve, his mental level would reflect all his successes. He would get full credit up to age eight, two-fifths credit at age nine, and one-fifth credit at age ten for a total mental level of eight and three-fifths years or eight years and seven months.

William Stern (1914) pointed out that the mental age is not a unitary measure of intelligence level but represents great variability between performances of different people. In his words:

> The full significance of this final value is disclosed only when we consider it in relation to other circumstances. It can evidently be related to other quantitative scales, like chronological age, school grade, and school standing, or we can find out how it varies with certain qualitative conditions, like social level, type of school, nationality, and the like.

Stern objected to the fact that the mental level did not consider the most important circumstance, chronological age. He, therefore, proposed that a ratio between mental age and chronological age be used so that a mental quotient would reflect the degree of a child's intellectual endowment. A quotient of one would indicate a normal level, a fraction would indicate feeblemindedness and an improper fraction, superior intelligence. Stern thus provided the reference point heretofore missing in the measurement movement.

It remained for Terman to supply the other steps necessary for meaningful psychological measurement. First, he revised the 1911 Binet scale, throwing out some problems and adding others, and established appropriate age levels by the simple criterion of requiring from two-thirds to three-fourths of a given age level of children to pass the tests successfully. Second, he adopted Stern's mental quotient, which he renamed the intelligence quotient, to express the degree of intellectual endowment. Third, he recognized that to be useful the scores had to represent accurately all of the people in the country who might be tested. Using census figures for his base, he drew a sample of children who represented an accurate geographical distribution and whose fathers' occupations were typical of the proportion of workers in the census figures. If 10 percent of the people in the country earned a living in the professions, 10 percent of the children in Terman's sample came from professional families. In 1916, Terman was quite certain that his standardization sample was representative of the population as a whole:

> It is believed that the subjects used for this investigation were as nearly representative of average American-born children as it is possible to secure.

The most significant discovery made by Terman was that in an analysis of the IQ distribution of 905 unselected children, ages three to fourteen, the percents earning particular IQs were:

IQs	%
56–65	.33
66–75	2.3
76–85	8.6
86–95	20.1
96–105	33.9
106–115	23.1
116–125	9.0
126–135	2.3
136–145	.55

This distribution of scores so closely resembles the normal probability distribution as to be practically identical. At last psychological measurement was a fact. The Stanford Revision of the Binet provides:

1. An equal unit scale. The difference between an IQ of 67 and 68 is treated as if it were the same as the difference between 100 and 101 or 151 and 152.
2. A mid-point score which represented typical performance.
3. An accurate sample of the population in terms of geography, socioeconomic level, age, and sex.
4. A statistic, the IQ, which lends itself to meaningful comparison both for individuals and for groups.

The unique contribution of the normal curve distribution characteristic of the IQ provides the real basis for meaningful comparison.

The Gaussian, bell-shaped or normal curve, sometimes called the normal probability distribution, has the property of identifying the percent of any distribution at any point from the average or mean. The application of this property to the IQ distribution allows us to place any IQ score in a percent relation to all other scores. Because of this, it is possible to judge accurately the degree of intellectual ability represented by any individual score.

Using an IQ of 100 as the average or typical score, the difference between any other IQ score and 100 gives an accurate representation of how different that score is from a typical score. However, a mere numerical difference does not tell us much. To know that an individual who earns an IQ of 90 is ten IQ points below average does not help us in judging his relative ability. We also need to know how he performs compared with the rest of the children in the country.

Fortunately, a statistical method exists which can answer this question of relative performance. It is called a standard deviation. Fundamentally, the standard deviation is an accurate method of determining not only the absolute difference between any score and its mean or average, but also the relative difference or deviation. The simplest formula for the standard deviation is:

$$S = \sqrt{\frac{\Sigma X^2}{N-1}}$$

where

> S is the symbol for standard deviation
> X^2 is the squared difference of a score from the mean $(X-M)^2$
> Σ is the summation sign
> N is the total number of scores
> $\sqrt{}$ is the square root operation sign

The formula means that the standard deviation may be found by squaring all of the differences between scores and the mean, summing or adding all the squared differences, dividing that number by the total number of scores in the distribution less one, and then taking the square root.

One of the uses of the standard deviation is in identifying the percent of scores within a given distance from the mean score. When the distribution is bell-shaped, within plus or minus ($\pm$) one standard deviation will be found 68.2 percent of the scores. Within ($\pm$) 2S, 95.4 percent of the scores will be found, and within 3S, 99.7 percent. Translating this fact into IQ distribution gives an accurate picture of the relative meaning of any IQ score.

On the 1916 edition of the Stanford–Binet, the total IQ distribution was found to have a standard deviation of 16. Since the mean score was 100, about two-thirds of the children tested earned scores of between 84 and 116 ($\pm$ 1S). Fourteen percent had scores between 68 and 84, 2.5 percent scored between 52 and 68, and .17 percent earned scores lower than 52. At the other end of the distribution, 14 percent scored between 116 and 132, 2.5 percent from 132 to 148, and .17 percent above 148.

Knowing these percentages, it was possible to state that anyone who earned a score below 52 had an IQ in the lowest .17 percent of the population. An IQ below 68 was in about the lowest 2.5 percent and an IQ of below 84 was in about the lowest 16 percent.

As was stated earlier, any measurement is always approximate. Many kinds of errors creep into any kind of comparison, and this is especially true of psychological measurement. In the case of a test like the Binet, facilities for testing may not always be the best. Likewise, the skill of the examiner as well as the motivation of the child being tested may both have an effect on the score obtained. This measurement error is a constant source of concern to those who give tests, and so generally is taken into account in any test administration. Nevertheless, an obtained IQ score which falls in the lowest three percent of the population distribution is a cause for concern. Whether an IQ below 70 is an indication of mental retardation is another matter.

Even though the 1937 revision of the Stanford–Binet was an updated and improved version of the 1916 edition, many psychological examiners were disturbed because the subtests were so heavily dependent upon verbal responses. Many deaf-mute children would be classified as mentally retarded because they earned low IQs due to their inability to speak. Observation of their everyday behavior demonstrated the ability to learn, to solve problems, to show good judgment, and to reason in their adjustment to environmental demands. Certainly, this is not the kind of intellectual behavior typical of mentally retarded children. Furthermore, many children who had been identified as retarded showed quite adequate behavior in nonverbal situations. For these and other reasons questioning the reliance on a test like the Binet for determining the total intelligence of people became a favorite psychological indoor pastime.

Spearman in England seriously challenged the notion on which the Binet test was based, the notion of sampling global intelligence. By means of correlational studies, Spearman demonstrated that only part of the intellectual functioning of people could be accounted for by the IQ scores. He therefore proposed a two-factor theory of intelligence. Fundamentally, he proposed that a general intellectual factor, or g, accounted for most of the performance on the various subtests, but that specific factors, s, made up the rest of the performance. Most important, he suggested that the general or global intelligence was partly verbal (v) and partly concrete (f).

Wechsler Tests

Although David Wechsler (1944) did not agree with Spearman's two-factor theory he was much influenced by the English statistician Spearman and W. P. Alexander when he set about to develop his own intelligence scale.

Wechsler recognized that any test was a sampling procedure which when pooled provided a measure of global intelligence. He recorded the importance of this fact in his analysis of Binet's work:

> One of the greatest contributions of Binet was his intuitive assumption that in the selection of tests, it made little difference what sort of tasks you used provided that in some way it was a measure of the child's general intelligence.

However, he identified the fundamental fault of the Binet test accurately when he commented on the use of the MA/CA ratio for a calculation of the IQ.

> From the theoretical point of view, the precise value of the denominator used, that is, whether the adult MA is taken as 14, 15 or 16 years, is of no consequence. They are equally fallacious in the sense that they assume that mental ability (as measured by tests) remains constant after any one of these ages. That unfortunately is precisely what most psychologists have assumed ever since the IQ was introduced. The result

has been that insofar as adult ratings are concerned, psychologists have been really not getting IQs at all; instead they have been calculating various indices of mental efficiency.

Wechsler pointed out that the MA/CA ratio was justified only if the obtained mental ages were linear, increasing at a constant rate with chronological age. He demonstrated that this is not so by graphing the original raw scores obtained at different ages on the Bellevue Intelligence scale. Instead of getting a straight line, he got a graph which began to curve sharply at about age twelve and continued to decline through the age of seventeen (which was as far as the graph went). The calculating of IQs from the MA/CA ratio was therefore unjustified.

Wechsler then turned his attention to a method which would provide a useful and justifiable system of comparing the intellectual ability of people at every age level. At first, he turned briefly to the method of physical measurement and attempted to define a zero IQ. This he identified as five standard deviations below the mean. Thoughtful consideration of the logic of zero or nothing IQ apparently made Wechsler abandon the concept as illogical:

> In point of fact this assumption is incorrect. A child at birth does not have zero intelligence nor for that matter zero chronological age. When a child is born it is already nine months "old" and manifests a certain amount of intelligence.

Instead, Wechsler used as a reference the scores of those individuals who fell in the middle fifty percent of the distribution. He called this spread of scores "average" and discovered that it represented one probable error around the mean of the distribution. With this procedure, a new dimension in psychological measurement was born; the deviation IQ. Wechsler summarized the advantages of the deviation IQ as:

> First, it dispenses with all assumptions as regards the precise relation between intellectual and chronological ratings of growth, and in particular, assumptions as regards the rectilinear relation between the M.A. and C.A. Secondly, in the calculation of adult IQ's it relieves us of the need to commit ourselves to any fixed average adult mental age. Each age defines its own adult denominator. Thirdly, the method

enables us to calculate IQ's which maintain the same meaning of the IQ namely, that of an index of relative brightness.

Having invented a measurement index which accurately reflected the relative brightness of people, the deviation IQ, Wechsler then turned his attention to the selection of items for his scale. Some two years were spent studying items contained in other tests and making new items which provided meaningful tests for a wide age span, and were suitable for a wide range of ability at any age level. Difficulties were myriad. For example, "Where is London?" was found to discriminate well between mental defectives and the borderline group, but not at all between average and superior groups. Likewise "What is the Koran?" did not discriminate at all at the lower levels (practically all failed it) but showed significantly higher percents passing it at the average and superior levels.

This work has resulted in perhaps the most usable scales ever developed for the classification of people according to relative brightness. The Wechsler Preschool and Primary Scale of Intelligence (WPPSI) is designed for children between the ages of four and six and a half; the Wechsler Intelligence Scale for Children (WISC) for children ages five to fifteen; the Wechsler Adult Intelligence Scale (WAIS) for people sixteen to sixty. The standardization population was as carefully chosen as that for the Binet. We can have every confidence that the scores are an accurate sampling of citizens in the United States between the ages of four and sixty from the point of view of geography, occupation, education and sex. The scales, although differing in test items at various levels, reflect a consistency in measurement, format, administration, scoring, and interpretation unequalled by any other scales.

Information. The range of information possessed by an individual is often thought to be a reflection of his cultural background or educational level. This test, however, has proved to be highly useful because the questions asked are related to the degree to which people are alert to the world rather than relying on specific information. The question "What is the average height of men and women in the United States?" requires the relating of observations for a meaningful answer reflective of alertness. "Who wrote Hamlet?" is specific and probably related to culture and education. The test items tend to be of the general rather than the specific variety.

Comprehension. This has sometimes been referred to as a test of common sense. Indeed, a question which asks, "What would you do if you found a letter that was already sealed, stamped and addressed?" would seem to elicit a straightforward answer, "Mail it." However, cultural mores also seem to play a significant role in some responses. Nevertheless, common sense or practical judgment seems to be dominant.

Arithmetical Reasoning. Although computational skill is highly related to culture and education, a question which probes "If eight men can finish a job in half a day, how long will it take one man to do the work?" requires a great deal more than simple computation. It calls for a careful assessment of the problem and no little judgment to determine the reasonableness of the answer.

Memory for Digits. The ability to repeat numbers from memory seems more like a circus trick than an intellectual exercise. Yet the actual reproduction requires the individual to develop some system of organization: grouping by twos or threes or finding some association which is suitable. This is even more apparent when the child must repeat numbers backwards. A retentive memory is not a demonstration of superior intellect, but memory is a requirement without which there will be no superior intellectual functioning.

Similarities. A person's ability to tell how air and water are alike makes it possible for examiners to identify the kind of thinking he can do. Distinguishing between superficial and essential likenesses reveals a depth or poverty of understanding of great significance not altogether culturally or educationally linked.

Vocabulary. As with the similarities test, not only the size but also the quality of a person's vocabulary become important considerations in a determination of intelligence. Furthermore, symbols are the necessary media for thinking. A large vocabulary may not be a demonstration of anything more than culture and education, but the manner in which a person defines words is also a measure of how he thinks.

One of the advantages of the Wechsler Scale is that some tests are grouped to provide a verbal IQ while others provide a performance

IQ. Generally, those tests which probe information, comprehension, arithmetic memory, similarities, and vocabulary are included in determining the verbal IQ. More properly, these tests appear to require a high level of ability to acquire and use symbol systems in abstract problem solving. This is, of course, the stuff that schools are made of. It comes as no surprise that a high relationship is found between verbal IQ and successful academic performance, school grades or learning to read. The often made assumption that a low verbal IQ is a demonstration of mental retardation cannot be legitimately accepted, however. This would be an example of using a quantitative score to arrive at a qualitative conclusion.

The performance or nonverbal tests of the Wechsler Scales involve primarily manipulative tasks.

Picture Arrangement. The task of arranging a series of mixed up pictures into a cartoonlike strip which illustrates a logical sequence requires more than accurate vision. It requires that the person must "catch on" to the story or idea represented. This orderly arrangement of discrete elements requires that the total situation must be comprehended first before any meaningful arranging can be done. Orderliness of thinking is a prerequisite for success.

Picture Completion. The test requires an individual to identify an essential part missing from pictures. To know that a smokestack is missing from a ship or an eyebrow from a girl's face requires considerably more than attention to details. It calls for the ability to detect a missing element essential to form or function. Discriminating between essential and nonessential elements is the important intellectual function here.

Block Design. The subjects are given from four to nine blocks colored red, white, and red/white and asked to reproduce designs presented on picture cards. Seemingly, success is possible when subjects can break down the design into component parts. Apparently the intellectual abilities of analysis and synthesis are both important in this test.

Object Assembly. This jigsaw puzzle type of test requires the ability to put together parts to form a meaningful configuration. The "catching on" function is not so important as seeing relationships between familiar elements.

Digit Symbol. Symbols paired with digits are reproduced using the numbers as stimuli. Ability to learn rapidly is certainly required, but so also is the ability to distinguish between essential and nonessential visual clues.

From the performance tests of picture arrangement, picture completion, block design, object assembly, and digit symbol such functions as comprehension, analysis, synthesis, seeing relationships, and distinguishing between essential and nonessential information can be observed. The performance IQ derived from the tests emerges as a measure of ability to deal with concrete materials in problem-solving tasks. Neither culture nor education seems to have as much influence in these tests as in the verbal part of the scale, although they certainly play some part. None of the tests could be considered completely culture-free. As in the calculation of the verbal IQ, the performance IQ is a deviation score representative of how an individual does in relation to his age peers. This is also true for the full-scale IQ which results from combining the verbal and performance parts of the scale.

Detecting Mental Retardation

Terman's original classification of intelligence according to the IQ used intervals of ten. This usage seems to be related to even number calculations of the MA/CA ratio. It should be noted that Wechsler acknowledged the legitimacy of IQ calculations from the MA/CA ratio whenever the empirical data demonstrated a linear relationship. Indeed, Wechsler's graph of mental growth for children between the ages of seven and seventeen did show such a relationship up to the age of about twelve. Since this is the case, the system used by Terman can be considered acceptable for children below the age of twelve. However, not all school children are below twelve years of age and many retarded youngsters are in elementary school even though their ages are considerably beyond twelve. Furthermore, Terman's classification stopped at IQ 70. The Terman and Wechsler systems were compared in this way by Wechsler (1944):

Classifications of Intelligence

Terman		Wechsler (ages 10–60)		
IQ	CLASSIFICATION	IQ	CLASSIFICATION	%
20–70	Definite feeblemindedness	65 and below	Defective	2.2
70–80	Borderline deficiency			
80–90	Dullness	66–79	Borderline	6.7
90–110	Normal or average intelligence	80–90	Dull normal	16.1
110–120	Superior intelligence	91–110	Average	50.0
120–140	Very superior intelligence	111–119	Bright normal	16.1
140 and above	Genius or near genius	120–127	Superior	6.7
		128 and above	Very superior	2.2

It is interesting that the actual percentage distribution secured by Wechsler so closely resembles the rather arbitrary convenience classification of Terman. The relative differences—below 70 for Terman and below 65 for Wechsler as the upper limit of defectiveness, and the 10 point range of Terman versus the 14 point range for Wechsler for delimiting borderline deficiency—do not present much cause for debate. Interestingly, the difference between Wechsler's 7 point spread for superior versus the 20 point Terman range is not only substantial, but could be a troubling problem for people who work in the area of gifted children. In the area of mental retardation the real problem which has arisen is whether the upper limit of mental retardation is 70 or 65 and also whether borderline deficiency scores (below 80) should not also be included in the classification of mental retardation. Further arguments have centered about the "real" meaning of the scores. Since the total standard deviation for the Binet is 16 and for the Wechsler 15, then a score of 84 IQ on the Binet is the equivalent of a score of 85 on the Wechsler. Additional fuel for discussion comes from being able to obtain verbal, performance, and full scale IQs from the Wechsler scales. Which is the best measure of intelligence, the most accurate for identifying mental retardation?

Such arguments have raged in the field of mental retardation for many years with little likelihood of reconciliation. Part of the difficulty stems from the question of whether a sampling of behavior in a one hour test can provide an accurate picture of the intelligence of an individual. Part revolves around the question of whether intelligence is genetically or environmentally determined (nature versus nurture). Part of the confusion involves whether mental retardation is purely an

intellectual problem, or whether social, adaptive behaviors are necessarily included. Still another difficulty is whether neurological pathology must be present in any firm diagnosis of mental retardation.
Finally, part of the difficulty revolves around the question of whether
the available tests measure intelligence in the first place.

As is well known, arguments occur when elements of truth favor
different points of view, when no firm elements clearly support one
position over another, and when the assumptions upon which the
arguments rest differ. The assumption that mental retardation is a
quantitative intellectual deficiency provides for most of the disagree-
ments. Even the rejection of a low IQ as the delineation of mental
retardation does not resolve the discussion. The lack of measuring
devices based upon the Piaget developmental levels leaves the field
dependent upon IQ tests for identification, albeit tentative. The best
that can be said is that a low IQ score is symptomatic of *probable*
mental retardation. A certain diagnosis can only be made on the
observation of an intellectual arrest at some level below Piaget's formal
or propositional thought. Since this is the condition of the field, we
have little alternative except to use whatever psychological measurement is available to find probable mental retardation and to guide the
teaching program. A firm diagnosis of the presence of the condition
must wait until chronological adulthood.

Other Identification Procedures

Certainly, the most acceptable instrument for obtaining an IQ
is a well developed and standardized individual test such as the Binet
or Wechsler. The impracticality of testing all the children in a school
system is demonstrated by the time factor alone. Generally, a psychometrician will need about half a day per child for testing, scoring and
interpreting. During a one hundred eighty day school year the maximum number of children who could be tested would be three hundred
and sixty. Even in a moderately sized school system of ten thousand
pupils (a community of 40,000 population), it would take nearly
twenty-eight years for one person to test all of the youngsters or,
conversely, twenty-eight full time psychometrists who did nothing but
give tests to examine all of the pupils in a single year. The situation

is patently absurd. School systems are forced to find more efficient methods for detection.

Many school systems call on teacher nomination and group tests to grossly identify those youngsters who are then referred for individual assessment. Teachers often use behavior which can be observed for guidance. Characteristics such as the following are cause for referral:

1. Poor memory
2. Short attention span
3. Dull
4. Immature
5. Difficulty in understanding
6. Limited vocabulary
7. Poor judgment

Some schools use group tests of mental ability. Most common are tests like the California Test of Mental Maturity, The Kuhlman Finch Test or the Test of Primary Mental Abilities. Although critical scores vary from school system to school system, an IQ of 85 or below or a percentile rank of 15 or below are frequently the alerting scores. Schools which do not use or are prohibited from using tests of mental maturity often turn to reading readiness tests for young children and grade level academic achievement tests for older children. Often used tests are the Iowa Tests of Basic Skills, the Wide Range Achievement Test, the Metropolitan Achievement test and the California Achievement Tests. Individual psychological assessment is generally sought for children whose achievement scores are one year or more below chronological age.

Individual Assessment

The purpose of individual assessment has typically been to identify the condition of mental retardation. Such a purpose is difficult to justify since a determination of the condition is not possible with present tests. What is possible is an indication of present intellectual functioning and a comparison of that efficiency with the performance of peers. Furthermore, educational planning can be based on accurate observation of the learning assets and liabilities of the child being studied.

It has long been recognized in educational circles that the mental age is the best single index of the levels of learning maturity of children. Since it is a single index, the mental age, by itself, is not completely dependable. Sensory efficiency, learning style, emotional maturity, motivation, prior experience, and physical vigor are significant contributors. Any assessment of learning potential should probe all of these factors.

MENTAL AGE

The Binet test scoring requires finding an MA. The system for doing so involves first finding a basal age. The basal age is the highest year level at which a child successfully passes all the test items. Second, the child is presented test items at succeeding year levels. Credit in months is given for successfully passed tests. Third, a ceiling is reached when a youngster fails all of the tests at a given age level. The mental age is the basal age plus the total months credit received for tests passed up to the ceiling. If a child passes all the tests at year eight, for instance, one test at year nine, one at ten and none at year eleven, his mental age would be $96 + 2 + 2 = 100$ months or eight years four months. This mental age is put into the formula $\dfrac{\text{MA}}{\text{CA}} \times 100 = \text{IQ}$. Thus, the Binet test gives both an MA and an IQ so both level and rate of mental efficiency are identified. The quality of thought is not determined by the scores. Expert psychological examiners can be quite accurate in identifying thought processes from observation of the kinds of responses given by the child, but these judgments are arrived at by inference; they are not inherent in the test scores.

The Wechsler tests do not provide an MA. Since Wechsler scores are points which cumulate for each subtest, they are not age scaled. Instead, the points earned by children of a given age have been tallied in a frequency distribution and converted to a standard distribution with weighted scores to make all frequency distributions conform to a single scoring system. In each subtest, the mean score is ten and the standard deviation is three. For the total IQ scores, the mean score is 100 and the standard deviation is 15. This method permits a meaningful comparison of the points earned by a child on any subtest with his age peers, and it provides the same comparison by IQ, for the Verbal, Performance, and Full scales. Because the Wechsler distribution approximates the normal curve, the score earned by a child can be accurately placed in a percent relationship to his peer. An IQ of 85, for example, means that about eighteen percent of his age mates earned scores equal to or lower than that and about eighty-one percent exceeded that performance. While it is not statistically legitimate to convert Wechsler scores to MAs, from a practical standpoint, it is often important to do so anyway. The justification for such a move is provided by the linear relation of MA and IQ up to the age of about twelve, the fact that any obtained MA needs to be interpreted in light of the sensory, experiential and motivational characteristics of the child, and the practical necessity of having a mental maturity level for an educational benchmark. A rather easy method of obtaining the MA is to apply the formula $\dfrac{CA \times IQ}{100} = MA$. A child of ten years with an earned IQ of 85 would have a mental age of about eight and a half years. Translated into grade expectancy (subtracting five from the MA) this would indicate that the child could be expected to understand academic work at about the middle third grade level in school. It should be reemphasized that this index of expectancy is only approximate, but it provides a very convenient point at which to start educational planning.

SENSORY ASSESSMENT

It has been well established in educational circles that the sensory efficiency of a child plays a significant role in his school performance. Fundamentally, the visual and auditory perceptual skills of the child are most important, but other senses augment these two transmission avenues. These two sensory areas, however, are most important and need to be examined for efficiency.

Visual Acuity. The simplest explanation for academic difficulty is vision. Not being able to see clearly certainly hinders academic performance. For this reason, tests of vision should always be included in a total child assessment. The visual area should be assessed by an eye specialist. Unfortunately, this is not always possible. In the absence of a thorough examination by an expert, a psychological examiner can do some screening to determine whether the visual functions are faulty.

Visual acuity may be examined by use of a Snellen chart. This chart consists of letters or *E*s of different sizes which have been standardized for reading at specific distances. Since the chart has been designed to be read to twenty feet, the visual acuity is expressed in fractions: 20/20 indicates normal acuity, 20/70 (a person sees at twenty feet what a person with normal vision can see at seventy feet) is indicative of impaired vision and 20/200 is legal blindness. The Snellen chart is useful for far point vision, but does not provide information on visual acuity for near vision, the distances at which reading of books or newspapers is done. Some psychometrists have made cards of letters which can easily be read at about eighteen inches by persons with normal vision. Youngsters with vision problems will move the cards closer to their eyes. Such action is cause for referral for a thorough examination to an expert on vision.

Acuity is not the only visual problem which needs assessing. Perhaps more serious are focusing, tracking, and orientation. These can be grossly assessed in a fairly simple manner. The examiner should face the child and hold a pencil or other small object about eighteen inches from the child's eyes, instructing the child to follow the tip of the pencil with his eyes while holding his head still. By moving the pencil toward the child's nose, the examiner can observe whether both eyes can turn in (hold focus) as the pencil tip approaches the nose. Similarly, at a distance of about eighteen inches the pencil can be moved horizontally, vertically and diagonally across the midline of the child. During all these movements the two eyes should track together. If they do not, referral to an expert on vision is indicated.

Auditory Acuity. Hearing acuity should be examined by an expert audiologist. Where this is not possible, screening with special recordings designed for group hearing testing can be used. Even in the absence of mechanical testing, informal methods can be employed. Whisper tests or coin click tests can provide a gross indication of auditory acuity. For the whisper or coin clicks, the child should be about twenty feet from the examiner with eyes covered or closed so he gets no visual clues to help him hear. The examiner instructs the child to plug one ear with his finger or an ear plug so hearing in each ear is tested independently. Having the child identify the number of times coins are clicked together or repeat the words whispered will give some indication of auditory efficiency. Any inaccuracies should be considered a reason for referral to a hearing expert for extensive assessment.

SENSORY EFFICIENCY

The fact that visual and auditory acuity are intact is still no sufficient reason for complacency. Learning through these sensory channels depends upon adequate sensory memory, discrimination, sequencing, and closure. A test which can provide information about sensory efficiency is the Illinois Test of Psycholinguistic Ability (ITPA).

THE ITPA

The ITPA was developed by Samuel A. Kirk and James McCarthy in 1961. In 1968, Kirk, McCarthy, and Winifred Kirk presented a revised test which consists of twelve subtests designed to function as a diagnostic rather than a classification tool. It is designed to delineate both specific abilities and disabilities in children so appropriate educational plans can be generated.

The tests deal with the psychological functions which operate in communication between individuals, as when the intentions of one person are transmitted to another and the second person receives these messages and acts on them. The tests deal with (1) the channels through which communications flow, (2) the reception, organization, and expression of messages, and (3) the organizing of information both simple and complex. The tests are point scales very much like the Wechsler scales and are scored in a similar manner.

Auditory Reception. Using questions like "Do airplanes fly?" and "Do canines manufacture?", the child reveals his ability to understand auditory questions which can be answered by "yes" or "no" or a nod or shake of the head. Does he understand what he hears?

Visual Sequential Memory. Using white plastic chips with black geometric designs, the child is required to reproduce from memory a sequence of chips shown to him for five seconds. The test probes "Can he see and remember?"

Auditory Association. This test uses analogy type questions like "Grass is green, sugar is _____" or "Years have seasons, dollars have _____" to discover whether a child can hear and understand relationship and associate that relationship to a similar situation. It requires a rather high level of understanding.

Auditory Sequential Memory. Similar to visual sequencing, this test places a high premium on the ability to remember numbers which are read to the child at the rate of one per half second.

Visual Association. As in the auditory association test, this test requires that the child understand the relationship between picture analogies. The pictures range from a bone with a dog to the relationship of two similar geometric designs.

Visual Closure. Hidden fish, shoes, bottles, hammers, and saws must be found by the child in pictures which are drawn in such a fashion that only part of the figure is visible (the tip of the dog's tail). Being able to draw inferences from only partial visual clues is the function tested.

Verbal Expression. Five objects are presented singly to the child (nail, ball, block, envelope, and button) for descriptions. The child should be able to identify by name, use, color, classification, shape, composition, major parts, number, comparison, and association. A high degree of intellectual integration must occur before this "see and tell" activity has much meaning.

Grammatic Closure. Action pictures serve as the stimuli for grammatical usage of tense and conjugation. Pictures range from a dog barking through a picture which has been hung to illustrate good, better and best.

Manual Expression. No verbalizing is required for these tests. Instead the child is asked to demonstrate what should be done with pictures of articles ranging from a hammer to a combination padlock. Various credits are given. For example, with an egg and eggbeater, breaking the egg, emptying the shells, discarding the shells, holding the eggbeater and turning the beater, all receive credit. Understanding of functions is the chief requirement for success.

Auditory Closure. Similar to visual closure, a child is required to identify whole words from partial sounds. These increase in difficulty from easy words like *da—y* to *ty—i—er* (typewriter).

Sound Blending. The ability to synthesize sounds separated in time is called for when the child is asked to recognize *sh-oo* as shoe, *l-i-t-l* as little, and various nonsense words presented in the same manner.

Auditory and visual reception, organizing and expression profiles are made meaningful by the use of Z scores. That technique essentially employs the same kind of percentage distribution as the normal probability curve and the deviation IQs of the Wechsler within an age range from four to ten. Fortunately, the test is useful for children over the age of ten because the mental age of the child establishes his level of psycholinguistic expectancy. A child of age twelve with an IQ of 75 would have a mental age of about nine. His ITPA scores would be judged relative to this Mental Age (9) rather than his chronological age (12). Furthermore, the test is designed to identify areas of weakness. If his scores were all above the norms except for one subtest, this finding would be significant because it would identify an area or channel of communication which could be a serious deterrent to his academic progress. Remedying of this weakness might enable the child to experience success in school rather than failure.

The identification of the rate (IQ) of mental growth, the level (MA), and weaknesses in reception, processing or expression of information is not a sufficient basis for developing an educational program. To discover that a child has difficulty in visual sequencing, for instance, does not tell why this weakness exists. The use of other tests may not answer the question of why, either, but the tests can pinpoint the level of visual–perceptual performance at which the child encounters failure.

Visual–Perceptual Failure

Marianne Frostig and her coworkers (1966) have devised a test of visual perception which probes five areas:

1. Perception of position in space. This ability, which shows itself in being able to differentiate letters which have the same form but differ in their positions, such as *b* and *d*, is examined with simple examples which increase in complexity. The figures are rotated and reversed in multiple choice test items.
2. Perception of spatial relationships. Geometric figures and designs must be located not only in relation to the child but also in relation to each other. Inability to do so seriously interferes with dealing with sequences of letters in a word or words in a sentence.
3. Perceptual constancy. Constancy in size and shape is essential if the child will learn to recognize words he knows in an unfamiliar context,

such as color or style of print. The test for this ability requires the child to draw lines around figures imbedded in geometric figures which include succeedingly greater amounts of irrelevant stimuli.

4. Visual–motor coordination. This test requires the child to draw a line between two figures within a path of successively narrowing width. Inability in this area is indicative of poorly directed eye movements as well as poor eye–hand coordination.

5. Figure–ground perception. Identifying shapes imbedded in competing shapes is essential if a youngster will be successful in the analysis and synthesis of words (syllabication and phonics).

Even though the Frostig tests do not provide information on why a child may have a visual–perceptual problem, unlike the ITPA, the Frostig tests identify a failure point. Remedial exercises have been developed which allow the youngster to start at, or a little below, his point of failure and to work at his own rate toward the elimination of the perceptual problem.

An alternative to the Frostig approach has been developed by Newell C. Kephart. Unlike Frostig, Kephart has a well developed theoretical framework for perceptual and conceptual development. Taking his cues from the neurological theory of Hebb (see Chapter 1), Kephart postulates a developmental information processing scheme not at all in conflict with the experimental findings of Piaget. (Chapter 5 has a more detailed discussion.)

As a base, Kephart believes the motor exploration of the world is the final arbiter of all further perceptual and conceptual development. The person is the focal point for all exploration since all sensations center in him. Touch, taste, smell, vision, and hearing are the channels of contact with the world but the individual's notion of the world is uniquely his own—the result of sensations brought to him by his sense organs.

Kephart believes that accurate perceptions must depend upon the motor explorations of the young child. All that he sees, smells, tastes or hears is related to touch. This is the motor–sensory exploration stage of development.

The perceptual–motor stage involves the relating of literally thousands of bits of perceptual information to the motor reality which the child has established in his first developmental stage. The perceptual–perceptual stage sees the child relating new perceptual elements to already established perceptual relationships. It allows him to fit new pieces of information into already developed perceptual schemes.

Perceptual–conceptual development is the relating of established perceptions to each other to form concepts. Even though each chair is different from every other chair, they have in common the elements of "chairness"—a base, seat and back.

Conceptual development is the relating of concepts to other concepts. It is the kind of thinking which allows a person to put materials he has read into his own words. The translation of one kind of information into another.

Conceptual–perceptual behavior accounts for bias. It is the ability of an individual to see only what he is tuned in to see. That "beauty is, altogether, in the eye of the beholder," simply means that perceptual sensations are translated into the viewer's own frame of reference.

Kephart and Roach have developed a test, the Purdue Perceptual–Motor Survey, designed to identify failure at any of the developmental stages. The tests include items dealing with balance and posture, body image and differentiations, perceptual motor matching, ocular control, and form perception. These tests are a useful extension of the Frostig materials because visual–perceptual failure identified by the Frostig tests can be corroborated in the Purdue survey, so that an accurate picture of the level of perceptual sophistication of a child is revealed. Quite often, remedial work must be initiated at a more basic level than that provided by the Frostig materials if a significant correction of the condition is to be effected.

Even though visual–perceptual–motor disability can be traced throughout the ITPA, the Frostig, and the Purdue Perceptual–Motor Survey, there is no presumption of causation. Some psychometricians employ tests like the Bender Gestalt, the Graham Kendall, or the Berry for further diagnosis. These tests require the child to reproduce from memory geometric designs of increasing complexity. Incomplete, rotated and reversed reproductions are often interpreted as evidence of minimal brain damage. The validation of this interpretation is far from established. However, even if it were possible to make a diagnosis of brain damage from the tests, remedial treatment would call for Kephart, Frostig, or ITPA derived lessons such as those developed by Bush and Giles or perhaps all of these. In this case, the label of brain damage provides no useful purpose. Labeling a problem as organic may have medical implications but it is doubtful that it is educationally useful (Gallagher 1957).

Auditory–Perceptual Failure

Problems of auditory memory, sequencing, discrimination, closure and sound-blending are well identified by the ITPA. Once auditory acuity has been eliminated as a possible cause of the difficulty, an examiner need not go beyond the ITPA itself for diagnosis. The tests for auditory efficiency can be interpreted as criterion tests. That is, the child either performs acceptably or he does not. If he demonstrates failure, then remedial work can be specific to the subtest failed. Bush and Giles have developed lesson plans appropriate for children from kindergarten to eighth grade which deal with each subtest of the ITPA. They are especially useful for classroom program planning.

Language Problems

Fundamental to all academic work is the efficiency of the language symbol system of a child. While language deficiency does affect the ITPA of a child, the test does not specifically probe this area. An experienced psychometrician can make quite accurate inferences about the child's language skills, but the test itself does not. Two tests which do probe this area are the Engelmann Basic Concepts Inventory and the Myklebust Picture Story Language Test.

Both of these tests are diagnostic in that they identify the level of language skill of the child. Remedial work can therefore start at the point of failure.

BASIC CONCEPTS INVENTORY

This test is designed to identify weakness in language usage at a basic level. It examines the ability of the child to understand the implied meanings of *or, and, not, if,* and *then* and also requires the child to demonstrate his ability to reason effectively. It is made up of three parts:

Part I requires the child to answer questions while viewing a series of nine pictures. The questions range from identifying (find the dog) to elimination (find the balls that are not white) to serial positioning (she is between a boy and a girl) to reasoning (there is a ball in one of these boxes. The ball is not in this box. Do you know where the ball is?).

Part II is made up of a series of statements and questions. The child is asked to repeat the statements verbatim and then answer the questions. For example, "Fends cannot crump." Say it. Then, what can't fends do?

Part III requires the child to identify a correct from an incorrect sequence of motor acts (clapping and slapping a table in patterns), repeat digits from memory and sound blend (flow-er).

Point scoring the Basic Concepts inventory is not so important as identifying those concepts the child fails to understand. In this sense, the test operates as a diagnostic test with remedial implications specific to the child's disabilities. It is presumed that a child must master all the concepts tested if he is to be successful in first grade work. Thus, the test serves to determine whether a child has the language concepts he will need to successfully negotiate first grade.

MYKLEBUST PICTURE STORY LANGUAGE TEST

This test is designed for use with children who can write. The main part of the test involves showing a picture to a child who then writes a story about the picture. The story is scored according to several criteria. First, the scoring uses an abstract-concrete scale with five levels of difficulty:

Level I   Meaningless language unrelated to the picture.
Level II Concrete descriptive, listing, categorizing, verb–noun combinations, one and two categories plus action are credited at this level. Such answers are typical of seven-year-old children.
Level III Concrete–imaginative. What the subject is doing plus some integration of the whole picture or the interaction of figures in the picture are scored at this level.
Level IV Abstract–descriptive. Sequences of consecutive events are typical of nine-year-olds. Twelve- and thirteen-year-olds generally give the figures a specific setting, give the picture a total setting, or add other figures within the setting described.
Level V   Abstract–imaginative. Fifteen-year-olds generally mention

either prior or future events while seventeen-year-olds remove the story from the picture by dealing with motivation, assigning a theme, or indulging in allegory.

In addition to the abstract–concrete scoring, Myklebust provides a scale of productivity by age equivalents for total words, total sentences, and the ratio between words and sentences. Syntax is assessed by type of errors (additions, omissions, substitutions, and word order) in terms of word usage, word ending, and punctuation. A syntax quotient is the ratio between the total units and the total correct. The chief advantages of the Myklebust test is the comparison of language production with that of age equivalents so it is possible to determine how much below average a child's language is. Remedial work can be quite easily geared to this scoring system.

Use of Test Information

One of the chief errors made by psychometricians in psychological assessment is that of expecting tests to make the evaluations. The tests provide for observation of behavior in a controlled setting, but diagnosis is a synthesis of information derived from the observations. This is done by the tester, not the test. Furthermore, the psychometrician determines which tests can provide the kinds of observations useful for a specific child. Therefore, the data which will be available to the psychometrician is limited by his skill in selecting the best tests to use. This puts the burden squarely on the shoulders of the examiner. He is the key to adequate examination, not the test.

The Case Conference

Interpretation of test results should be a group project. A screening and placement committee should be composed of a physician or nurse, a social worker, a school psychologist, the child's teacher, a speech pathologist, a special education representative, and the school principal. This is a minimal listing. Other experts who may have pertinent observations to contribute should be enlisted as needed. Sometimes the child's parents or guardians may need to be included, but more often they should be seen by the committee chairman after the committee has considered all the available evidence and decided on a course of action.

Most case conference committees evolve a set of procedures which are useful to them and which lead to effective decisions. While these vary from group to group they generally cover specific items common to all the committees.

The foremost consideration is a determination of the child's potential for academic work. The committee must decide whether the IQ scores earned by the child provide a reliable indication of his intellectual efficiency. Such a decision is basic to educational planning. This is where the debates on the relative merits of the verbal versus the performance versus the full scale IQ originated. The decision on the reliability of the IQ scores can probably never be certain, but some intelligent discussion can reduce the uncertainty. Sensory acuity problems in either vision, hearing, or both can be expected to interfere with test performance. Lack of motivation, poor concentration, and over-anxiousness will all operate in a negative way. A child who is uncertain or fearful in the examining setting or a hostile child will typically do poorly. It should be noted that while these variables tend to interfere with test performance, they also are inhibitors of classroom learning. The finding that an IQ score is not a reliable index of intellectual efficiency does not mean that special educational provision will not be beneficial for the child. It may mean that something other than or in addition to special class placement is required. In every case, the committee must decide on a tentative estimate of the level of understanding which can reasonably be expected. That is, the committee must be able to decide the academic level at which instruction can be expected to be successful. A useful index is to subtract five from the mental age. For instance, if a child of eight has an IQ (judged by the committee to be a fairly reliable index) of 75, his mental age would be about six, $\frac{8 \times 75}{100} = 6$. Five subtracted from six equals one. It would be the committee's decision that the child would probably be able to be successful with beginning first-grade level work.

The second decision should be one of learning style. Profile scores from the ITPA can help identify the skill with which the child can accept, process, and give information. More fundamentally, the ITPA can provide clues as to the visual and auditory skills of discrimination, memory, sequencing, and closure possessed by the child. Areas of relative strength can be used for channels of instruction. Areas of weakness need remedial work. However, remedial decisions can be greatly improved by further examination. In the visual areas, the Berry, Frostig, and Purdue tests can be used to pinpoint failure so remedial work can start at a point which will assure the success of the instruction. In the auditory areas the ITPA subtests are more efficient; however, the auditory areas are affected by the language skills of the child. Since the ITPA does not provide much information on language, tests such as the Basic Concepts Inventory or the Myklebust Picture Story Language Test can be used to identify an instructional level at which to start a program.

The third decision is that of appropriate placement. This decision must take into account the prior decisions on instructional level and learning style. Here, the facilities of the school system must be matched to the needs of the child. In addition, ancillary services, such as medical attention, speech correction, and counseling for either the child or his family may need to be provided. Often the services of community agencies may be needed to supplement the school offerings. Clearly, representatives from the community agencies whose cooperation is solicited deserve a full account of the committee deliberations and decisions in the decision areas.

Finally, program plans should be formulated. These plans are left until last because they depend upon the instructional level, learning style, and placement decisions. The program should identify clearly stated behavioral goals, how they may best be sought, and precisely when and how evaluations of progress are to be initiated and evaluated. Often it is possible to identify priorities and even alternative courses of action which can be tried in cases of failure. While no one plan will be suitable for all children, the law of parsimony should be invoked to govern all plans. That is, the simplest possible procedure should be tried first and evaluated. Subsequent plans will, therefore, have the benefit of identifiable cause and effect relations. In this way the committee can be relatively sure that specific variables do or do not play a part in the child's learning problems.

An alternative procedure advocated by some program planners is to start at the most basic level at which failure occurs in any developmental system: visual–motor–perceptual, auditory–perceptual, and language. This assures that the child will not miss any developmental steps. Actually, both procedures can be instituted simultaneously. Most children with learning problems will have developmental gaps. Intelligent evaluation of progress will allow program planners to attend to difficult problems and skip irrelevant procedures. This is good for both the child, his teacher, and the reputation of the school system.

Any child who demonstrates a low IQ when he first appears in school should be provided an intensive tutoring program for at least a year or two. The program should be based on the identification of the most critical performance deficits of the child, so that every effort can be made to increase his learning efficiency. Assignment to a long-term adjusted program should not be made until efforts to eliminate the learning problems have proved futile. Only then should the curriculum be adjusted to accommodate the difficulties.

References

Anastasi, Anne, *Psychological Testing*, 3d ed. New York: The Macmillan Company, 1968.

Bush, Wilma Jo and Marian Giles, *Aids to Psycholinguistic Teaching*. Columbus, Ohio: Charles E. Merrill Books, Inc., 1969.

Engelmann, Siegfried, *Basic Concepts Inventory*. Chicago: Follett Educational Corporation, 1967.

Frostig, Marianne, Welty Lebever, and John R. B. Whittlesey, *Tests of Developmental Perception*, rev. ed. Palo Alto, California: Consulting Psychologists Press, 1966.

Gallagher, James J., "A comparison of brain injured and non-brain-injured mentally retarded children on several psychological variables." *Monograph Society for Research in Child Development*, 1957, Vol. 22, No. 2.

Jastak, J., S. Bijou, and S. Pastak, *Wide Range Achievement Test*, rev. ed. New York: The Psychological Corporation, 1965.

Kephart, Newell C., *The Slow Learner in the Classroom*, 2d ed. Columbus, Ohio: Charles E. Merrill Books, Inc., 1971.

Kirk, Samuel A., James J. McCarthy, and Winifred D. Kirk, *The Illinois Test of Psycholinguistic Abilities*. Urbana, Illinois: University of Illinois Press, 1968.

Lindquist, E. F. and A. N. Hieronymus, *Iowa Tests of Basic Skills*. Boston: Houghton Mifflin Company, 1956.

Myklebust, Helmer R., *Myklebust Picture Story Language Test*. Los Angeles: Western Psychological Services, 1965.

Roach, E. G. and Newell C. Kephart, *The Purdue Perceptual Motor Survey*. Columbus, Ohio: Charles E. Merrill Books, Inc., 1966.

Sarason, Seymour and John Doris, *Psychological Problems in Mental Defiency*, 4th ed. New York: Harper & Row, Publishers, 1969.

Spearman, C., *The Abilities of Man: Their Nature and Measurement*. New York: The Macmillan Company, 1927.

Stern, William, "The Psychological Methods of Testing Intelligence," tr. by G. M. Whipple, *Education and Psychological Monographs*, 1914, No. 13.

Terman, L. M., *The Measurement of Intelligence*. Boston: Houghton Mifflin Company, 1916.

Tiegs, Ernest W. and Willis W. Clark, *California Achievement Tests*. Los Angeles: California Test Bureau, 1950.

Wechsler, D., *The Measurement of Adult Intelligence*, 3d ed. Baltimore: Waverly Press, 1944.

CHAPTER 3

Causes of Mental Retardation

If the estimate of 3 percent of the population falling in the classification of mentally retarded is applied to the United States, some 7,000,000 people would fall in this category. This figure cannot be verified because no universal system for identification has been accepted. Furthermore, it is most unlikely that a country which jealously guards the right to privacy would ever institute a testing program for everyone. However, figures from England, Holland, the Scandinavian countries, and a few surveys of states (Hawaii) and specific counties in the United States report incidence figures which are strikingly similar. Classification by degree of severity is also rather uniform even when differing methods of data collection and arranging are used. A consistent total of 3 percent is generally accepted with some 2 to 2½ percent included in the mild and moderate divisions (educable), about one percent in the severe, and a fraction of a percent profoundly retarded. In gross numbers, about 6,000,000 would be considered educable with perhaps 750,000 trainable and 250,000 profoundly retarded. Those individuals falling in the age range of interest to educators can be estimated to comprise about twenty percent of the total group. Even this very rough estimate indicates that there are about 1,200,000 who would be eligible for educational provisions in public schools which have a goal of fostering independent adult behavior, 150,000 who may be capable of semi-independent behavior, and 50,000 children whose lot in life would be total care.

While not precise, the percentages of classification by severity roughly parallel the number of individuals for whom a cause of the condition can be specified with some confidence. That is, those individuals in whom retardation is profound or severe are usually found to exhibit physical symptoms which relate to the cause or causes of the retardation. The less severe the retardation, the less the likelihood of accompanying physical pathology. Thus, the approximately 1,200,000 youngsters who are seen in schools typically offer few clues to the possible causes of the condition.

The very size of the group with uncertain cause for retardation has led many educators to question the necessity of teachers being knowledgeable about medical aspects of retardation. It is obvious that a physician must be quite familiar with genetic, anatomical, physiological, and systematic pathology as they relate to either medical treatment or prevention but teachers are involved in behavior modification remote from medical concerns. Furthermore, the vast majority of the teachers seldom come in contact with severe and profound conditions and, therefore, have no real need for knowing much about them.

While we grant the validity of these two arguments, there are some other considerations which cannot be overlooked. First, there is the possibility that some kinds of neurological damage may be found to be better treated by one educational program than by another. Such a relationship has been suggested by Strauss (see Chapter 5). If this is found to be even partly true, then a knowledge of causes may be important to the educator. Second, anyone who considers himself a professional in a field should have at least a conversational knowledge of all major aspects of his chosen field. Third, as more educators are called upon to function as members of interdisciplinary teams, it becomes critical that the team members have a common language which will aid rather than impede communication. Fourth, teachers often find themselves called upon to visit parents. The ability to detect family members who may need referral to medical resources could be of critical importance in some circumstances. More crucial may be the need to provide accurate information to the parents. In the majority of parental encounters, it may be that no causative agent can be detected. In this circumstance accurate information about what the condition does *not* represent may be greatly valued. Considerable knowledge is necessary before authentic elimination of possibilities can be realized.

Classification Systems

SYMPTOM CLASSIFICATION

Clinical descriptions provide the easiest approach to classification. Because the characteristics used for classification are those which can be easily seen, no very elaborate techniques of diagnosis need to be employed. For the most part, descriptions of the anatomical and the physiological characteristics are sufficiently different among the various conditions that there is little danger of either overlap or confusion. Unfortunately, the clinical descriptions often refer only to observable characteristics and so sometimes hide the causes of the condition. In other instances, certain anatomical and physiological conditions are not detectable by casual observation, but need various laboratory tests for confirmation. In addition, the severity of the condition is not always apparent from the looks of the child. Webber (1962) classified the clinical groups into cretins, mongoloids, hydrocephalics, and microcephalics. Because these represent children who show gross anatomical and cranial differences the children are easy to identify, but the classification system falls far short of including all of the more than two hundred different known causes of the condition.

ETIOLOGICAL CLASSIFICATION

Attempts to classify by cause started as early as Bolton's classification of 1912. It was the opinion of this physician that mental retardation was characterized by an insufficiency of neurons and neuroblasts and that the retarded were of two kinds: (1) those with primary amentia caused by factors operating on the fertilized ovum, and (2) those with secondary amentia whose causation was from factors operating at or after birth. Although the factors operating were not identified, at least Bolton called attention to time as a critical consideration in a classification system.

Tredgold (1922) proposed (1) amentia due to inheritance, (2) amentia due to environment, (3) amentia due to both heredity and environment, and (4) amentia without discernible cause. By 1956, Tredgold had modified his classification, adding subgroups to the two main groupings of primary and secondary amentia. He proposed:

1. Primary amentia
   a. Simple
   b. Genetic
2. Secondary amentia
   a. Deprivative
   b. Traumatic
   c. Infective

While the distinctions among subgroups are difficult to make, Tredgold did suggest specific factors of genes, deprivation (presumable sensory), trauma, and infection. This, at least, was a substantial start toward a usable system.

Kirk and Johnson (1951) used the classifications of (1) brain injury, (2) physiological disturbances, (3) hereditary factors, and (4) cultural factors. While no great precision was represented in this system, Kirk and Johnson did point out that culture was a significant factor in causing retardation.

In 1959 a committee on nomenclature was appointed by the American Association on Mental Deficiency. This group developed a classification system which tried to recognize all of the possible causes of the conditions in general categories and allow subcategories of specific agents to be grouped together for classification. The major categories were:

1. Infection
2. Intoxication
3. Trauma or physical agents
4. Disorders of metabolism, growth or nutrition
5. New growths
6. (Unknown) prenatal influences
7. Unknown or uncertain causes with structural reactions manifest
8. Uncertain (or presumed psychologic) cause with the functional reaction alone manifest

The AAMD system was designed to be flexible enough to allow any new causative agent to find a home in one of the categories. At the same time, the categories were those which could be agreed upon by medical, psychological, educational, and sociological professionals. It retains the areas of infection and trauma, and adds intoxication, metabolism, new growths, and three unknown categories for prenatal, structural, and psychologic agents. Hereditary influences were dropped as a category, presumably because specific genetic factors seldom are identifiable as a single cause (there appear to be few or no genes specific to mental retardation), and because some genetic problems such as phenylketonuria manifest a metabolic defect.

The AAMD system has great utility, but it does not consider the time factor to which Bolton called attention. However, a way of using the AAMD system in a time sequence is possible by discussing etiology in developmental periods: prenatal (before birth), natal (at or during birth), and postnatal (anytime after birth). This method of presentation preserves the integrity of the AAMD classification of causes while allowing the additional perspective which comes from adhering to a life progression sequence. Furthermore, it seems a little easier to understand since nearly all of the causative categories can be identified at virtually any stage of life. However, it is virtually impossible to stick to a strict period sequence and, furthermore, the time period at which an agent is operative may have a significantly different effect than at some other time. Trauma, for example, in the prenatal period may be devastating to a developing embryo, yet have little residual effect on an adult. Because time cannot be ignored, the following discussion follows a relative time sequence with some deviation allowed for a discussion of unique problems.

Human Growth

Conception, the start of a new life, may also be the start of retardation. Within the fertilized egg are all the basic potentialities of development and the blueprint for the construction of a completely unique person, unlike any other ever born or ever to be born.

From this single living cell eventually some twenty-five quadrillion cells will form a human being. This is possible because of three qualities of the cell: first, metabolism, the ability to grow by converting food into living matter and to derive energy by a breakdown of some of the food; second, cell duplication, the ability of a cell to divide in such a way as to yield two exact duplicates of itself; and third, cell differentiation, the ability of cells to become altered so as to best perform specific functions.

Each cell consists of two main parts, a nucleus which contains the vital genes which control cell activity and growth, and the cytoplasm where most of the metabolic processes take place. Normally each cell nucleus (except that of the sex cells) contains twenty-three pairs of rodlike bodies called chromosomes. The chromosomes are made of protein and the genes. Genes are in the form of a double helix of deoxyribonucleic acid (DNA). The helix is formed by a double strand of sugar and phosphate with cross-connecting bases. Although there seem to be only four bases in DNA (adenine, cytosine, guanine, and thymine), the different combinations of these bases provide variations in the genes. The genes send instructions to the cytoplasm by way of a chemical messenger from the nucleus. The chemical messenger is ribonucleic acid (mRNA).

The mRNA encounters globular structures in the cytoplasm called ribosomes which decode the messages and produce the particular protein needed. The amino acids which form the protein are brought to the ribosomes by a second kind of RNA, called transfer RNA (tRNA), which attaches itself to the active part of the mRNA at the ribosome. Essentially cell activity stems from the DNA which codes the mRNA which in turn is decoded by ribosomes to form enzymes (proteins in the cytoplasm which cause chemical changes to occur without themselves being involved in the change). Obviously, any missing amino acid or the wrong amino acid in the sequence of an enzyme could seriously alter cell functions.

The multiplication of cells is made possible by the ability of cells to divide to and form identical replicas of themselves. This duplication is accomplished by mitosis. A second type of division, meiosis, takes place to form sex cells.

In mitosis, the long, slender chromosomes become duplicated and then become much shorter and thicker by a process of coiling. They then line up in a row in the center of the cell and separate with one of each kind of chromosome going to either end of the cell. The entire cell then divides to form two new cells, each capable of all the cell activities and cell division of the original cell. Geometric multiplication

(1, 2, 4, 8, 16, 32, and so on) accounts for the development of the twenty-five quadrillion cells which make up the mature human being.

Serious consequences can arise as a result of the unequal distribution of chromosomes in the formation of reproductive cells (meiosis). Two divisions are involved in meiosis, but there is only one duplication of chromosomes, so the final cells have only half as many chromosomes as are found in body cells. In the first division the genes and chromosomes become duplicated, as in mitosis, but the duplicated chromosomes do not separate. Hence, two cells are formed with only 23 chromosomes each, although each of these is a double chromosome. In the second division there is no gene nor chromosome duplication, but the double chromosomes separate so that there are four cells, each with 23 single chromosomes.

On rare occasions there is nondisjunction of chromosomes during meiosis—the two paired chromosomes fail to separate, so that two go to one cell and none to the other. This gives one reproductive cell with 24 chromosomes and one with 22. Such reproductive cells can result in a fertilized egg with one too many, or one too few chromosomes. Dire consequences can result, as we shall learn later.

Also, pieces of a chromosome may break off and become lost, resulting in a shortened chromosome lacking in some of its genes. This is known as a deletion. On other occasions the piece broken off may become attached to another chromosome. This is known as a translocation. Both of these conditions can upset the balance of genes and have serious effects on a developing embryo.

Cell differentiation seems to be possible because the genetic code of the DNA in the cell is activated by the position of the cells. That is, as cells multiply, some cells become covered by other cells. Food material brought to the inside cells triggers different instructions than that brought to outside cells. Thus, groups of cells which receive similar instructions develop special functions different from all other cells. This differentiation of activity results in the development of skeleton, skin, organs, and other body parts. All cells in the body have the great majority of their possible functions inhibited.

Not only is position important in determining cell functions, but time also plays a part. Cells which have been transplanted from one part of the body to another, if transplanted early, take on the characteristics of the surrounding cells. If the transplanting occurs later, the cells retain their original functions and characteristics. Seemingly, the biochemical coding is susceptible to responding to new instructions only up to a point (Spemann 1938). Should intervention such as diet control be started late in a child's life, the possibilities for dramatic change become minimal.

Prenatal Causes

Chromosome abnormalities which are associated with mental retardation were not known of until microbiologists developed techniques for identifying different chromosome pairs in 1956. The study of cells with high powered microscopes enables the researchers to classify and arrange the chromosome pairs according to size and shape so that they can be numbered. Pair number one is the largest while number twenty-two is the smallest. The sex chromosomes make pair twenty-three. This arranging of pairs, called karyotyping, makes it possible to analyze chromosomes for possible abnormalities.

It was just such comparing which led Lejeune to discover that children with Down's Syndrome (Mongolism) had an extra chromosome. The actual discovery was like a chapter out of a detective story.

In 1866 Dr. Langdon Down, a British pediatrician, identified newborn children who did not look like members of their own families, but who were strikingly similar to each other in appearance. Dr. Down was familiar with Charles Darwin's theory of evolution and apparently believed that man descended from lower forms of life, slowly evolving from simple form to his present complex physiological and anatomical form. Down further believed that all races represented evolutionary stages of development with the Black races the most primitive, the Asiatic races the next and Caucasians the most advanced.

As Dr. Down observed the children who resembled each other but not their own parents, he described them as:

> I have been able to find among the large number of idiots and imbeciles which come under my observation, both at Earlswood and the out-patient department of the Hospital, that a considerable portion can be fairly referred to one of the great divisions of the human family other than the class from which they have sprung. Of course, there are numerous representatives of the great Caucasian family. Several well

marked examples of the Ethiopian variety have come under my notice, presenting the characteristic malar bones, the prominent eyes, the puffy lips, and retreating chin. The woolly hair has also been present, although not always black, nor has the skin acquired pigmentary deposit. They have been specimens of white negroes, although of European descent.

Some arrange themselves around the Malay variety, and present is their soft, black, curly hair, their prominent upper jaws and capacious mouths, types of the family which people the South Sea Islands.

Nor have there been wanting the analogues of the people who with shortened foreheads, prominent cheeks, deep-set eyes, and slightly apish nose, originally inhabited the American Continent.

Because these children had the oriental slant to their eyes and because they seemed to have a similar appearance, he reasoned that they must have some kind of developmental experience in common. He, therefore, deduced that they represented a particular stage in evolutionary history, the stage of the Mongoloid race which he thought more primitive than the Caucasian. He named the children Mongoloid children and attributed their cause to a throwback or arrest of development at the mongolian level of evolutionary change. Thus, Mongoloid children were considered a mistake of nature.

Benda (1946) wrote the first authoritative book on the condition. Based upon his extensive experience as Superintendent at the Wrentham Institution, he presented a wealth of behavior, learning, and medical detail about the children. The persistent theme in Dr. Benda's book included the mystery of why these children from such diverse backgrounds should look alike. By the 1940s the evolutionary theory of race was no longer accepted. Furthermore "Mongoloid" children had been found among Negroes, Chinese, Japanese, and among Mongolians. It scarcely seemed suitable to tell a Mongolian mother that she had a Mongoloid child.

Benda apparently reasoned that since the children looked alike they probably had some developmental factor in common. As he searched through his mass of record details, he was struck by the fact that many of the children were either premature births or that they were much smaller than typical normal births or both. He was also drawn to the fact that the children had other anatomical features which seemed immature by comparison with normal children. Benda soon became convinced that the condition represented children who were not as mature as their age peers, so he named them "unfinished children." The children had a rate of growth, both physically and mentally, that was somehow slower than normal. Thus, Benda identified the common factor in their development as a slow growth rate rather than evolutionary arrest as Down had.

By 1950 Penrose in England had rejected both the evolutionary arrest theory of Down and the "unfinished children" theory of Benda. His line of inquiry consisted of a great many comparisons of physical characteristics of Mongoloid children with normal children. As he pursued these comparisons, he discovered what he thought was some similarity between the hand and finger prints of the children and the hand and finger prints of their parents. Extending his identification of physical signs, he found some parents who had thickened epicanthic folds, saddle nose, heavy jowls, and other signs similar to those of the children, but the parents were not, themselves, Mongoloids. Penrose reasoned that some genetic factor was surely involved, but he did not know what because none of the data fitted into Mendel's theory of inheritance through dominant and recessive genes.

It was not until karyotyping of chromosomes was discovered that Lejeune (1966) was able to pinpoint the factor common to all Mongoloid children—chromosome abnormality. His discovery of an extra chromosome number 21 led to naming the condition trisomy 21. It was at first thought that nondisjunction or a failure of the chromosomes to divide properly during mitosis was the condition common to all Mongoloid children. Thus, first reports indicated that Mongoloid children had 47 chromosomes rather than 46. Subsequent studies by other cytologists soon showed that a few mongoloid youngsters had only 46 chromosomes. An extra 21 was attached to one of the longer chromosomes. It, therefore, was apparent that translocation could also be involved and that mongoloid children were not all alike except that all have extra chromosome material. It seems that there are at least three kinds of chromosome problems among Mongoloid children: translocation, nondisjunction, and mosaicism. Because there is no chromosome problem common to all Mongoloid children, the various names which have been used to describe them have been largely discarded. Terms like Mongoloid, unfinished, and trisomy 21 have been discarded in favor of Down's syndrome. It is a curious twist of events that efforts to find some common developmental history for over 100 years have, after a successful effort, resulted in a return to naming the condition after the physician who first described it.

Recently Turkel (1970) has attempted to treat the condition of Mongolism biochemically. This approach has its roots in Zimmerman's use of glutamic acid in the 1930s. However, Turkel's approach has a better rationale and is more extensive. Briefly, Turkel bases his treatment on the belief that the chromosome excess in Mongoloid children affects the metabolistic functions of the cells because DNA codes are out of balance. Using a probe which he designed, Turkel analyzed which of the metabolites are not being properly eliminated from the cells and then prescribes fifty-one specific chemical agents to counter the toxic effects of the interference of accumulated materials on efficient cell functioning. Although his experimental procedure is quite new, and therefore not yet validated, clinical reports are quite encouraging. The morality of this tampering with chromosomes raises serious questions. Until these questions of ethics can be satisfactorily answered, it is probable that this line of experimental inquiry will be quite limited.

As a by-product of the search for clues to the origin of Down's syndrome, cytologists have identified other conditions in which chromosome abnormality is present. Klinefelder's syndrome is that of a male with a generally effeminate figure and other effeminate characteristics. The presence of an extra X chromosome which is believed to be a result of nondisjunction of the sex chromosomes during meiosis has led to calling the condition trisomy X. However, Turner's syndrome in females, which is the counterpart of Klinefelder's syndrome in males, is actually an absence of the X chromosome (the chromosome count is 45) yet it results in infantile sex characteristics of the female. Since reference to the presence or absence of the X chromosome tells little about the condition, the practice of naming the condition after its discoverer seems to be not only just but useful. In any case chromosome abnormalities have been identified as important in the field of mental retardation and will probably come in for considerable attention by future scientists, especially in reference to the causes of nondisjunction and translocation in mitosis and meiosis.

INFECTION

Prenatal infections, or infections of the mother during pregnancy, are of critical concern in the prenatal period. Regardless of the source, the infection may cause an inflammation of the cells and a destruction of those cells which are infected. If the infection is in the cells of the spinal cord and brain, the cells do not regenerate and brain damage results. If the infections occur early in the pregnancy greater damage usually results than if it occurs later, and, generally, if the infection is severe the damage is greater. Although Asian flu, chicken pox, hepatitis, and mumps contracted by the mother during pregnancy are suspected of being linked to mental retardation, the relationship is supported by only flimsy evidence. Other infections are directly responsible and therefore, deserve discussion.

The causes of infectious diseases are bacteria, viruses, and protozoa. Often it is difficult to find an effective preventive measure, because different strains of the various infective agents require specific vaccines or other treatments to produce immunization, but great progress is being made by determined scientists.

German measles or rubella was first identified as a possible cause of birth damage by two epidemiologists, Collman and Stoller (1962) in Australia. Alerted by a large number of children with birth defects including vision and hearing loss, cardiac abnormalities, and mental retardation, they discovered an outbreak of German measles of epidemic proportions coincided with the early stages of the pregnancies of the mothers. Further investigations confirmed the suspected link and the discovery that if women contract the disease within the first three months of pregnancy from 10 to 85 percent of the children born will be damaged. Furthermore, this is one of those unusual diseases in which the seriousness of the mother's illness is not a good clue to the amount of damage the child may suffer, so that the attending physician is not able to decide on the basis of the discomfort of the mother whether the unborn child may or may not be damaged. Legalized abortion, therefore, cannot be sought without raising a great many legal and moral uncertainties.

For these and for other reasons the United Cerebral Palsy Association underwrote the cost of research to discover a vaccine against rubella. Subsequent support by governmental agencies enabled public health scientists to develop, test, and distribute an effective vaccine which is now distributed to school children nationwide.

Another viral infection which has not received much attention because it was believed to be quite rare is cytomegalic inclusion body disease. This infection of the salivary glands of the mother is thought to be transmitted through the blood of the mother to the blood of the child and is believed to be a factor in some cases of hydrocephalus, microcephaly, blindness, deafness, convulsions and intercranial hemorrhage. Efforts at prevention are not great at present, but the increasing suspicion that the disease is at the root of many more cases of damaged children leads to the hope that the disease may come under greater scrutiny in the future.

Bacterial infections of the mother may also take their toll of offspring. Perhaps the best known is syphilitic infection. While at one time syphilis was considered the second greatest cause of mental retardation, legal requirements for premarital blood tests and prenatal clinic blood tests have resulted in early detection and treatment, so that only rarely are cases of mental retardation caused by syphilis now encountered. Nevertheless the danger is real and cannot be dismissed. Furthermore, the damage does not usually become apparent until the child is about ten years old (slightly earlier for boys than for girls) and produces gross neurological symptoms of progressive intellectual deterioration and ultimate death. It is a dangerous, destructive, and unnecessary disease.

Toxoplasmosis, a disease caused by a parasite, is probably the most damaging of all the infectious diseases. The mother may show almost no evidence of being ill, yet the embryo suffers severe damage. Unlike in the viral infections, the fetus is more susceptible to damage during the last half of the pregnancy period rather than in the beginning stages of growth. The parasite enters the mother's body probably through food and the protozoan parasite apparently invades the fetus from the blood stream of the mother. Treatment with sulfa and other drugs seems to be effective, but unless it is started early, the child may suffer considerable damage.

Although microcephalus, hydrocephaly, epileptic seizures, and psychomotor disturbances are frequent consequences of the disease, the most common residual is an abnormal condition of the choroid coat of the eye and retina. This most often is observed in addition to one or some of the other pathologic conditions mentioned. Damage is serious both physically and intellectually.

TRAUMA AND PHYSICAL AGENTS

Because extremely good protection is afforded the fetus by its position in the mother during pregnancy, the incidence of mental retardation due to trauma or physical agents from the prenatal period is very small. However, some danger still exists. Obviously, accidents of an automobile or motorcycle where the mother receives a severe blow to the abdomen can cause fetal damage. Likewise, the more severe the blow and the earlier the pregnancy the greater the probable damage.

Somewhat less obvious is the possible damage which can result from X-ray and other radiation. If either X-ray or radium is used in large amounts, as in the therapeutic treatment of cancer in the mother, substantial damage may be done the fetus. This damage is done directly to the unborn child, and is not the result of transmission from the mother. Furthermore, germ cells may be damaged in the fetus so that hereditary defects may result in the child's offspring. While some of the effects of radiation are known, many are not yet completely understood. As we enter an age of increasing uses for nuclear power, it may be that previously unknown relationships will be uncovered.

Insufficient oxygen to the fetus may also be a cause of mental retardation. Since oxygen is supplied the fetus through the blood supply of the mother, conditions in the mother such as heart trouble, severe anemia, or interferences with the arterial system could all reduce the oxygen supply. Without sufficient oxygen the cells may die or function at a subnormal level. Destruction of the cells in the central nervous system results and brain damage is the consequence.

INTOXICATION AND ALLERGIC REACTIONS

While it is recognized that certain chemicals, serums, and drugs may directly affect the fetus, more common is the damage which can be done as a result of reactions which arise in the mother to various kinds of foreign agents. Improper or incomplete elimination of the toxics may cause such conditions as toxemia of pregnancy. During the later stages of pregnancy toxic substances accumulate in the mother and are believed to be transmitted to the fetus through the placenta. The actual mechanism of the condition is not fully known, but endocrine system imbalance and metabolic disorders are suspected as the operating factors. In any event, the fetus absorbs the toxins in roughly the same proportions as the degree of severity of the toxemia in the mother.

The same kind of damage to the fetus can result from intoxicants and poisons ingested by the mother during pregnancy. It has been well established that heavy cigarette smoking by the mother is linked to smaller than average birth weight of children. Whether this is causative is not known. It is known that alcoholic mothers often have children afflicted with malformations and degenerative brain tissue. Recently, the rapid rise of narcotic and drug usage is causing great concern. The actual effects of the use of marijuana, heroin, cocaine, and morphine as well as the synthetic hallucinogenic substances by pregnant mothers is not established, but studies of the effects on laboratory animals are underway and the results, so far, are frightening.

Poisons ingested by the mother also take their toll in the unborn child. Lead, mercury, manganese, arsenic, and carbon monoxide poisoning have been shown to be causative factors. In addition, lesser known poisons such as lye and caustic compounds are equally dangerous.

The sensitivity of mothers as shown in allergic reactions to certain biochemical substances is also related to mental retardation. Perhaps the best known maternal sensitization reaction is that of Rh incompatibility. When a union occurs between an Rh positive father and an Rh negative mother where the child, because of the dominance of the Rh positive factor, is Rh positive, the mother's body reacts to Rh positive blood, which escapes from the child through the placenta into the blood stream of the mother, by producing antigens. As the supply of antibodies builds up in the mother, some penetrate the placenta and attack the blood supply of the fetus. Usually two or more pregnancies must occur before serious damage is done to the fetus, but sometimes damage is sustained in an initial pregnancy. The result of the antibody activity is a destruction of red blood cells and yellowish-red bile secretion called bilirubin is deposited in the cells of the skin and the brain causing a yellowish color of the skin. This is referred to as jaundice. When the level of bilirubin reaches 20–25 milligrams per 100 cubic centimeters of blood, brain damage occurs. This condition is called kernicterus. Fortunately, kernicterus can be prevented by replacing the contaminated blood of the child with whole blood by transfusion. Although transfusions are typically not performed until after a child is born, Liley in 1961 perfected a technique for intrauterine transfusion which is rapidly being adopted in medical circles. The development of a vaccine to prevent Rh negative mothers from becoming sensitized has been proceeding with excellent results. The vaccine, Rh immunoglobulin (Rhogam), may soon be used universally, so that mental retardation from this source may disappear.

ENDOCRINE DISORDERS

Failure of the endocrine glands (thyroid, parathyroid, pituitary, thalamus, adrenal, and pancreas) to function properly may be a causative factor in mental retardation. Although knowing that a gland malfunctions is important for treatment purposes, one still may have no knowledge of why the gland does not perform satisfactorily. In some instances the problem may be metabolistic which has a root problem in genetics. In other circumstances the problem may be disease or trauma or some combination. This area is further complicated by the fact that advances in biochemistry allow for discoveries of new interrelationships which may be associated with mental retardation in as yet undiscovered ways. The emerging knowledge in the field has a redeeming feature: biochemical problems typically respond to biochemical solutions, so that as new problems are identified, ready-made solutions are often available. Nevertheless much uncertainty about cause and effect currently exists.

The best known of the endocrine problems associated with mental retardation is cretinism. A typical cretin is short and stocky with stubby fingers and toes. Usually cretins have a broad face and their thickened eyelids and short necks add to the broad appearance of the face. The universal characteristic, however, is a chronic lethargy and in most cases cold, dry skin which feels much like bread dough.

The causative agent in cretinism is a lack of the hormone thyroxin, secreted by the thyroid gland. This can result either from an absence of the gland itself or from improper functioning of the gland. Since the thyroid secretions play an important role in regulating the speed of all cellular activity, any malfunction has a significant effect on life processes. Interestingly, cretinism is rapidly disappearing, not because of any concerted program, but rather as a result of increased iodine intake in diet. The universal use of iodized salt and the improvement of packaging and shipping of seafoods have made it possible for persons living in areas where little iodine exists in a natural state in the soil (primarily the midwestern states) to enjoy an iodine rich diet. The major consequence of these dietary improvements is in the improved functioning of the thyroid gland and a subsequent reduction in the number of children born with cretinoid characteristics. Although we may rejoice at the result of this happy circumstance, it is sobering to contemplate the consequences of dietary deficiency. Diet control of pregnant women and newborn children looms as a major area for attention in the prevention of mental retardation.

In the newborn child, if a cretinoid condition is discovered, the progressive course of the destruction can be arrested by injections of thyroxin in the child. Although extensive damage may be prevented, it is questionable whether all aspects of brain pathology can be. It seems likely that at least some neurophysiological impairment will be manifested, but it will be less than that sustained by untreated children. However, because of the success of both prevention and treatment of thyroid dysfunction, there is every hope that other glands in the endocrine system will eventually be equally responsive to treatment.

METABOLIC DISORDERS

The inability of a child to produce enzymes necessary for metabolizing food substances can be a factor in mental retardation. The actual mechanism is a breakdown in the digestive process and the resulting accumulation of waste substances in the cells of the body including the brain. The basic reason why children do not secrete the needed enzyme is probably genetic, but why there should be defective or missing genes is not known. Furthermore, while the breakdown is in metabolizing the food substances, the effect is a toxic one. For these reasons, errors of metabolism can be thought of as genetic, biochemical, or toxic, all of which are probably partly correct. The types of problems which occur include failure to metabolize lipids (fats), amino acids, carbohydrates, or calcium. Each results in specific types of disorders and each probably is controllable by diet or other biochemical means. Unfortunately, the field is so new that not very great progress has been made in either early detection or treatment. In those few areas which have received attention, the results have been nothing short of dramatic; in most the areas, however, little has been done.

Lipids. Hurler's disease is probably the best known of the lipid disorders. The condition is often called Gargoylism because the physical deformity resembles that of gargoyles found as statuary on many European public buildings. Usually children appear to be normal at birth, but after five to six years of failure to effectively metabolize the fats, the accumulation of mucopolysaccharide throughout the body results in an individual of short stature, protruding forehead, bushy eyebrows, coarse features, short lobsterlike fingers, and a semi-crouching stance. Generally, there are accompanying organ difficulties of the liver and spleen and sometimes cardiac and eye problems. As in most metabolic disorders, the condition is usually progressive with little hope for improvement.

Another lipid disorder is Tay-Sach's disease or amaurotic familial idiocy. While this is more common among children of Jewish parents (some 50 to 60 percent of the cases have Jewish parentage) it is by no means exclusive of other backgrounds. Tay-Sach's disease shows a considerable accumulation of ganglioside in the brain, but the most noticeable characteristic is a cherry-red spot on the retina of the eye. Quite often convulsions and spastic paralysis which become progressively worse with time are also present. Treatment attempts have so far been futile, but it is quite likely that advances in biochemistry may promise more hope for the future.

Amino Acids. Probably the most highly publicized of all the metabolic disorders is phenylketonuria or PKU. The condition stems from failure to metabolize phenylalanine because of an absence of a liver enzyme. This results in excessive amounts of phenylalanine and an alternate product, phenylphyruric acid, which are only partly excreted in the urine. During the fetal period, the mother's liver enzyme keeps the level normal. After the child is born, as he begins to take milk, there is a sharp rise in the phenylalanine level and the condition can be detected within a week after birth. The sharp odor of the urine of the child is usually the alerting symptom, and it is also possible to detect the condition through blood tests. If the condition is untreated, the children become irritable, typically have blond hair and blue eyes because pigment formation is interfered with, and become progressively more mentally retarded. Fortunately, mental retardation can be prevented by eliminating phenylalanine from the diet. This condition is the finest example of the remarkable results which can be achieved when early detection and treatment are combined.

Calcium. Fanconis syndrome or idiopathic hypercalcemia is characterized by extensive calcium deposits in the brain. This extremely destructive condition is probably due to a sensitivity to vitamin D and a subsequent inability to metabolize calcium. Other similar conditions may show such symptoms as dwarfed stature and demineralization of the bones, but it is the calcium deposits in the brain which do the damage.

Carbohydrate. The best known of the carbohydrate metabolism disorders is galactosemia. This inability to metabolize galactose, a derivative of lactose (milk sugar), results in vomiting, diarrhea, and colic in the newborn infant quickly followed by extreme malnutrition. Fortunately, the condition can be detected by a urine test, and effective treatment involves the elimination of lactose and galactose from the child's diet.

Closely related to galactosemia is glycogen storage disease, a failure of the body to produce the enzyme necessary for glycogen synthesis. Fortunately, this condition also is controllable through diet; unfortunately, since it is a rare condition, it often is undetected until after considerable damage accrues to the child.

CRANIAL ABNORMALITIES

Disorders which are recognized by abnormal head size, shape, or appearance cannot be strictly included in the time sequence of prenatal conditions. Although the causes probably originate in the prenatal period, often the conditions are not recognized until some time after a child is born and, therefore, could be included in the postnatal period. Since the conditions are unique, and could have any one or several sources, the conditions are included in the prenatal group.

The most often mentioned of the cranial anomalies is hydrocephalus. The name literally means water on the brain. This is a classic example of misnaming since the condition involves an excess of cerebrospinal fluid (not water) and the fluid is usually trapped in ventricles inside (not on) the brain. In the normal course of living, cerebrospinal fluid is manufactured in ventricles located inside the cortex of the brain. A kind of pressure valve releases the fluid allowing it to circulate around the cortex and through the spinal column. When the valve fails to function, the pressure builds up inside the brain forcing it to become enlarged and often causing severe damage. Although there are many variations of the failure to distribute the cerebrospinal fluid properly, (such as failure to absorb the fluid, forcing pressure on the outside of the cortex) the actual causes seem to be related to prenatal infections, intoxications, radiation, and the like; there is no one cause and effect relationship yet established. All of the children have an abnormally large head above a normal size face. This distortion of the bones of the skull is the chief identifying characteristic. In addition, there are frequent associated disorders of vision, hearing, speech, and motor coordination.

If allowed to persist unchecked, severe brain damage and death can result. Fortunately, an operative procedure has been developed which can arrest the build up of pressure by releasing the fluid from the brain. This involves inserting a pressure valve, called a shunt valve, and plastic tube into the ventricle, then running the tube either into the jugular vein or into the heart or abdominal cavity. In either procedure, the mechanical valve opens as fluid pressure builds up and releases the excess fluid so it can be circulated via the blood stream. The procedure effectively prevents further brain damage. However, it should be noted that the shunt valve would not be inserted until after the condition is identified, and that identification is not made until it is observed that the bones of the skull are abnormally large. By this time, it is probable that some brain damage has already been suffered. The shunt valve procedure can effectively prevent further damage, but it cannot compensate for damage already done.

A condition often referred to as the opposite of hydrocephaly is microcephaly. Actually, it is a condition in which the brain fails to develop to normal size, so that the bones of the skull are not pressured to expand. The consequence is a normal face development capped by a receding forehead and a very small or conical skull. At present it is believed that microcephaly may in some cases be genetically transmitted, or it may result from prenatal infection, radiation, some toxics, or injuries. Exactly what the causative agent in any specific case may be is not certain. Furthermore, there is no known cure or even arrest. At the present time prognosis for the condition is not very hopeful. The cause is difficult to determine, there is no known cure, and prevention does not seem possible.

Hypertelorism is a condition in which the child has a wide separation of the eyes due to maldevelopment of the sphenoid bone at the base of the skull. The whole forehead is thrust forward and the skull is wide and flat. Often the distance between the eyes is so great they may appear to be on the sides of the head. Just what the cause may be is not presently known. Neither does there appear to be any effective treatment.

Tuberous sclerosis refers to a condition in which nodules of a potato-like consistency appear as a butterfly shaped rash on the face. Internally, the nodules form on the brain causing severe damage. Accompanying the nodules are tumors in the internal organs as well as in the retina of the eyes. The condition is believed to be genetically transmitted.

Although there are many other medically interesting conditions, most are so rare as to be seldom encountered outside of medical settings. For the most part, those which have been discussed are the more commonly occurring conditions.

Natal and Postnatal Periods

During the period of birth, mental retardation can occur as a result of many causes. The birth process itself can be a traumatic experience, especially in prolonged (72 hours or more) or in very short (20 minutes or less) delivery. Breech delivery, forceps accidents, umbilical cord strangulation, and the like may seriously injure the child. Fortunately these difficulties are rather rare and so the vast majority of children are born relatively unscathed. Occasionally damage does occur, but only occasionally.

After a child has been born, he is vulnerable to many of the potential causes of retardation that were discussed in the prenatal section. Poisons, accidents with head injuries, poor diet, infections, and lack of oxygen all may take a toll. Each may be serious in its own right, but two kinds of infection are particularly destructive, meningitis and encephalitis.

Meningitis is an infection of the protective membranes which cover the brain, the meninges. The infection may result from different causes including virus, bacteria, or protozoa, but the effect is an inflammation which destroys the protective membranes and cells in the central nervous system. One problem associated with the infection is that it often occurs in epidemic form, affecting many people in a given geographical area. A second problem is that specific cases may affect different membranes so different kinds and extent of damage occur. At present, attempts at either prevention of the infection or limiting the extent of damage have not been very successful.

Encephalitis is similar to meningitis, except that instead of the membranes being infected, the brain itself is inflamed. Encephalitis is caused by a viral infection and often occurs in epidemic proportions, but there appear to be several different types, each probably associated with a specific viral strain. Lethargic, St. Louis, Japanese, and equine encephalitis refer to the behavior or origin associated with the infection. Equine, for example, is believed to be harbored in horses and spread to people by mosquitos. Fortunately serums have been developed for prevention and treatment. Unfortunately, the infection develops so rapidly that some damage is apt to occur before the treatment can be effective. At least it is possible that universal immunization may some-day be an accomplished fact, and mental retardation from this source may disappear.

CULTURAL–FAMILIAL RETARDATION

Causes which can be pinpointed and described account for only about 15 percent of the total retarded population. The remaining 85 percent do not have a readily identifiable cause and so are classified as cultural–familial in origin. Not only is this the largest group, but the individuals so classified are the least retarded, falling in the moderate and mild or educable categories. In IQs they range from the high 40s to 80 or 85.

The term cultural–familial implies that the cause of the retardation is to be found either in the culture or in hereditary characteristics or some interaction between the two. The usual practice is that if no cause for the retardation is obvious, the condition is classified as cultural–familial. Thus, the cultural–familial classification emerges as an example of negative assignment. It is the label pinned on a youngster when no other cause can be found. It is often referred to as the waste-basket, the category into which any case is dumped which does not exhibit the characteristics which allow precise classification by cause. Despite the virtual uselessness of the term for any purpose—etiology, sociology, psychological, or educational planning—from an educational viewpoint it is important at least to try to identify causative elements.

Heredity. Gregor Mendel's theories of the transmission of parental characteristics through dominant and recessive genes, first found application to mental retardation in the writings of Henry Goddard. When he was Superintendent of the Vineland Training School in Vineland, New Jersey, Goddard found a retarded patient named Ruth whose ancestors could be traced through four generations to a soldier in the Revolutionary War of 1776. Goddard called the man Martin Kallikak (which literally means good and bad), because Martin apparently great-great-grandfathered two families. *The Kallikak Family* (1912) was Goddard's description of the two families and his attempt to relate the genetic theories of Mendel to the field of mental retardation. According to the account, the side of the family which eventuated in Ruth was started as a result of the union of Martin Kallikak and a barmaid (presumed by Goddard to be mentally retarded). The progeny were thought to have inherited mental retardation from the barmaid mother and a recessive gene for retardation carried by Martin Kallikak. This recessive gene which allowed a dominant characteristic to appear when paired with the recessive genes from the mother was believed to be responsible for four generations of retarded persons. Goddard's proof of mental retardation was a long family record of social failure ranging from shiftlessness and drunkenness to crimes of violence.

The contrasting study resulted from the marriage of Martin Kallikak to a girl from a reputable family. This union started four generations of solid citizens. Because no social incompetence was evident in this side of the family tree, Goddard concluded that mental retardation was a recessive characteristic which could be transmitted genetically, but would not appear unless a similar recessive gene was furnished by the other parent.

The seemingly incontrovertible evidence of two sides of a family tree with a common male founder, one side nearly totally socially incompetent, the other nearly all pillars of society, was enough to convince many people of the validity of the genetic basis of mental retardation. Fortunately, many modern writers (Wallin 1955, Kirk 1964) have called attention to the fact that Mendelian theory cannot account for social depravity, that there is no proof the barmaid was retarded in the first place, and that environmental influences were not accounted for at all on either side of the family. These criticisms have helped serious scholars to more precise examination of both heredity and environment. Particularly, it is now certain that intellectual behavior cannot be traced to a single gene either dominant or recessive in either the father or the mother or both. As a corollary, social incompetence is no more the inevitable consequence of mental retardation than is social competence the birthright of the gifted.

With the demise of the dominant–recessive inheritance theory of mental retardation, references to the role of heredity in retardation came largely from the studies of identical twins reared together and reared apart. Newman, Freeman, and Holzinger (1937) demonstrated that correlations of IQ scores among siblings were about .50, identical twins reared together, .88, identical twins reared apart, .70, fraternal twins reared together, .63, and fraternal twins reared apart, .50. Erling-meyer-Kimling and Jarvik (1963) in their summary of research on the hereditary basis of intelligence concluded that heredity can account for about half of the intellectual performance. Reed and Reed (1970) identified the intelligence of parents and related this to the percent of children who were mentally retarded. When both parents were retarded, of 217 children examined, 85 or 39.5 percent were retarded. When one parent was retarded, of 1736 children 195 or 11.2 percent were retarded. When neither parent was retarded, of 7035 children only 64 or 0.9 percent were retarded. Citing the report of Kemp (1957) that where the mother was retarded, of 352 children, 112, or 31.8 percent of the children earned IQs of less than 75 and another third scored between 75 and 90, as well as Akesson's (1961) report from Sweden that 53 percent of the brothers and sisters of retarded children were also retarded, they make a strong case for sterilization as a way of preventing mental retardation. It is the contention of Reed and Reed that from a third to a half of the number of retarded persons could be eliminated through sterilization. Support for this position comes from the report of Heber, Dever, and Conry (1968) that 45.4 percent of the mothers who had IQs below 80 produced 78.2 percent of the retarded children found in their sample.

However, even if the relationship of the correlation of identical twins reared apart is accepted as the contribution of heredity to intellectual functions, the .70 correlation means that only about half of the total functioning can be considered hereditary ($.70 \times .70 = .49$). Other factors contribute the additional 51 percent. Furthermore, in Akesson's study, while half of the siblings were retarded, half were not. Heredity, therefore, cannot be isolated as the sole culprit.

Environment. Jensen's (1969) excellent review of the nature of IQ identifies many of the environmental factors which affect intellectual performance. These include both the physical and the social environment of the child. Such things as a protein-rich or protein-poor diet are part of a growing child's physical environment. So also are birth

weight, birth order, and multiple births. The social environment includes emotional interaction, child rearing practices, family values,
family models, and whether language is used as a medium for thought
or primarily for behavior control. In addition, in the social environment, the kinds of intellectual behavior which are encouraged because
the parents reward them are of critical importance. Essentially, children
tend to repeat behaviors which have a favorable consequence and to
eliminate acts which do not bring them satisfaction. Thus, consistent
reinforcement of intelligent behavior tends to fix a pattern of behaving
intelligently while inconsistent rewarding, ignoring, or punishing this
behavior tends to cause the child to refrain from repeating the acts.
Similarly, the finding by Sears (1957), that creative thinking in young
adults is associated with a rich childhood fantasy life which has been
encouraged by parents, identifies another crucial area of the social
environment.

Jensen has suggested that environmental influences act as a
threshold much as nutrition is a threshold for physical growth. It is
his contention that a diet rich in proteins, vitamins, and minerals is
necessary for optimum growth but will not influence physical height
much beyond the genetically determined limits set by the genes contributed by the parents and grandparents. Short ancestors have short
children and a rich diet will not make them tall. Severe nutritional
deprivation, however, can significantly stunt growth. Likewise, severe
social and sensory deprivation can have a limiting effect on intellectual
development, but an environment rich in sensory and intellectual
stimulation cannot overcome the genetic limits with which a child is
born.

This rather compelling argument is far from settled, but results
from early intervention programs such as those of Kirk (1958), the
Jensen report of the Gray and Klaus studies (1966) and the Durham
Education Improvement Program (1966), and the review of programs
by Bereiter and Engelmann (1966) indicate gains among culturally disadvantaged children averaging no more than 10 IQ points. Obviously
if the average is about 10 IQ points, then roughly half of the children
showed lesser gains than 10.

At present, it would appear that even massive environmental
intervention efforts will not result in IQ gains of very noticeable proportions. However, mental retardation is defined in this book as a

condition of intellectual arrest below Piaget's level of formal or hypothetical thought. None of the studies have used this description. They have dealt only with IQ scores. Since IQs are presently not translatable into levels of thinking, it appears that there is no ready conclusion which can be drawn regarding the effect of environment on mental retardation among the cultural–familial group. No doubt there is a relationship, but it is presently obscured.

A suggestion by Jensen may be seriously considered as an alternative to inaction, however. That is his finding that learning style is considerably influenced by training. Working with children who came from low and middle socioeconomic backgrounds, Jensen argues that simple association type learning, which he calls Level I, develops rapidly in both socioeconomic groups. Level II learning (which he calls conceptual or cognitive learning) develops more slowly, reaching prominence between the ages of four and six, but is consistently more evident in the performance of the middle socioeconomic status children. Furthermore, typical educational procedures emphasize understanding relationships (cognitive tasks) rather than simple learning relationships (associational tasks). In learning that $2 + 2 = 4$, for instance, cognition requires the understanding that a set of two combined with another set of two equals a set of four and that the sets of two must have certain identical properties in common or they will not combine. At the associational level, $2 + 2 = 4$ can be taught as a conditioned response with no understanding. Jensen believes that since Level I thinking is a strength of the lower socioeconomic group children, educational methods should depend upon this ability. It is interesting that teachers of mentally retarded children have emphasized concrete teaching methods for several decades, not because of any theoretical orientation, but because experience has demonstrated the effectiveness of the approach. It is comforting to find this time-honored practice now being supported by research evidence.

More important, however, Jensen's description of Level I associations is strikingly similar to Piaget's sensory-motor and intuitive thought while his Level II or cognitive learning is similar to the concrete-operational level of Piaget. It is unfortunate that Jensen's work has been confined to young children since it could easily be speculated that if his children could be studied for another six to eight years, he might discover the same phenomenon observed by Piaget; the emergence of even more complex thought processes.

Summary

It has been pointed out in this chapter that a very small percent (about 15 percent) of the total population of the retarded have causative factors which can be clearly identified. The remainder (some 85 percent) have obscure etiology. The educational significance of this large group is not completely obvious. To be sure the cultural–familial group is the largest, least limited, most like the nonretarded in appearance and behavior and most likely to appear in public school. From a treatment point of view, it now seems plausible that fully half of the retardation is due to some inherited mechanism which makes it impossible for them to effect the neurological change necessary for developing more complex thought processes with maturation. Whether educational intervention can materially affect the condition is not certain. It is certain that educational methods can be consistent with their level and style of learning and therefore be effective in imparting knowledge and satisfactory behavior patterns. Whether the abstract thinking ability of the youngsters can be improved is an unanswered question. The absence of well designed teaching strategies can have a stunting effect on learning, but whether the presence of even excellent teaching can overcome the limited thought processes is at present doubtful.

Perhaps an illustration from botany is not too far-fetched to consider. For the maximum development of any plant, a seed needs liberal supplies of water, sunlight, minerals, fertilizer, and optimum temperature. Yet massive applications of any one or combination of these elements will not increase either the size or quality of the plant very much. On the negative side, deficiencies in the supplies of any of the elements—continued cold temperatures, lack of sunlight, water shortage, mineral or fertilizer lacks—can have a serious effect on plant growth. As a parallel in intellectual growth, the absence or restriction of any of the environmental influences may have a seriously limiting effect on intellectual development. But adequate exposure will allow development only within the range imposed by the inherited limitations of the child. At present this amounts to only about a maximum of half of his final functioning level and is quite probably much less. That is, environmental stimulation does not appear to be capable of making it possible for all children to develop the kinds of thought processes described by Piaget as those of hypothetical or formal thought.

This capability seems to be governed by hereditary endowment and may, therefore, someday be influenced by biochemical intervention. Until such a day dawns, as professional educators it appears that we must attend to providing as rich environmental influences as we can as early and continuously as possible even though our efforts will probably not be completely successful.

References

Atlas of Mental Retardation Syndromes. U. S. Department of Health, Education and Welfare, Social and Rehabilitation Services, Rehabilitation Services Administration, Division of Mental Retardation, July 1968.

Benda, Clemens E., *Mongolism and Cretinism.* New York: Grune & Stratton, Inc., 1946.

Bereiter, Carl and Siegfried Engelmann, *Teaching Disadvantaged Children in the Preschool.* Englewood Cliffs, New Jersey: Prentice-Hall, Inc., 1966.

Bolton, J. Shaw, Richard J. A. Berry, and R. G. Gordon, *The Mentally Defective: A Problem in Social Efficiency.* New York: McGraw-Hill, Inc., 1931, p. 137.

Carter, Charles H., *Medical Aspects of Mental Retardation.* Springfield, Illinois: Charles C Thomas, Publisher, 1965.

Collman, R. D. and A. Stoller, "Epidemiology of Congenital Anomalies of the Central Nervous System With Special References to Patterns in the State of Victoria, Australia." *Journal of Mental Deficiency Research,* Vol. 6, 1962.

Down, J. Langdon H., "Observations on an Ethnic Classification of Idiots," in Thomas E. Jordan, ed., *Perspectives in Mental Retardation.* Carbondale, Illinois: Southern Illinois University Press, 1966.

Erlingmeyer-Kimling, L. and Lissy J. Jarvik, "Genetics and Intelligence: A Review." *Science,* Vol. 142, No. 3598, 1963, pp. 1477–1478.

Goddard, Henry H., *The Kallikak Family.* New York: The Macmillan Company, 1912.

Heber, Rick, *A Manual on Terminology and Classification in Mental Retardation.* Monograph Supplement to *The American Journal of Mental Deficiency,* Vol. 64, No. 2, Sept. 1959.

Heber, Rick, Richard Dever, and Julianne Conry, "The Influence of Environmental and Genetic Variables on Intellectual Development," in H. J. Prehm, L. A. Hamerlynck and J. E. Crosson, *Behavioral Research in Mental Retardation.* University of Oregon Press, Rehabilitation Research and Training Center in Mental Retardation, 1968, pp. 1–22.

Jensen, Arthur R., "How Much Can We Boost I.Q. and Scholastic Achievement?" *Harvard Educational Review,* Vol. 39, No. 1, Winter 1969, pp. 1–123.

Kirk, Samuel A., "Research on the Education of the Mentally Retarded," in Harvey A. Stevens and Rick Heber, eds., *Mental Retardation: A Review of Research.* Chicago: University of Chicago Press, 1964.

Kirk, Samuel A. and G. Orville Johnson, *Educating the Retarded Child.* Boston: Houghton Mifflin Company, 1951.

Lejeune, Jerome and Raymond Turpin, "Chromosomal Aberrations in Man," in Thomas E. Jordan, ed., *Perspectives in Mental Retardation.* Carbondale, Illinois: Southern Illinois Press, 1966, Part 7, pp. 210–220.

Liley, A. W., "Liquor Amnii Analysis in the Management of the Pregnancy Complicated by Rhesus Sensitization." *American Journal of Obstetrics and Gynecology*, Vol. 82, No. 6, 1961, pp. 1359–1370.

Newman, H. H., F. N. Freeman, and K. J. Holzinger, *Twins: A Study of Heredity and Environment.* Chicago: University of Chicago Press, 1937.

Penrose, L. S., "Observations on the Aetiology of Mongolism." *Lancet,* Vol. 267, 1954, pp. 505–509.

Reed, Sheldon C. and Elizabeth W. Reed, "Who Are the Parents of the Retarded Children?" *Focus on Exceptional Children*, Vol. 1, No. 8, January 1970, pp. 5–7.

Sears, R. R., E. E. Maccoby, and H. Levin, *Patterns of Child Rearing.* Evanston, Illinois: Row, Peterson, 1957.

Spemann, H., *Embryonic Development and Induction.* New Haven, Connecticut: Yale University Press, 1938.

Tredgold, A. F., *A Textbook of Mental Deficiency*, 7th ed. Baltimore: The Williams & Wilkins Company, 1947.

Turkel, Henry (anonymous), "A Treatment for Mongolism—Stymied by FDA." *Prevention*, March 1970.

Wallin, J. E. Wallace, *Education of Mentally Handicapped Children.* New York: Harper & Row, Publishers, 1955.

Webber, Elmer W., *Educable and Trainable Mentally Retarded Children.* Springfield, Illinois: Charles C Thomas, Publisher, 1962.

Winchester, A. M., *Concepts of Zoology.* Princeton, N. J.: D. Van Nostrand Company, Inc., 1970.

Zimmerman, F. T. and B. B. Burgemeister, "Analysis of Behavior Patterns Following Glutamic Acid Therapy," *Archives of Neurology and Psychiatry*, Vol. 81, 1959, pp. 639–648.

CHAPTER 4

Psychological
Aspects
of Retardation

Behavior characteristics attributed to the mentally retarded have generally reflected the sophistication with which people were able to make comparisons. Before the development of tests like the Binet and Wechsler, comparison with age peers was necessarily limited to unsystematic observation of pretty gross behaviors. Words like dumb, stupid, ament, incompetent, foolish, childlike, defective, deficient, subnormal, feebleminded and dull, eloquently testify to the poor regard accorded the condition. From a scientific standpoint they are frustratingly vague. The impossibility of precisely matching two people on dullness or stupidity or childlikeness is certainly a deterrent to serious study. Classification by common consensus does little to further research.

With the arrival of the Stanford revision of the Binet, the descriptions became more meaningful. Mental retardation was identified as below average performance on the tests. Therefore mentally retarded persons demonstrated poor memory, vocabulary, reasoning, judgment, foresight, association, and logic by comparison with their age peers. David Wechsler's tests allowed professionals even greater precision by including the verbal skills in which the retarded demonstrated limited information, poor comprehension, few arithmetic skills, difficulty in describing similarities, restricted vocabulary, and problems remem-

91

bering numbers. In performance they were inept at completing pictures, arranging pictures into a related story, putting colored blocks together to form a design from a picture, putting together picture puzzles, and associating forms with numbers.

It is curious that even with the specific scores from the subtests of the Wechsler available to researchers, no catalog of limitations seems to have tried to find the upper limit of information or comprehension demonstrated by ten-year-old children with IQs of 75 or 50 or 25. Limitations have been expressed only as relative deviations through the IQ score, but it might be helpful if the kinds of information, comprehension, and other lacks were identified. Such a cataloging might at least point some directions to better understand the reasons for the deficiencies. Even better, it might provide information which could lead to greater insights into the nature of the condition. What has persisted has been an imprecise noting that the retarded are inferior to average youngsters in memory, language, information, understanding, reasoning, judgment, foresight, association, and problem-solving. No one has indicated by how much or in what ways.

Learning Characteristics

Descriptions from the writings on the condition of mental retardation vary from some or a few of those characteristics to rather elaborate and detailed lists. One of the most complete is presented by Ingram (1953). Drawing from over 30 years of observation and work, she grouped the educable retarded by chronological age and listed characteristics in motor, social, and mental trait areas. Under mental traits she listed:

CA—5, 6, AND 7

Mental ages equal to three- to five-year-old average children.
Slow perceptions and associations.
Poor quantity and quality of ideas.
Not curious about people or things.
A "now" sense of time.
Able to name only one or two objects in a picture.
Complete a man with only one or two details.

Rote memory for four digits or for a short sentence not successful until about CA of 7.

Cannot count to 4 or 5 until about CA 7.

Colors not recognized until CA of about 7.

Vocabulary from 25 percent to 50 percent below average.

Define objects by use.

Can discriminate forms like square, circle and triangle.

Can do simple puzzles by CA 7.

Can copy a square and circle but not a diamond.

CA—8, 9, AND 10

With an MA of 6, they can learn to read.

Poor memory for images.

Poor logical memory.

Time is associated with events, for example, 12 o'clock, lunch.

Do not understand similarities and differences.

Vocabulary is from 25 percent to 35 percent below the eight-year-old standard.

Still define objects by use.

Picture descriptions are naming or actions.

No self-criticism—any response is acceptable.

Cannot associate so have difficulty adapting to new situations.

CA—11 AND 12

Mental ability similar to seven- to nine-year-olds.

Increasing ability to concentrate.

Rote memory good.

Still poor memory for images.

Still poor logical memory.

Can tell time.

Poor association of months with seasons.

Emerging concern with "what" and "why."

Better definition of objects.

Concrete description of pictures—no interpretation.

Self-criticism is increasing but success is still an elusive concept.

CA—13, 14, 15, 16, AND OLDER

Mental ability equivalent to eight- to ten- or eleven-year-olds.

Good memory.

Comparison, generalization, and abstraction weak or lacking.

Definition of abstract words cannot be formulated.
Striking lack of creative imagination.
Adverbs not commonly used.
Vocabulary of 7,000 to 9,000 words compared with 15,000 for average child.
Increasing ability to learn in practical situations.
More adequate adaptation in new situations.
Better observation of details of the environment.
Greater general interest.

No IQ ranges were presented by Ingram, so it is difficult to know just what these descriptions mean. It is doubtful that an eleven-year-old with an IQ of about 50, for example, would be capable of telling time with the same precision as an eleven-year-old with an IQ in the high 70s. From the viewpoint of MA alone, the MA of one would be about five and a half while the other would be over eight and a half. A difference of three years in mental age is apt to be quite significant, especially in academic performance. Despite that criticism, Ingram has given serious attention to the job of providing some indication of the level of mental activity appropriate to given chronological ages. This practical listing has served to give teachers behavioral expectations which have made education practices realistic.

In 1958, Goldstein and Seigle provided a description of the characteristics of educable mentally retarded children which attempted to deal with both the nature and some of the consequences of the condition. Primary characteristics were identified as those which are built into the child. His low IQ as a rate of learning and his low MA as a level provided the key for all the educational provisions. Consequences of the primary characteristics or perhaps corollaries to them were such things as frustration, self-devaluation, and specific learning disabilities. The learning disabilities were identified as a tendency to oversimplify concepts, poor ability to generalize, short memory and attention span, limited incidental learning, and restricted language. The educational program presented was specifically aimed to strengthen these weaknesses and to circumvent those areas which did not respond to the efforts to strengthen.

The departure of Goldstein and Seigle from traditional listings is most significant because they concentrated almost exclusively on learning dimensions. After identifying the IQ as an indicator of rate and MA for level of learning, the specific learning disabilities they examined were the traditional ones which have been the primary research domain of educational psychologists for over half a century. They aimed at providing guiding principles which teachers could use as a base for educational efforts. If a child were poor in incidental learning, then those knowledges and behaviors typically learned by nonretarded children rather incidentally would need to be presented in an appropriately planned manner, or the child would be denied the opportunity to learn. That is, his retardation almost guarantees serious gaps in his knowledges and skills because he will not learn well from his environment, and if the school curriculum does not include things usually learned incidentally by other children, the net effect of this double neglect can be serious.

Other learning disabilities which generalize their effects were apparently seen by Goldstein and Seigle as more important considerations than simpler behaviors like reasoning and seeing likenesses and differences, because they are basic to all learning. In defense of earlier writers, it should be noted that prior to 1960 very little actual research had been done to find out about the learning behavior of the retarded, and therefore information on the phenomena of transfer, incidental learning, memory, attention, and association was not available. Nevertheless, Goldstein and Seigle were perceptive enough to apply basic learning data to program development. This made their work something of a milestone in the field.

By 1968 several other authors had extended the work of examining the behavior of retardates relative to learning behavior. Smith (1968) provided a most comprehensive analysis of research on learning behavior as a basis for clinical teaching. After reviewing research in each of the areas of learning Smith comes to specific conclusions and then suggests how teachers may circumvent the deficit discussed. In regard to short-term memory he says

> The literature strongly suggests that retarded youngsters exhibit significant weakness. . . . Their ability to store auditory or visual material over a few seconds or minutes is decidedly poor.

Long-term memory is seen by Smith as one of the few areas in which a weakness is not apparent. In his words:

> Long-term memory deficits in retarded individuals have not been observed when comparisons were made with intellectually normal sub-

jects. . . . Generally, retarded youngsters were able to remember material as well as normal subjects if (1) they have overlearned the fact or concept beyond a minimal criterion level and (2) they have had an opportunity to reinforce this learning through constant use.

Discrimination learning studies typically requires the person to choose from a group of things or objects which have some specific characteristics in common. Although these typically are color, shape, symmetry, or position, an almost endless variety of possibilities can be used. Smith concludes that in this area:

> The studies which have contrasted retarded and normal children in discrimination learning are inconsistent in the directions of their findings.

and then adds a note that:

> caution should be exercised in generalizing these findings to all populations of retarded youngsters since, in many cases, trainable-level children were used as subjects in these studies. The applicability of these findings to the educable child remains somewhat speculative.

Learning set, or learning to learn, is demonstrated by any individual when he is able to show that practicing solving problems of one type reduces his time or errors in solving similar but somewhat different problems. Retarded children do learn to learn. In Smith's view:

> The ability to establish a learning set seems to be directly related to MA, (however) the retarded children seem to be slower in establishing a learning set (than normal children). (*parentheses added*)

Incidental learning, the learning of something to which attention is not directed specifically, is believed by Smith to be related only slightly to the condition of mental retardation.

> Although the retarded appear to have the potential for making use of stimuli which are incidental to a direct task, the empirical evidence . . . is fragmentary.

These conclusions from the review of relevant research by Smith in the areas of memory, discrimination, learning set, and incidental learning are quite similar to other reviews (Ellis 1963, Robinson and Robinson 1965, Stevens and Heber 1964). The continuing theme of inferior learning performance displayed by the retarded is evident in all the reviews of research. However, most of the reviews treat only the conclusions or findings of the studies and are not detailed concerning the conditions under which memory, for instance, is deficient. To understand the psychological aspects of mental retardation it is appropriate to review recent studies in a little more detail.

MEMORY

When memory is studied, an individual is required to learn something. Sometime later he is tested to find out how much he remembers. The first task in memory investigation therefore involves learning. Learning in turn requires a person to pay attention to some stimuli and to discriminate between relevant and irrelevant stimuli. Furthermore, to remember it is necessary to arrange information in some manner for storage purposes. What appears to be a simple matter of comparing the memory of the retarded with the nonretarded becomes an enormously complex job of comparing the part played by attention, discrimination, information arranging (often called clustering) for storage and retrieval immediately as well as after a considerable passage of time to the total area of memory.

Two theories invented to clarify the presumed poor memory of the retarded were the "leaky bucket" and the "peanut brittle" theories. The leaky bucket notion held that information leaked out of the retarded in equal amounts regardless of what kind of information it was. The peanut brittle theory held that some kinds of information were retained, but that some other kinds were not. Before much formal research got underway, both theories were discarded because they were global and did not deal with the specific elements of memory.

Probably the first really significant finding came from the work of Zeaman and House (1963). These two investigators became interested in learning styles and launched a whole series of studies in this field. One of their discoveries was that when learning curves were reversed so they revealed the number of trials needed to reach the desired level of learning, mentally retarded children made a great many errors of a purely random nature. Once they seemed to "catch on" to what was required, they learned as rapidly and skillfully as nonretarded children. Further study of this phenomena convinced Zeaman and House that retarded children were not able to direct their attention to find the right cues to allow them to learn. They therefore felt that one of the major characteristics of retardation was an attention deficit. This was demonstrated in studies which showed that retarded youngsters were inferior in short-term memory, but equal to other children in long-term retention.

Ellis (1963) observed the same phenomenon but explained it in different terms. He felt that since short-term memory required a sufficiently strong stimulation of the neural cells to cause them to become excited electrochemically, a central nervous system which was inferior would not be as sensitive as one which was intact. He therefore speculated that mentally retarded children suffered from a deficient stimulus trace and therefore demonstrated poor short-term memory because the stimuli could not register their impact on the neural cells of the brain. The good long-term memory of the retarded simply meant that the materials had been presented long enough or strongly enough to overcome the stimulus trace deficit. His contention was given considerable support when Baumeister, Hawkins, and Davis, (1966) found that retarded youngsters learned considerably better under conditions of five to seven second stimuli exposure than under one to four second exposure. Such a finding does not, however, rule out the possibility that better attention focusing can take place in five to seven seconds.

Arguments over whether Zeaman or Ellis is correct, whether the problem is psychological or physiological, learned or constitutional, qualitative or quantitative, are futile. They can only be settled by further research. What is not arguable is the fact that retarded youngsters waste more time in random, trial and error efforts than do normal children in the initial stages of learning, but once they find out what to do they learn at the same rate as their peers. In memory studies, retarded children do more poorly than normal children because they learn less in the same period of time. Indeed Logan, Prehm, and Drew (1968) found that retarded and normal children were equally good in recall when adjustment was made for the amount learned in the first place. From the foregoing discussion it can only be concluded that the retarded are not deficient in either short- or long-term memory if they have a sufficient opportunity to learn the materials in the first place.

Another aspect of memory has to do with the manner in which individuals store information. Although good agreement can be found to support the notion that various systems are used to reduce the amount of information to be remembered, it was believed that the retarded did not typically use information reduction systems very effectively. Stedman (1963) was one of the first to study this problem with the retarded. In association learning tasks, he found that the retarded did impose a system on the materials to be learned, but they used contrast and coordination whereas the normal children used more abstract methods' such as actions, synonyms, and superordinate sets. Spitz (1963) did a series of studies in the same area and reported that providing the retarded with verbal labels for classifying helped them remember. Then Madsen and Connor (1968) found that the retarded used clustering and information reduction as well as normal college students when the available categories were known to them.

Many other studies related to the memory area provided additional information. Like normal children, retarded youngsters had difficulty learning when items were highly similar, when interpolated materials were introduced, when no opportunity for practice was given, and when competing stimuli were presented. And like normal children, overlearning improved retention, and distributed practices were superior to massed presentations.

From the information presently available it appears that retarded children spend more time than normal ones making random errors before they catch on to what they are supposed to do, and have few category labels, especially of the more abstract variety, to use for clustering data for storage; but when they find out what they are supposed to do, and when they have labels available, they can learn as rapidly, reduce information as efficiently, store as well, and remember as accurately as normal children. They are just as susceptible as normal children to interference such as competing stimuli, retroactive inhibition, lack of opportunity for overlearning and practice, but are no more so. The time-honored report of poor memory does not seem to be true. The deficit appears to be an inefficiency in the initial aspects of learning which can be explained either by an attention problem (psychological), or a deficient stimulus trace (physiological), and a problem in using abstract systems for categorizing and storing information. Their ability to learn and remember is decidedly related to mental age.

TRANSFER

The ability to transfer is often referred to as learning set, generalization, or learning to learn. Smith's review of the literature led him to the conclusion that transfer was related to mental age and slower for retarded than for normal children. However, the voluminous literature on transfer in the field of educational psychology clearly demonstrates that transfer can take place in two ways: either by application of identical elements, or by use of principles. Identifying elements in new situations which are identical to those from previous experience apparently cues behavior which has been successful in the past, thus allowing a person to use previous experience in present solutions of problems. This is generally considered a concrete, non-abstract, and relatively uncomplicated procedure. Applying a known principle to the solution of a hitherto unmet problem allows for considerably more flexibility of application, but requires a high degree of abstraction ability. Curiously, only one study has dealt with the method of transfer. All the other studies have been concerned with whether the retarded do transfer. They do. Orton, McKay, and Rainey (1964) however, taught two groups of educable retarded youngsters to read Roman numerals. One group was taught by a rote method, the other was taught the principle upon which the numeral system is based. Later they were given Roman numerals to read in large numbers which they had never seen before. The group which had been taught by rote did better than the group which had learned the principle. Apparently transfer by identical elements was easier for the retarded than transfer by application of principle. Although the issue suffers from limited data, it appears that the retarded do transfer and that they use the mechanism of identical elements rather than principle. Furthermore, the characteristics of proneness to frustration and self-devaluation discussed by Goldstein and Siegle can be understood readily as resulting from a failure set or negative transfer. That is, life experience which has been filled with inadequate performance can quickly make a person gun-shy of new encounters. The expectancy of failure and the ability to recognize rather quickly the cues of early stages of failure can lead to reduced efforts for success. Thus both failure proneness and self-devaluation may not be based on generalization by principle, but rather on the accurate recognition of the identical elements of failure from previous failures.

INCIDENTAL LEARNING

The presumed inability of retarded children to learn incidentally has been one of the most persistently noted characteristics. Even though Goldstein and Siegle mention this as a deficit, a study by Goldstein and Kass (1961) does little to support such a claim. Retarded children were shown a picture for one minute during which time they were instructed to point out all the 2s in the picture. Later they were asked to recall all the things that were in the picture. Their ability to recall those incidental items in the picture was compared with young, bright children whose mental ages were equal to those of the retarded. The retarded recalled more items but because they were less accurate than the bright children, the total scores for both groups were equal. Likewise Oliver (1963) and Singer (1964) did not find the retarded inferior in incidental learning. Finally, Williams (1968) examined the ability of retarded children to associate written numerals with pictures and dots and found no evidence of deficient incidental learning.

In view of the evidence that the retarded are not inferior in incidental learning one wonders why this theme of inferiority persists. A possible explanation may lie in the nature of the subject matter usually included in discussions of incidental learning. Most often matters of morals, values, manners, and bits of common knowledge are presumed to be the things learned incidentally. In middle-class culture these common elements are so taken for granted as to be considered obvious. A somewhat closer look at child rearing practices reveals that these subjects are not so incidental as is often supposed. Great care is taken to assure that middle-class children say "Please" and "Thank you," that males rise at the entrance of women, and that amenities are observed. Punishment of violators of social mores is swift and rewards are sure. In addition, models of adequate behavior are plentiful with parents, relatives, and friends playing adult roles with consistency and certainty. It would be difficult for a child in such an environment not to know quite a lot about current political, national, and athletic heroes. In such an atmosphere rules of participation are constantly emphasized and the ethic of accomplishment is a pervading fact of life. Children from less affluent backgrounds not only are often deprived of adequate models after whom they can pattern behavior, but are more often subjected to inconsistent reinforcement in child rearing practices. Often they have their experiences outside the home severely restricted because their available life space includes little beyond the boundaries reached by the local methods of transportation. Added to these restrictions is the fact that language is typically used to satisfy the affective needs of the moment. Because of this, information bits commonly available in middle class homes may seldom be discussed in lower class ones. It is difficult to estimate the crippling effect of such language restriction on the intellectual development of children, but it must be substantial. It may also contribute to the restricted fund of information attributed to the retarded and add its contribution to the persistent notion of limited incidental learning of the retarded.

It appears that the characteristic of limited incidental learning is not properly assignable to the retarded. Instead, it would be more appropriate to consider deficiencies in general information, rules of courtesy and the like in relation to cultural background differences. Interestingly enough, even though the retarded do not show a deficient ability to learn incidentally, the schools still must do what they can to compensate for the limited cultural influences in the backgrounds of many of the children. In short, they still need to treat the children as though they show deficient incidental learning.

SOCIAL LEARNING

The self-concept of any individual is dependent upon his success or failure in daily living. Cromwell (1963) has pointed out that the evaluation of success or failure is very much a personal matter contingent upon the meaningfulness to the individual of the consequences of his behavior. The problem became a focus for research attention when Ringelheim (1958) used a digit symbol task in which the retarded children were required to finish 50 boxes. Half the children were stopped 10 short of the goal; the other half were allowed to reach the goal. Ringelheim found that even in the face of objective failure, the children who were stopped short did not perceive of their performance as being a failure. Subsequent studies aimed at determining the meaningfulness of failure to the retarded. Heber (1959) found the retarded worked harder for a high value incentive than for a low value one, thus demonstrating they could and did recognize differential values. The MAs of the youngsters studied by Ringelheim were about 4 or less while those in Heber's study were only slightly higher. Chinn and

Kolstoe (1969) studied the effects of a promise of a reward, a low tangible and a high tangible reward on concept-switching tasks. They found the children showed no difference in performance under the three reward conditions. However, the children in this study had MAs of about seven.

It appears that at lower mental ages, there is little discrimination of values. By the time the children have MAs of seven, however, they are able to attach their own meaning to rewards. This looms as a most significant finding since mental age appears to be the critical element in a child's assigning meaning to rewards.

The relationship of mental age to meaningfulness of rewards provides an explanation of two other questions of motivation which were raised by Cromwell—approach-avoidance and locus of control.

The locus of control got its first systematic attention when Zigler investigated a notion proposed by Kounin (1941) that retarded children had difficulty switching from one activity to another because of psychic rigidity. Kounin had borrowed the idea from Lewin (1940) who suggested that the boundaries between psychological fields for the retarded could account for stereotype or rigid behavior. After a series of studies, Zigler (1965) came to the conclusion that the rigid behavior of the retarded was due to their desire to prolong contact with adults, so that their performance was actually dictated by whatever strategy seemed likely to bring them adult attention. Zigler felt that deprivation of satisfactory emotional interaction because of home or institutional environment triggered the reaction and gave rise to children whose behavior control came from outside influences. When Cromwell and his students (1963) developed an instrument for measuring whether behavior was influenced more by internal or external factors, a host of studies using internal locus of control (ILC) and external locus of control (ELC) children were pursued. Perhaps most significant was a study by Bailer (1960) reported by Cromwell (1963). This investigator found that ILC correlated with mental age about .55 but that it seemed to emerge at a somewhat later age than it does for normal children.

One of the difficulties encountered by Cromwell and his students was that they found few of the young retarded children who were success-strivers. That is, they did not seem to be motivated to do those things which would lead to success in problem-solving. Bailer's results, however, provided an explanation. It appeared to Cromwell that young children and those with low mental ages reacted on a pleasure-approach and pain-avoidance principle. With increased mental maturity they responded to the success-striving and failure-avoiding principle, but because they experienced a considerable amount of failure they tended to adopt primarily failure-avoiding strategies. The mental age therefore was definitely related to the locus of control; internal control became dominant as rewards became meaningful, that is, as they recognized failure and success. For young children failure was defined as lack of approval from adults; hence their behavior reflected ELC. Only later was the locus of control internalized. This was ably demonstrated by McGee (1968). In an ingenious study this investigator used a modified shooting gallery to test the effects of feedback information of a controlled nature on the shooting accuracy of retarded children. Using educable retarded children aged ten to thirteen, he presented different patterns of scores which were rigged by a remote control button on the machine. Among the more significant findings were:

1. Performance in response to successful or failure scores was highly variable for those children whose IQs ranged from 50 to 58.
2. Performance was highly predictable for the group from 68 to 75 IQ.
   a. Shooting accuracy declined after continued increased scores.
   b. Shooting accuracy declined after continued decreased scores.
   c. Shooting accuracy increased under conditions of moderate success or failure.

Thus it appeared that those children whose mental ages were below seven demonstrated little response to objective feedback information of success or failure. Those children whose mental ages were above seven apparently had learned to internalize success and failure and so responded to feedback information on how well or badly they were performing in the same manner as normal children do.

In the social sphere Festinger (1957) provided a general social theory which held that individuals strive for self-evaluation and that in doing so they compare their own performance to that of other persons who are similar to themselves. People who are different are generally shunned because the comparisons do not provide accurate feedback information. The application of Festinger's theory of social comparison to the mentally retarded was made by Reynolds (1960).

Reynolds speculated that the mentally retarded would probably be imprecise and frustrated in their own self-evaluation because there would be few people of their own ability level with whom they could compare their abilities and attitudes.

In a test of this thesis, Kuehn (1969) used a modified Asch (1956) technique in which youngsters were shown a line of a certain length as a stimulus and asked to choose from among three other lines the one which was the same length as the stimulus line. The trick in the procedure was that each child was asked to identify his best friend. During the actual experiment he was told which line his best friend had chosen so it was possible to identify the degree to which he would conform to choices made by his friend. Kuehn found the retarded youngsters (CA ten to fifteen, IQ 40–90 with a mean of 68) to be both inefficient and inaccurate in their judgments and to show virtually no conformity behavior. Thus it would appear that at least at this age level the retarded did indeed behave as Reynolds predicted they would, but they did not seek each other's company as Festinger's theory would predict. In short, inadequate social behavior seems to be a corollary of mental retardation and would appear to be a most important aspect in need of educational focus. In other words, retarded children need to be taught to make social comparisons. Since this seems to be related to internal locus of control, it would appear that mental age might be a significant influence on successful learning. While no definitive information related to this question is presently available, it seems safe to speculate that the mental age of about seven may mark the dividing line between probable success and failure.

In summary, it appears that:

1. The learning of the mentally retarded is mental age specific.
2. Initial learning is haphazard but once they understand what is to be done they learn at the same rate as normal children of similar mental age. Whether this initial learning problem is psychological or physiological is not yet established.
3. Their learning style is concrete. Information reduction and gathering for storage purposes is apt to be based on obvious relations such as contrast and coordination rather than the more abstract systems like action, synonyms, and superordinate sets.
4. They are just as susceptible to learning interferences from the presen-

tation of similar materials, interpolated information, competing stimuli, and lack of practice as other children.

5. They transfer by identical elements rather than principle.

6. They learn incidentally as well as normal children of equal MA, but their cultural backgrounds tend to make them appear to be deficient in behavior amenities and this has made them appear to be poor in incidental learning.

7. They pattern their behavior on the pleasure-pain principle up to about a mental age of seven, but adapt the success-striving versus failure-avoiding strategy beyond that level. However, there appear to be few success-strivers compared to failure-avoiders. This is probably a consequence of a history of failure.

8. Social inadequacy is a pervading corollary of mental retardation.

The foregoing list of characteristics must be considered only tentative. At the present stage of knowledge the research support is merely suggestive and will probably remain so until research studies are superseded by research programs. The interactions among chronological age, mental age, IQ, child rearing, and environmental influences have not been studied at all. Furthermore, the possible effects of educational intervention by various techniques and at various ages are also unknown. Great progress has been made in understanding the psychological concomitants of mental retardation since 1960, but efforts so far are minuscule by comparison with what still remains to be done.

Theories of Behavior

How people behave and what rules or principles govern behavior have been the focal concerns of psychologists ever since psychology divorced itself from speculative philosophy in the middle of the 1800s. As groups of like-minded psychologists have crystallized their techniques of the study of man's behavior, schools of thought have developed their unique explanations of behavior. While each theory treats behavior in general and does not attempt to cover mental retardation by itself, the theories have necessarily been expected to be applicable to this aspect of human behavior also. Although there is no shortage of theories from which to choose, the dominant theories and therefore those which have been applied to the retarded include dynamic, Gestalt or sensory, and various aspects of behavioristic psychology.

DYNAMIC PSYCHOLOGY

Freud has developed probably the most elaborate of the dynamic descriptions of behavior. In his various writings he has been concerned with human development in nearly all its dimensions, but primarily in personality. Fundamental to all behavior Freud believed that Eros, a striving for life, and Thanatos, a death wish, provide the basic motivation for behavior. This energy is directed by three structures. Primitive drives emanate through the id which is the seat of the animal instincts. The superego was described as a stern and inflexible conscience—the source of moral and ethical behavior. These competing forces are mediated by the ego which is the structure through which the individual maintains a balance between the primitive drives and conscience in the day-by-day reality of living. This system of checks and balances operates throughout the lifetime of the person and although the emphasis changes as a function of the developmental level of the person, the basic drive is broadly sexual. At the most basic level the source of satisfaction is oral. Not just the physical area of the mouth, but also the acts involved with eating are included. As the child develops, satisfaction shifts to the anal region, including anal activity and control. The phallic stage of development finds the child deriving satisfaction from the physical sex organs. During the next developmental period, the latency period, areas of the body as a primary source of satisfaction are superseded by exploring and discovering the self. Intellectual as well as physical activities provide the avenues for discovering who one is and what he can do. The final stage of development is the genital stage. Here adult sex activity is the primary role for behavior.

It is Freud's contention that moving from one developmental stage to another is a traumatic experience. Indeed, some individuals may never accomplish satisfactory adult role behavior while others may regress to infantile developmental stages under conditions of severe or prolonged stress. Since Freudian psychology deals with the dynamics of behavior, it is quite understandable that much use is made of abnormal behavior patterns and the theory itself has undergone modifications to make it fit observed clinical and experimental observations.

White (1959–1960) rejects the basic motivational drives of Eros and Thanatos, submitting that the basic drive which motivates all people is the striving for competence, or to use his word "effectance." Effectance is the need to investigate, explore, try out, and control the environment. Furthermore, although he accepts the developmental stages of Freud, White maintains that moving from one stage to another may not be traumatic, because the child is exercising a new kind of control over his environment and thereby demonstrating his effectance or competence. At the adult level, sex as a pervading force must move over to make room for competence as expressed in one's work. However, like Freud, White contends that some individuals may never exercise satisfactory effectance in adult roles and some may regress to previous developmental levels in the face of stress. Since White's theories derive from Freud it is small wonder that they are quite similar. It should be noted that the emphasis on cultural rather than purely biological drives is typical of other interpreters of Freud, but White is somewhat more extreme than some others, for example, Karen Horney (1950).

Mental retardation from a Freudian point of view has been discussed by Robinson and Robinson (1965). These two authors speculate that the retarded would probably show a reduced life energy, that the development from stage to stage would be slower than normal, that each stage of development would probably be accompanied by greater trauma, and that impulse control would probably be deficient because the ego would be weak. Although debating these speculations would not seem particularly fruitful because of lack of empirical evidence, another interpretation could be considered. If Freud's biological basis of behavior is accepted, there would be no compelling reason to believe that the mentally retarded would be very much different in their development from anyone else. That is, they would not be expected to have a reduced source of life energy, be any slower in their movement from one developmental stage to another, nor suffer any more trauma moving from stage to stage than anyone else. Where they could be expected to have difficulty would be in impulse control and during the latency period when intellect supersedes sex. However, if White's notion of the pervasiveness of the need for effectance is accepted, then the retarded would be expected to have great difficulty in development because competence has an intellectual component running through it and mental retardation is, fundamentally, a condition of intellectual incompetence.

At a basic level Freud believed that unconscious desires of the id persistently seek the pleasure satisfactions of the moment. These desires are fundamentally sexual and amoral, so they are constantly evaluated for appropriateness by the superego and when deemed to be inappropriate are held in check or channeled into other more accept-able behaviors by the ego. The suppression of primitive desires Freud termed repression. However repression is only partly successful because the unconscious urges continue to try to assert themselves and to circumvent the ego control. The most usual circumstance for revealing repressed desires is in dreams either day or night. Even in dreams the amoral desires are disguised. That is, dreams have both a manifest and a latent content. The manifest content is the coherent story of the dream itself which generally reflects those things and events experi-enced by the individual during his waking hours. The latent content is often the wish fulfillment expressed as symbols such as doors, bal-conies, and gardens representing females, while candles, snakes, and the like represent males or seemingly innocent events represent wished for forbidden encounters. Even slips of the tongue, names not remem-bered, and tasks or appointments forgotten are deemed to be related to repressed desires.

Because of the conflict between unconscious desires and repression, rational thought is given very little credit by Freud for affecting or controlling behavior. If this is correct, then mental retardation would not appear to be a special case of human behavior except where intellect plays a part in disguised wish fulfillment. Freud identified defense mechanisms or substitute behaviors used instead of desired behavior to reduce frustration: aggression, denial, introjection, regres-sion, isolation, reaction formation, projection, and sublimation were identified as the major defense mechanisms.

Aggression can be either direct or indirect. Direct aggression is physically assaulting the object or person concerned. Indirect aggres-sion may involve making snide or nasty remarks about someone or it may be demonstrated by berating an innocent bystander. In any case, some verbal or physical violence is displayed.

Denial is typically illustrated by a little boy who has been called stupid responding by shouting, "I am not." It may, however, be considerably more subtle as in the instance of pretended sophistication in worldly affairs or a fund of superficial information which passes for knowledge or understanding. Fundamentally there is a thread of pretense which underlies the behavior.

Introjection is the process of adopting into the self other persons or things so that what happens to these things or people is personally felt. Joys or sorrows, triumphs or tragedies experienced by others are as sharply poignant as if they had happened to the person himself. This living through others has the definite advantage of allowing one to be selective.

In regression an individual returns to forms of behavior which had been satisfactory at an earlier developmental level. Often described as childish, regression implies behavior which is essentially inappropriate at the time and circumstance in which it occurs.

Isolation is a form of withdrawal in which the person simply refuses to be drawn into social interaction which may prove painful. At a more personal level, refusing to talk to others or even to leave home may be the principle behavior.

Reaction formation is seen when the person does the opposite of what he may wish to do. A hated person becomes the recipient of unrequited solicitation and concern; a desire for aggressive action is masked by meek and timid demeanor.

Projection in a sense is the opposite of introjection in that the person's deficiencies are identified not in himself but rather as residing in others. Generally this is accompanied by consistent criticism leveled at the behavior deficiency itself, as in a hypocrite refusing to attend church because "Those people are all hypocrites."

Sublimation is the displacement of an instinctual urge into socially approved effort. Strenuous athletic participation as a way of sublimating the sex drive is probably the most common example. To sublimate effectively, however, one must at least recognize the social acceptability of one kind of behavior and the unacceptability of another. This, at least, requires an intellectual recognition not necessarily employed in other defense mechanisms.

Anna Freud in discussing defense mechanisms makes a reference which has clear implications for mental retardation:

> It may well be that before its sharp cleavage into an ego and an id, and before the formation of a super-ego, the mental apparatus makes use of different methods of defense from those which it employs after it has attained these levels of organization.

She then suggests a hierarchy starting with regression at the lowest level followed by projection and introjection, and finally by repression and sublimation. It would seem to do no violence to her list if aggression and denial were equated in complexity with regression while projection, introjection, withdrawal, and sublimation formed a higher level grouping. That is to say, one would rather expect the retarded to employ regression, aggression, and denial with ease, but to have some difficulty in the use of projection, introjection, withdrawal, and sublimation because of the intellectual components of the mechanisms.

In summary, the principal area in which mental retardation cannot be adequately accommodated by Freudian theory would be in the kinds of defense mechanisms employed. Should striving for effectance as proposed by White be assumed to be the basic drive rather than the biological drives as suggested by Freud, it is obvious that mentally retarded individuals would appear to be at a distinct disadvantage by comparison with normal persons. However this would assume that the retarded are competent to judge accurately their incompetence relative to normal people. Since there is considerable doubt that this assumption is viable, it seems that dynamic psychological theory should be applied to the retarded with great caution.

GESTALT PSYCHOLOGY

Prior to 1910, nearly all study of human behavior was patterned after the extraordinarily successful methods of the physical sciences. Atomic weights and the periodic table provided a model which allowed the arranging of chemical elements in an orderly fashion. Psychologists apparently felt that human behavior could also be reduced to similar elemental units which could then be subjected to the same kinds of manipulations and predictions which were so useful in chemical formulae and physical laws. This belief was given even further credence when biologists presented a careful classification system of plants and animals in terms of phylum, class, order, family, genus, species and subspecies, or variety. Since man could now be precisely placed in a complexity relationship to other animals, animal experiments were granted a mantle of acceptability of great moment. That is, man was assumed to be capable of nearly all the behaviors observed in all animals of less complexity than man plus behaviors, such as speech, which were not possessed by lower animals. By describing animal behaviors accurately, and subtracting these behaviors from the observed behaviors of man it would be possible to extract those things which make man human.

In order to arrive at a delineation of humanness, however, it was necessary to identify the elements or basically irreducible units of behavior much as the elements in chemistry could be distinguished from compounds. This was elemental psychology, the study of basic behavior units. It encompassed such diverse areas as the study of instincts, reaction time and stream of consciousness reports. Experience, it was contended, was made up of the sum of the elemental units which were fused, blended or associated into something meaningful.

About 1910 Wertheimer investigated the "phi phenomenon"—the fact that two lines separated by space and physically stationary when exposed successively at a given rate will appear as a moving line. This is the same phenomenon which makes moving pictures "move" even though they are physically only a series of still pictures. Wertheimer and his colleagues reasoned that the phi phenomenon could not be explained as consisting of the simple sum of its elemental parts. It had to be understood in its wholeness or totality, not as discrete elements. They went on to develop Gestalt psychology which became a protest movement against all the schools of established psychology.

According to Heidbreder (1933):

> The protest was neither mild in character nor limited in scope. The new school demanded nothing short of a complete revision of psychology.

The term Gestalt was apparently used in two ways. First it was used to refer to a property of something such as shape or form. Second, it was used to refer to an entity in which shape or form was only one of its attributes. In any case since there is no exact equivalent for this German word in the English language, several synonyms such as shape, form, and configuration have come into common usage. While none is completely acceptable, it appears that the word "form" is probably the least objectionable. In most instances the term Gestalt is used to refer to the unique relational properties which make a thing recognizable, such as a theme in music or the squareness of a cube.

As the movement gathered momentum, the Gestalt psychologists extended their investigations to include the study of other perceptual phenomena similar to the phi. The fact that we see and recognize a square table regardless of the angle from which it is viewed is another case which proves that our perceptions are something more than a simple adding or fusing of the sensations received. Extension of this recognition to other instances, such as distance and size, led the Gestalt psychologists to contend that the whole is greater than the sum of its parts, and that perception involves the organizing and relating of sensations into a meaningful form.

Once the Gestalt psychologists rejected the elemental interpretation of sensations, they were led to a wholeness theory of brain excitation. This theory held that sensations excited the brain as a total electrical field and these sensations were thus interrelated because the brain operated as a unit. Further extension of the theory led to the speculation that when a child was born, the neural relationship potential was already intact and needed only experience to provide meaning.

In addition, these workers came to accept a new form of thinking which had not been considered previously. This they called insight. They explained insight as the seeing of relationships which were new or unique without any apparent or systematic or even logical deductive or inductive preceding activity. The sudden solution to problems, the recognition of order in apparent chaos, the detecting of similar elements in seemingly dissimilar arrangements, were believed to emerge because all parts of the brain were interconnected and simultaneously stimulated. Thus the commonly observed "ah ha!" solution to puzzles was granted a scientifically acceptable explanation. In so doing, they did not completely reject the idea that learning could occur as a result of simple conditioning, but they did contend that the mere elaboration of S–R bonds could not and did not account for insight.

The electrical field explanation of brain function was little changed until 1949. At that time D. O. Hebb published a theory of neurological function which grew out of his work on experimentally induced neurosis in rats. Hebb had observed that when rats were stimulated to action and then prevented from carrying out that action that they exhibited bizarre behavior of an uncontrollable nature. He reasoned that the controlled behavior was a reflection of total excitation of the brain, but that controlled behavior could only result when well differentiated and fairly limited numbers of neural cells and connections were involved. From this, Hebb developed his theory of perceptual organization which is currently the most widely accepted explanation of brain function.

Hebb believed that at birth the brain is made up of billions of neural cells which have no or little specific assignment of activity. The first observed behaviors of children reflect this lack of differentiation in that the child reacts in a massed or global manner. That is, his reaction to pain is a total reaction involving all the parts of his body. As the infant matures, the child begins to be more selective. He learns, for example, at the sight of a bottle at feeding time to begin reaching and sucking movements which he has discovered to be successfully related to relieving the discomfort induced by hunger. In like manner, other and more elaborate behaviors develop in response to additional sensations he encounters.

The explanation of total neural excitation proposed by the Gestaltist psychologists could not account satisfactorily for differentiated behavior because the rather specific behaviors seem to involve only a few rather than a great many brain cells. Furthermore, it seemed more likely that the same group of behaviors were somehow related and therefore were probably controlled by activity in a localized area of the brain rather than involving all of the billions of neural cells which made up the brain. Hebb, therefore, proposed that the development of the organization of behavior consists of the excitation of groups of related cells which respond to fairly specific sensory stimulation relayed to them by the nerves from the receptor organs. Visual stimuli, for example, are probably only generally excitatory to the newborn infant. As the child sees the same things repeatedly the stimuli become meaningful and he develops responses which are relevant to those stimuli as, for instance, the reaching at the sight of his bottle.

The basic mechanism for this differentiated behavior is called a cell assembly. The cell assembly is a group of adjacent cells which become related through repeated excitation by sensory stimulation. Visual stimuli, for instance, are channeled to the visual area of the brain and cause an electrochemical reaction to occur in the cells. Repeated sensations cause groups of adjacent cells to react (fire), so that a consistent reaction (reverberating circuit) occurs each time the same or a similar visual sensation is received. This consistent neural reaction to sensory stimuli makes it possible for the individual to perceive what he is seeing as something which has been seen before, and thus to recognize the object. Sensory perceptions, therefore, are possible because groups of adjacent cells become related by repeated sensory excitation and fire in an orderly manner thus forming a reverberating electrochemical circuit or cell assembly.

The elaboration of cell assemblies into sequential activities is called phase sequence. Essentially this is an intercellular relationship among cell assemblies which makes possible orderly behavior such as the sequence of motor movements in walking or the recognition of forms like squareness. Phase sequence can explain the phi phenomenon, but it does so on a differentiated rather than a global basis.

The most complex level of neural activity is called phase cycle or superordinate association. Phase cycle is an integrative activity in which the cell assemblies and the various intercellular associations may be called upon to make a selective contribution to the total ongoing activity. Both phase sequence and phase cycle apparently take place through the enlargement and multiplication of synaptic knobs, so that the transmission of excitation can go from the cell assemblies through synaptic bridges to the associative structures. Problem-solving may thus involve individual perceptions, sequential perception and concepts, and the arranging of bits and pieces of information to produce a new set of relationships among the neural connections. This may be analogous to building a house. The cell assemblies can be thought of as the nails, boards, bricks, and other elements for building, which need to be made first. The use of the elements to form the foundation, walls, floors and roof would be analogous to phase sequence. The total house, like phase cycles, results when the elements and related parts are integrated into a meaningful structure. Obviously this is a rough analogy, but is probably not too far-fetched to be reasonable.

In order for Hebb's theory to be workable, some controlling mechanism must be involved. This is believed to be the hypothalamus at the top of the brain stem. It acts as a switchboard allowing sensory stimuli to be channeled to the correct area of the brain, and in return channeling neural impulses to the proper organs and muscles for the execution of desired behavior.

Although this explanation of neurological function does not explain behavior, it does explain how the behavior of human beings is physiologically possible. Moreover, while Hebb's theory refutes the Gestalt notion of total electrical field function of the brain, it can accommodate the phi phenomenon as well as insight. The phi phenomenon can be explained as a function of phase sequence, in that independent perceptions (cell assemblies) are related in a meaningful sequence of form. Insightful thinking is possible because superordinate associations or perceptions and concepts from different cell assemblies and sequences are related in new ways through the integrated circuitry of the neural cells. The quarrel between Hebb's theory and Gestalt theory is only in how perceptions develop, not in the way the perceptions function once they have been formed.

An attempt to relate Hebb's theory to the condition of mental retardation was first made by Benoit in 1959 commenting on the effective use of large materials used by Itard and Seguin in teaching retarded children he explains:

> . . . Hebb's theory assumes that the spread of stimulation at the sensory surface is associated with a more abundant excitation in the higher centers of the nervous system, and that perceptual structures arise more readily; superordinate structures emerge more easily because there is then a greater number of points at which interfacilitation can take place.

Benoit suggests not only using large things for teaching perceptions, but also a multisensory approach precisely because it increases the number of points at which interfacilitation can take place. At the same time he explains the success of a simplified approach with children whose perceptual processes are destroyed by brain damage because:

> . . . attention is controlled through the delivery of facilitation from one organizational structure to another. Accordingly, the successful induction of new learning may require the elimination or minimizing of irrelevant stimuli, until interstructure facilitation has been developed enough to permit the easy channeling of in-coming stimulation to the appropriate organizational structures.

Kephart has focused on the learning tasks of children who have suffered brain damage. He contends that these children have inadequate or undeveloped synaptic bridges for developing basic cell assemblies. Accordingly, his teaching approach aims at the development of intact reverberating circuits by carefully controlled redundancy exercises. This involves the repetition of perceptual exercises using a vast variety of media so that the perceptions will generalize to the more complex activities of phase sequence and phase cycle. Thus Hebb's theory has been applied to the teaching of children who have difficulty developing cell assemblies and superordinate associations as well as children whose neural connections are incomplete or inefficient because of brain damage.

BEHAVIORISM

At about the same time that the Gestalt psychologists sought to revolutionize the field through their studies of apparent motion, John B. Watson emerged from an intensive study of the behavior of animals to declare that the only legitimate way to study man was as an animal and therefore with the techniques used to study animals. His new school of study, behaviorism, rejected any attempts to study man from the inside. Stream of consciousness reports, feelings, the phi phenomenon or anything which suggested a dualism of mind and body were considered outside the realm of legitimate study. The focus was only on behavior.

Watson was not only highly influenced by his own study of animals, but also by the conditioned reflex studies of the Russian psychologists, particularly Pavlov. Conditioning was believed to be the mechanism through which all learning took place. In the original experiments of Pavlov, a bell rang simultaneously with the presentation of a meat powder. It was discovered that eventually the experimental dogs salivated when the bell was rung even without the meat powder being present; the bell became a cause of the salivation response. Watson came to believe that all large units of behavior were simply elaborations of the original stimulus–response connections. Two outgrowths of the movement were particularly important, first, the objective character of the data collected, and second, the fact that the data was quantified.

Objectivity and quantification greatly enhanced the scientific respectability of the psychological data collected. Furthermore, the drive for objective data increased the reliance on statistics, not only for comparative information, but also for designing the studies in the first place. The inclusion of statistical methods in turn made it possible to engage in experimental studies designed to provide if–then, cause–effect, or stimulus–response information.

By the 1940s the stage was set for behaviorist psychologists to attempt to systematize the field. This was first proposed by Clark L. Hull at Yale. Borrowing from statistical methodology for relational data and the logical positivist philosophers, Hull attempted to identify psychological laws which applied to animal behavior. Hull proposed that the behavior of animals reflected learning and that learning was demonstrated by repeated behaviors which became habitual. He expresses this relationship as sH_R or habit strength. Working backwards from learning curves obtained under various conditions of learning, Hull and his students derived the mathematical formulae which fitted the curves obtained and deduced from the formulae the effects of several variables on the speed of learning. The basic formula of sH_R was N^{10}, where N was equal to the number of reinforcements given the animals. He subsequently found that if the animals were deprived of food or water for long periods of time and so made very hungry or thirsty, this increased their speed of learning. Therefore the variable D or drive equal to the amount of deprivation had to be included in the equation. Likewise the magnitude of the reward (K) and the delay in presentation of the reward (J) affected the learning. The basic formula for predicting the speed of learning was expressed as the excitatory potential of the animal: $sE_R = sH_R \times D \times K \times J$. Other variables which affected learning were investigated in much the same manner and included in the basic formula in an attempt to derive mathematical laws which apply to all animal learning, including that of the animal man.

Unfortunately learning is expressed as drive reduction; that is, when a thirsty animal is given water, this reduces his excitatory potential and it is obvious that not all human behavior can or is rewarded by giving a person food or water. So far, the experimental work has been largely done with animals. Where application has been made to humans, it has largely been an attempt to find out whether the laws derived from animal learning apply and how. At the present time, no universal set of laws has been discovered.

Certainly the effect of behaviorism on the study of man has been substantial. Nearly all of the experimental work in psychology uses the techniques of control developed by the behaviorists. Also, statistical analysis requires that groups of people rather than individuals be studied, so that experimental studies have attended to group behavior. In addition, the effort to study the effect of a single, uncomplicated variable rather than many variables has added a kind of exactness to psychological study previously neglected.

The application of behaviorism to mental retardation has been most extensively done by Cantor (Ellis 1963). In a series of studies Cantor and his colleagues used a curve-fitting approach, a comparative approach, and a noncomparative approach. Cantor summarizes the application of the theory to the study of mental deficiency by saying:

> To the extent that such research helps to verify any of the various Hull–Spence postulates, or to show in what fashion they are inadequate, to this extent will behavior theory benefit from the activity and to whatever extent behavior theory benefits, the understanding of defectives' behavior cannot help but be improved, assuming, of course, some degree of fruitfulness in the Hull–Spence approach.

It is precisely at this point that Skinner and his followers part company with the Hull–Spence approach; on the question of fruitfulness. Behaviorists who work in the Skinnerian domain confine their attention exclusively to the stimuli and responses. They studiously avoid any discussion of intervening variables or hypothetical constructs used to explain the relationship between the stimuli and responses. Instead they concentrate on observing the behavior consequences produced when stimuli are manipulated. Although the operant conditioning group is interested in S–R connections, their interest is somewhat different. For example, they pay little attention to drive reduction as reward. The primary characteristic of a reward is any event or object which either increases or decreases the frequency of a response. As such, rewards become highly personal and encompass an almost endless list of events or objects which qualify as modifiers of behavior.

The actual principle of operant conditioning is quite simple: behavior is increased or decreased as a function of its consequence. Positive reinforcers are those consequences which increase the frequency of behaviors. Negative reinforcers are those consequences which decrease frequency of behaviors. In practice, rewards are given to a child when he has done what the experimenter wishes him to do, as a positive reinforcement, in the expectation that this will increase the frequency of the desired response. Withholding the reward in situations where nondesired behavior occurs helps to extinguish (eliminate or decrease) the nondesired act. Aversive rewards as punishment for undesirable behavior are also used for negative reinforcement, to extinguish a response.

Operant conditioning, behavior modification, and contingency reinforcement are all names for the same technique. Although the procedure derives from behavioristic psychology, it differs in some important ways. First, the behavior attended to is the response, not the S–R connection. Second, the technique is applied to individuals, not groups. Third, elaborate research designs are not generally used. Fourth, statistical analysis involving probability is not a necessary part of the procedure. Because of these differences, it may appear that operant conditioning is many light years removed from the scientific rigor of behavioristic research. Such is not the case. Even though this is applied psychology, the technique is as precisely applied as in any comparative study.

The application involves three phases: identifying the behavior, gathering baseline data, and consequating the response. Each requires accurate observation and complete objectivity. To use the technique successfully the behavior to be modified must be an overt act of some kind. This can be a positive act such as hitting someone or it can be negative such as not looking at a book. Inferential behavior descriptions such as "seems hostile" or "immature" or "low frustration tolerance," do not lend themselves to the method. Furthermore the circumstances which precede the overt behavior need to be carefully noted because they may be reinforcing the behavior and will need to be controlled. Once the behavior which is to be modified is pinpointed, it is necessary to determine whether this is rather isolated behavior or whether it is part of a chain of related behaviors and if so whether it is at the beginning, in the middle or at the end of the chain. If a behavior is to be changed, its temporal position will have a great influence on whether to deal with it directly or whether to concentrate on some other behavior in the chain.

Once the behavior to be modified has been identified, it is necessary to gather baseline data. Fundamentally this is a count of the frequency with which the behavior occurs. However, counting by itself does not provide an accurate indication of frequency unless it is converted to some meaningful ratio. Thus number of times per minute in successive samples of observations in a given time interval will need to be recorded. Since this is the base used to determine whether the behavior modification has been successful, it is obvious that the same kind of ratio must be used in later stages of the procedure to find out if the rate of behavior occurrence has actually changed.

Consequating the behavior effectively demands equally precise techniques. First of all, a reward has meaning only to the individual. What may be meaningful to anyone depends entirely upon his personal likes and dislikes. Furthermore, even within our likes, each of us likes some things better than others and even these likes may change in value under different circumstances. While a T-bone steak may be highly rewarding to a hungry man, it is not seen as very desirable after one has just finished eating a big dinner. Rewards, therefore, must reflect meaningfulness. Because of this, experimenters have used rewards which range from edibles to toys, money, tokens, smiles, pats on the head, and even free time in which a person can pursue his own activities. Second, the rewards must be issued only a little at a time so the behavior being reinforced is sustained. These considerations of what and how much are critical to the success of the procedure.

The actual consequating of the behavior must follow immediately after the behavior. Thus a systematic delivery system is mandatory. In addition, the issuance of rewards on different schedules generates different curves of learning so the practitioner has to decide whether rewards will be given 100 percent of the time, 50 percent, a third of the time, or on a random or intermittent schedule. In practice, at the beginning of the procedure, rewards are usually on a 100 percent schedule. As the behavior is modified, a partial reinforcement schedule is maintained. Then when the behavior becomes fairly stable, intermittent reinforcement is used. Furthermore, at the beginning usually highly desired rewards such as food are used with social rewards such as praise being gradually introduced to replace the tangible rewards as the behavior stabilizes.

Unless accurate records are kept and compared with the baseline data there is no way one can tell whether the procedure is succeeding or not. Rigorous attention to all details throughout the entire sequence of activities and constant checking of progress require the utmost objectivity. Furthermore, the effectiveness of different kinds of reward and different schedules of reinforcement in effecting behavior change, and the interventions required to sustain the change call for scrupulous monitoring. Data collection is therefore as scientifically respectable in this procedure as in any other. Theory building is not a necessary part of the procedure because the operant conditioning psychologists attend only to what is effective in changing behavior and what conditions facilitate change, not on determining why. Laws of behavior are empirically determined and therefore do not need to fit a hypothetical-deductive theory system.

The application of operant conditioning to the mentally retarded has been extensive and universally successful. Lindsley (1964), Haring and Schiefelbusch (1967), Lovett (1967), Homme (1966), Spradlin (1963), and Walker (1969) have written in great detail on the successful application to the retarded. However, the fact of retardation is an irrelevant consideration because the relative IQ is an intervening variable which does not affect the procedure. The technique is applicable to lower animals and to all levels and conditions of man, so it is as usable with the retarded as any other group. Above all, it is fruitful in changing behavior. Because of this it is attracting a host of followers, particularly among teachers who find it most applicable to children whose classroom decorum is troublesome and disruptive. One limitation is evident, and that is that while the technique is useful in modifying overt behavior, there is virtually no data relating the effectiveness of the procedure to the development of higher thought processes. That is, those cognitive functions which are used in problem solving at a hypothetical or propositional level have apparently not been systematically studied to determine the applicability of the technique. Until such time as its usefulness in this area is demonstrated, the technique will have to be considered useful but limited.

SUBJECTIVE BEHAVIORISM

In 1960, Miller, Galanter, and Pribram published a treatise which rejected the concept of the behavioristic reflex arc as a controlling unit of behavior. Some doubt had been cast on the adequacy of stimulus–response connections even with elaborations as early as 1931. At that time Lashley's attempts to find a relationship between the impairment of specified abilities and related brain injuries indicated a given part of the cerebral cortex was not related. He did find a relationship between the amount of destruction and the degree of impairment but not the location. This apparently meant that more complex performance requires a larger amount of operating brain tissue than do simple acts so, logically, the reflex arc could not be considered the controlling unit of behavior. Other objections to behaviorism stem from the fact that it does not consider the study of consciousness within the legitimate realm of psychology. This, in essence, poses a mind–body dualism; anything associated with mental behavior is highly suspect unless it can be shown to be related to the body. Studies of intelligence, aptitude, attitudes, and moods, which require the conceptualization of mental variables for adequate examination, were either ignored or reduced to overt behavior terms if they were dealt with at all. In no sense could man as the master of his fate or captain of his soul be accommodated in behaviorism. Man was the victim of his reflexes and the environmental circumstances in which he dwelled. As disconcerting as this conceptualization of man might be, it was not so objectionable as the assertion that behavior was a fit subject for study, but how one feels, believes, or thinks is not.

Miller, Galanter, and Pribram began their criticism of strict behaviorism by trying, vainly, to explain hypnotism, instincts in animals, individual differences in intellect, aptitude, attitude and feeling, and mental illness in a behavioristic schema. As they failed in this endeavor, they concluded that the reflex arc was an inadequate mechanism for accounting for behavior. Their speculations led them to the consideration of other possible mechanisms. After considering all of the possibilities from Gestalt and dynamic psychologies, they settled on the feedback loop or servosystem as the only feasible explanation. Fundamentally, they rejected the reflex arc because (1) it could not account for mental phenomenon, (2) it was helplessly mechanistic, (3) it could not explain personal variability in behavior, and (4) it did not account for self-initiated behavior.

As they continued their criticisms, they came to believe that somehow the human organism has his own unique view of the world, that he interacts with the world on his own terms, that he determines his own course of action and that he continually tests the effectiveness of his actions against the criteria of whether they are satisfactory to him.

If they are not, he then modifies his behavior in a manner determined by himself to achieve a satisfying result.

In order to make it possible for a feedback loop explanation of behavior control to operate, the human organism itself became the center of the system. Miller, Galanter, and Pribram proposed that each person develops an Image of the world which is the total of his needs, desires, knowledge, and thought processes. The Image is relatively stable, but since the Image is influenced by learning, it changes as a function of experience. The individual is not the same yesterday, today, tomorrow, and always, but change usually takes place gradually enough that his personality is recognizable from one time to the next. The Image works like a thermostat or many thermostats in that it sets the standards or expectancies for the person, determining to what he will pay attention. Each person sets his standards by Plans which are consistent with his Image and which are roughly analogous to "set." They are the goals of the person and at any given moment may be simple or complex, immediate or long range, fixed or flexible, sketchy or elaborated.

The operating mechanism for the whole system is the feedback loop called TOTE. This is an acronym made up of the first letters of Test, Operate, Test, Exit which Miller, Galanter, and Pribram believe carry the information in the feedback loop. TOTE is described as the means by which sensory information is carried from the receptor organs to the brain where it is tested against the standards of the Image for congruity. If the sensory information is in harmony with the expectancies of the individual, the ongoing activity of the person continues according to the Plans which initiated it. If there is an incongruity between the feedback information and the standards, the organism acts to reduce the incongruity (operates). The effect of the action is again tested and if the incongruity is reduced the unit exits. Since every sense impulse is evaluated, thousands upon thousands of TOTE units must be handled simultaneously and/or sequentially and each unit would be intimately influenced by the energizing of every other unit. Changes in Plans and therefore in standards can be immediately effected so the organism can be completely in touch with the world. It should be noted, however, that the world each individual is evaluating is uniquely his own because his expectancies are determined by his own Image of the world. What may be seen by someone else as inappropriate behavior may be completely acceptable to oneself and vice-versa.

Even though research validation of the Miller, Galanter, and Pribram formulation is as yet unavailable, there are a number of compelling reasons why the theory should not be summarily rejected before it is fairly evaluated. First, the theory retains the principle of reinforcement as a facilitation of behavior and ignoring as a method of extinguishing behavior. Therefore the pleasure–pain principle and success-seeking versus failure-avoiding behaviors, including internal and external locus of control, are viable constructs. Second, the theory emphasizes that meaningfulness is a personal variable which determines whether a reward has value. Third, conditioning as a method of learning is retained, but so also are insight and other conceptual relational ways of learning. Fourth, it admits all elements of human activity as suitable for scientific study. Perhaps its lack of exclusivity in the proper subject matter of psychology is its most redeeming feature.

There are also some distinct advantages to the conceptualization:

1. It replaces the inadequate reflex arc behavior control unit with the feedback loop servosystem which can account for self-initiated behavior.
2. It is a dynamic explanation of behavior. At the center of the conceptualization is the recognition that each person has a unique perception of the world but that the perception is a product of the development and experience of the person. Change is therefore an acknowledged central characteristic of people.
3. It can accommodate the major tenets of other schools of psychological thought without serious distortion. For example, the behavioristic conceptualization of intervening variables, (delay of reinforcement, weight of the reward) can be interpreted as affecting the standards of the individual. In Freudian terms, the Image can be likened to the ego. From a Gestalt point of view, the relational aspects of perception become focused through the feedback testing procedure.

These three pluses by themselves recommend the subjective behaviorism of Miller, Galanter, and Pribram.

An application of this behavior theory has been advanced by Kolstoe (1970) in a book on teaching educable mentally retarded children. Central to the application is the assumption that the standards of mentally retarded children would be different from those of the nonretarded only where an intellectual component is involved. In the biological needs for air, food, water, sleep, elimination, and movement there is no reason to predict differences between the retarded and nonretarded. The same would hold true in the area of emotional needs. A difference could be expected in the uniquely human activities like language, learning and thinking. The book on teaching the retarded therefore emphasizes the development of the perceptual, conceptual, language and thinking processes of the retarded and those other behavior areas in which cognition plays a role. Throughout it emphasizes the dynamic and relational aspects of behavior, utilizing the feedback loop concept as the controlling mechanism.

References

Asch, S. E., "Studies of Independence and Conformity: A Minority of One Against An Unanimous Majority." *Psychological Monographs*, Vol. 70, 1956, pp. 1–36.

Baumeister, A. A., W. F. Hawkins, and P. A. Davis, "Stimulus–Response Durations in Paired-Associates Learning of Normals and Retardates." *American Journal of Mental Deficiency*, Vol. 70, No. 4, 1966, pp. 580–584.

Benoit, E. Paul, "Toward a New Definition of Mental Retardation." *American Journal of Mental Deficiency*, Vol. 63, No. 4, 1959, pp. 559–565.

Boring, Edwin G., *A History of Experimental Psychology*. New York: Appleton-Century-Crofts, 1929.

Cantor, Gordon N., "Hull–Spence Behavior Theory and Mental Deficiency," in Norman R. Ellis, ed., *Handbook of Mental Deficiency*. New York: McGraw-Hill, Inc., 1963.

Chinn, Philip C. and Oliver P. Kolstoe, "Concept-Switching Task Performance as a Function of Rewards." *Journal of Experimental Education*, Vol. 37, No. 4, Summer 1969, pp. 21–25.

Cromwell, Rue L., "A Social Learning Approach to Mental Retardation," in Norman R. Ellis, ed., *Handbook of Mental Deficiency*. New York: McGraw-Hill, Inc., 1963.

Ellis, Norman R., "Stimulus Trace and Behavioral Inadequacy," in Norman R. Ellis, ed., *Handbook of Mental Deficiency*. New York: McGraw-Hill, Inc., 1963.

Festinger, L., *A Theory of Cognitive Dissonance*. New York: Harper & Row, Publishers, 1957.

Freud, Anna, "The Mechanisms of Defense," in Eugene L. Hartley, Herbert G. Birch and Ruth E. Hartley, *Outside Readings in General Psychology*. New York: Thomas Y. Crowell Company, 1950.

Freud, Sigmund, *An Outline of Psychoanalysis*. New York: W. W. Norton & Company, Inc., 1949.

Goldstein, Herbert and Corinne Kass, "Incidental Learning of Educable Mentally Retarded and Gifted Children." *American Journal of Mental Deficiency*, Vol. 66, No. 2, 1961, pp. 245–249.

Goldstein, Herbert and Dorothy Seigle, *The Illinois Plan for Special Education of Exceptional Children: A Curriculum Guide for Teachers of the Educable Mentally Handicapped*. Circular Series B-3, No. 12, Springfield, Illinois: State Department of Public Instruction, 1958.

Haring, Norris G. and Thomas C. Lovitt, "Operant Methodology and Educational Technology in Special Education," in Norris G. Haring and Richard L. Schiefelbusch, *Methods in Special Education*. New York: McGraw-Hill, Inc., 1967, Chap. II, pp. 12–48.

Haring, Norris G. and Richard Schiefelbusch, *Methods in Special Education*. New York: McGraw-Hill, Inc., 1967.

Hebb, D. O., *The Organization of Behavior*. New York: John Wiley & Sons, Inc., 1949.

Heber, Rick F., "Motor Task Performance of High Grade Mentally Retarded Males as a Function of the Magnitude of Incentive." *American Journal of Mental Deficiency*, Vol. 63, No. 4, 1959, pp. 667–671.

Heidbreder, Edna, *Seven Psychologies*. New York: Appleton-Century-Crofts, 1933.

Homme, Lloyd E., "Human Motivation and Environment," in University of Kansas Symposium, *The Learning Environment: Relationship to Behavior Modification and Implications for Special Education*. Kansas Studies in Education, University of Kansas Publications, School of Education, Vol. 16, June 1966.

Horney, Karen, *Neurosis and Human Growth*. New York: W. W. Norton & Company, Inc., 1950.

Hull, Clark L., *Essentials of Behavior*. New Haven, Conn.: Yale University Press, 1951.

Ingram, Christine P., *Education of the Slow Learning Child*, 2nd ed. New York: The Ronald Press Company, 1953.

Kephart, Newell C., *The Slow Learner in the Classroom*. Columbus, Ohio: Charles E. Merrill Books, Inc., 1960.

Kolstoe, Oliver P., *Teaching Educable Mentally Retarded Children*. New York: Holt, Rinehart and Winston, Inc., 1970.

Kounin, J. S., "Experimental Studies of Rigidity: I. The Measurement of Rigidity in Normal and Feebleminded Persons," *Character and Personality*, Vol. 9, 1941, pp. 251–273.

Kuehn, George I., "A Comparison of Sociometric Status and Conformity in Educable Mentally Retarded Children." Unpublished doctoral dissertation, University of Northern Colorado, 1969.

Lashley, K. S., "The Studies of Cerebral Function in Learning: The Retention of Motor Habits after Destruction of So-called Motor Areas in Primates," *Archives of Neurological Psychiatry*, Vol. 12, 1924, pp. 249–276.

Lewin, K., *A Dynamic Theory of Personality*. New York: McGraw-Hill, Inc., 1935.

Lindsley, Ogden R., "Direct Measurement and Prosthesis of Retarded Behavior." *Journal of Education*, CXLVII, 1964, pp. 62–81.

Logan, D. R., J. Prehm, and C. J. Drew, "Effects of Unidirectional Training on Bidirectional Recall in Retarded and Non-Retarded Subjects." *American Journal of Mental Deficiency*, Vol. 73, No. 3, November 1968, pp. 493–495.

Madsen, Millard D. and Katherine J. Connor, "Categorization and Information Reduction in Short-Term Memory at Two Levels of Intelligence." *American Journal of Mental Deficiency*, Vol. 73, No. 2, September 1968, pp. 232–238.

McGee, Jerry E., "The Effects of Induced Failure and Success on the Sequential Performance of Educable Mentally Retarded Children." Unpublished doctoral dissertation, University of Northern Colorado, 1968.

Miller, George, Eugene Galanter, and Karl Pribram, *Plans and the Structure of Behavior.* New York: Holt, Rinehart and Winston, Inc., 1960.

Oliver, W. C., "A Comparative Study of Incidental Learning of Educable Mentally Retarded and Intellectually Normal Children." Unpublished doctoral dissertation, University of Northern Colorado, 1963.

Orton, Kenneth D., B. Elizabeth McKay, and Dan Rainey, "The Effect of Method of Instruction on Retention and Transfer for Different Levels of Ability." *The School Review,* Vol. 73, No. 4, 1964, pp. 451–461.

Ringelheim, D., *Effects of Internal and External Reinforcements on Expectancies of Mentally Retarded and Normal Boys.* Ann Arbor, Michigan: University Microfilms, 1958.

Reynolds, Maynard C., "The Social Psychology of Exceptional Children. III. In Terms of the Interaction of Exceptional Children With Other Persons." *Exceptional Children,* Vol. 26, 1960, pp. 243–247.

Robinson, Halbert B. and Nancy M. Robinson, *The Mentally Retarded Child.* New York: McGraw-Hill, Inc., 1965.

Singer, R. V., "Incidental and Intentional Learning in Retarded and Normal Children." Unpublished doctoral dissertation, Michigan State University, 1964.

Smith, Robert M., *Clinical Teaching: Methods of Instruction for the Retarded.* New York: McGraw-Hill, Inc., 1968.

Spitz, Herman, "Field Theory in Mental Retardation," in Norman R. Ellis, ed., *Handbook of Mental Deficiency.* McGraw-Hill, Inc., 1963.

Spradlin, Joseph E., "Language and Communication of Mental Defectives," in Norman R. Ellis, ed., *Handbook of Mental Deficiency.* New York: McGraw-Hill, Inc., 1963.

Stedman, Donald J., "Associative Clustering of Semantic Categories in Normal and Retarded Subjects." *American Journal of Mental Deficiency,* Vol. 67, No. 5, March 1963, pp. 700–704.

Stevens, Harvey A. and Rick F. Heber, eds., *Mental Retardation: A Review of Research.* Chicago: University of Chicago Press, 1964.

Walker, Hill M. and Nancy K. Buckley, *Modifying Classroom Behavior: A Manual of Procedure for Classroom Teachers.* Department of Special Education, University of Oregon, 1969.

White, Robert W., "Motivation Reconsidered: The Concept of Competence." *Psychological Review,* Vol. 66, 1959, pp. 297–333.

Williams, Eddie H., "The Effects of a Readiness Activity on Incidental Learning among Educable Mentally Retarded, Normal and Gifted Children." Unpublished doctoral dissertation, University of Northern Colorado, 1968.

Zeaman, David and Betty J. House, "The Role of Attention in Retardate Discrimination Learning," in Norman R. Ellis, ed., *Handbook of Mental Deficiency.* New York: McGraw-Hill, Inc., 1963.

Zigler, Edward, "Mental Retardation: Current Issues and Approaches." Unpublished paper, 1965.

CHAPTER 5

Educational
Efforts

Education has been an instrument for change in every society which has figured in recorded history. In some civilizations the educational programs concentrated primarily on training the young to carry on the vocations of their elders. Other societies made sure that the knowledge of one generation was faithfully transmitted to the next. It was not until after the renaissance in Europe that education was recognized as a necessary tool in the pursuit of the fullest development of the self.

In the United States, education has been granted a place of honor in our national priorities ever since the earliest colonial days. The Protestant settlers provided schools almost as soon as they built houses, so that their children could learn to read and write. Apparently the chief reason for their concern for literacy was religious. The Protestant revolt taught that each person's relationship with God was personal. Since the search for this personal relationship depended upon holy scripture, it was mandatory that everyone could read the Bible. The practical test of literacy therefore was whether one could read well enough to be able to interpret the lessons of the Bible for personal guidance. Thus most of the early educational efforts stemmed from Protestant religious needs but were aimed at self-development.

As this country grew and prospered, it soon became evident that education had many more uses than purely religious ones. Trade, commerce, farming, and government depended upon the skills and knowledge of homegrown leaders. Since there was no established class system which furnished leaders, competent individuals came to be selected by their fellow colonists and placed in positions of trust. It did not require any great perceptive ability to recognize that a high degree of literacy was mandatory for all but the most routine leadership roles. Soon educational opportunity for all became the birthright of every citizen.

The architects of the American revolution recognized that if political power was to be wielded effectively it was necessary to assure that those in power were educated. Since this new experiment in government placed political control in the hands of the people themselves, it was mandatory that each citizen be informed and knowledgeable. Thus universal education became the instrument which would insure that people could learn about issues and select capable representatives to govern them. A country which espoused life, liberty, and the pursuit of happiness for everyone pinned its very existence on the faith that informed citizens would be the product of a system of universal education.

It is most fortunate that the founding fathers framed the preamble and the constitution in terms which were both humanitarian and vague. Because they did not attempt to define liberty, equality, and happiness, each new generation has been obligated to provide contemporary interpretations of what these terms mean. Thus the laws, rules, regulations, and practices reflect the current conditions of society and remain as modern today as they were at the time they were written. Each generation has provided its own interpretation of the terms, but no generation has seen fit to abolish them. Throughout the history of this country the concepts have changed, but educators have remained faithful to the trust of applying education to develop people who can manage their own lives, who revere liberty, and whose purpose in life is the pursuit of happiness.

As a corollary to the American experiment of equal educational opportunity for all, has been the recognition that a viable society is dependent on the maximum development of each individual in that society. Education has therefore accepted the responsibility for doing three basic things: (1) transmitting knowledge so that each generation can profit from the wisdom of the past, (2) providing a basis for vocations so that people will be equipped to earn a living, and (3) providing for self-realization so each person can develop his unique abilities and interests to the maximum. Sometimes these functions of education may interfere with one another, but most often they complement each other. In any case, each individual is free to decide which purpose he will pursue: cultural heritage, vocational preparation, self-development, or some combination which suits him best.

One result of the multipurposes of education is that education has come to be regarded as a smorgasbord from which one may choose his own diet. Such a conceptualization of education may be acceptable if all persons are presumed to have equal potential for benefiting from the offerings and equally good judgment in their ability to select wisely. That these assumptions are not warranted, has led to one of the great and continuing dilemmas in education—the relationship of individual differences and equal educational opportunity.

Prior to World War I, the opportunity for education was generally available, but no one was required to attend school. Not only was attendance permissive, but there was also no requirement as to how long one was expected to stay in school. The result of this condition was a rather casual attitude toward school: you could go if you wished and leave when you liked. The fluid boundaries of the Western part of this country encouraged those who did not wish to try to prepare themselves to fit into the relatively highly structured Eastern culture where education was a requirement for successful participation, to seek their fortunes in those personal contests with nature—farming, ranching and mining—where educational requirements were minimal.

In the period immediately following World War I several events combined to change education. The industrial revolution had brought about a shift in population concentration from rural to urban living. Cities which became the centers of industry began to experience the problems and complexities which arise when large numbers of people are crowded together into a small place, and educational systems were faced with larger numbers of children than had ever been encountered before. During the actual war years, youngsters who did not adjust well to the schools found it easy and patriotic to find jobs in the war industries, so they were not really a problem. Demobilization, however, was a sudden upheaval. Literally millions of soldiers were dumped into civilian life within a period of a very few months to look for jobs.

As war production ceased, jobs became scarce and this country found itself with a huge surplus of workers where returning war heroes were competing for a dwindling number of jobs with large numbers of adolescents who had been enjoying great prosperity from war industry employment.

Many solutions were tried. The most notable were those involving education. At the college level, a G.I. bill provided financial support for veterans who wished to attend school. This solved the employment problem for thousands of veterans by taking them out of the labor market until industry had a chance to convert from war production to civilian production. At the elementary and high school levels, child labor laws prevented many youngsters from quitting school to seek work, and compulsory school attendance laws caused many children to appear in school who might not have attended very long if any other options had been open to them. This also had the effect of easing the surplus labor pressure.

During World War I a unique problem was encountered in the military. This was a crucial need for leaders who could be trusted to be in charge of groups of men who knew very little about the art of soldiering. The solution to the problem was to select people who could learn quickly and put them through a concentrated program of leadership training, but the question of how to find people who had this ability to learn quickly loomed as a formidable one. The answer was found in psychological tests. Group tests, the Army Alpha test for soldiers who could read and the Beta test for those who could not, were developed, tried out, and found to be useful all in an incredibly short period of time. The men who scored high on the tests did learn rapidly and were good leaders. This development assured the respectability of psychological tests and they became an accepted part of our culture.

The gathering of nearly the entire population of children in the single institution of the nation's schools made individual differences in ability suddenly and painfully apparent. Coping with children with a wide range of ability and interest in academic tasks became a major problem for teachers. Now that school attendance was compulsory, even children of the most limited ability somehow had to be accommodated. Once again psychologists were called upon to help, but this time the psychological tests were needed to select those children who learned slowly and inefficiently rather than those persons who learned quickly, so they could be given an educational program more in keeping with their abilities.

As dissatisfaction with a universal educational diet for persons of widely differing intellectual digestive capacities grew, educators turned to programs which had been successful with children of limited abilities to see if they could be used in public schools. The programs they found had been successful largely in Europe although some few were being used in America. Thus, most of the early attempts at education of the retarded in this country were copies or modifications of programs which had been started in Europe as early as 1800.

Jean Marc Gaspard Itard: 1774–1838

Itard lived in Paris during a time of lively philosophical controversy between the nativists and sensationalists over the nature of man. The nativists held that man's abilities were determined by heredity and that because these abilities were fixed they would emerge almost regardless of the kind of environment a person grew up in. The sensationalists believed that each person was the product of his environment. Taking their lead from the writings of John Locke, they believed that each person's mind at the time of his birth was a *tabula rasa*, a blank paper to be written on by experience. Experiences, to the sensationalists, were the sensory impulses which were heard, seen, smelled, felt, or tasted in man's daily living. Man's innate perfection became warped by his contacts with an imperfect world, so man himself became what the world made him. To the nativists, education was important only for those persons who had inherited good abilities to begin with, but should never be wasted on the ill endowed. To the sensationalists, education was viewed as an important instrument for modifying behavior; important almost to the point of sacredness and certainly not to be taken lightly.

Itard also grew up in a time of military conscription. Since he came from a business family, he at first prepared to go into business, but as the threat of conscription became more real, he abandoned his business career plans to become an assistant surgeon on the medical staff of the Institute for Deaf Mutes under the direction of Jacob

Rodriguis Pereire. Apparently Itard was an able physician; in any case he published a treatise on diseases of the ear in 1821. More important, as he witnessed the responses of his deaf-mute charges to educational efforts, he became more than ever convinced that man was very much a victim of his environment and that education was a powerful tool for shaping behavior.

In 1799 a wild savage was captured in the woods of Caure by hunters. He subsequently escaped, but was captured a short time later when he was seen entering an abandoned house and was trapped in it. He was delivered to the Abbé Secard Bonaterre, Professor of Natural History in the Central School at the Department of Averyron for study. Bonaterre judged the boy to be about eleven or twelve years old, totally devoid of any redeeming human qualities and so much a curiosity that he called in all his professional friends to see him.

When Itard first saw the boy he described him as a:

> . . . degraded being, human only in shape; a dirty, scarred, inarticulate creature who trotted and grunted like beasts of the fields, ate with apparent pleasure the most filthy refuse, was apparently incapable of attention or even of elementary perceptions such as heat or cold, and spent his time apathetically rocking himself backwards and forwards like the animals at the Zoo. A 'man-animal' whose only concern was to eat, sleep, and escape the unwelcome attention of sightseers.

Subsequently the boy was named Victor and was known as the Wild Boy of Averyron. Finally, the eminent Pinel himself diagnosed Victor as an incurable idiot. Itard, however, was not so convinced. His work with deaf-mutes had demonstrated that many of them who had been believed to be hopeless showed remarkable progress once they were exposed to an educational program. He thought that perhaps Victor was only wild and untaught, and that his arrest of development resulted from never having learned how to be a human being. Nevertheless, Itard was not, at first, much interested in working with Victor.

Bonaterre, however, saw the possibilities of a great experiment and encouraged Itard to work with Victor by pointing out:

> . . . here is a boy who knows nothing. If he has innate ideas it should be possible to evoke them by proper stimulation. If his mind is an empty tablet it should be possible to make impressions upon it by applying the appropriate stimuli.

Apparently the excitement of such a challenge appealed to Itard because he accepted Victor as a pupil and set about to test the validity of the sensationalists' theory.

Itard embarked on a five-point program: (1) to interest Victor in social life; (2) to awaken his nervous sensibilities; (3) to extend the range of his ideas; (4) to lead him to the use of speech; and (5) to induce him to employ simple mental operations.

SOCIAL TRAINING

Victor had spent his whole life doing just what he pleased, namely eating, sleeping, running in the fields, and being idle. Itard believed that this manner of existence did nothing for intellectual development and, in fact, simply made Victor more indolent. He, therefore, established a routine for Victor which he tried to make more attractive than the carefree life Victor was used to. One way to do this was to use both praise and food for reinforcers. Rather than to allow Victor to eat at whatever time pleased him, Itard guarded the food carefully and set regular times for eating, gradually presenting meals farther apart and having fewer of them, until Victor was eating on schedule like other people. Furthermore, he made mealtime a happy time which Victor soon came to enjoy so that he apparently did not mind having that aspect of his life regulated.

At the same time, Itard established a sleeping routine at night. Essentially this meant that Victor was not allowed to sleep whenever he felt like it. Instead he was kept awake during the day and allowed to sleep when others slept. This also seemed not to be resented by Victor. A third part of the program involved establishing a routine of activities. Essentially, this resulted in cutting down on the amount of time available to Victor to simply run in the fields. As these excursions were restricted, he was placed on an activity schedule which served to carry the other parts of the program so that Victor ate, slept, worked, and played on much the same schedule as other people did.

SENSE TRAINING

Although Victor had shown himself to be quite insensitive to heat, cold, and pain, Itard began his sense training program using these senses. Whether Itard believed these to be the basic senses, or whether they were believed to be the easiest to train, or whether the lack of communication made vision and hearing difficult to train, is not known. In any case, Itard used the approach–avoidance principle of pleasure and pain as a basic teaching strategy nearly 150 years in advance of its articulation by modern psychologists.

Victor was clothed warmly during the day and covered well when he went to bed. In addition he slept in a cold room and his clothes were placed across the room from where he slept. Therefore when Victor awoke in the morning he had to go from a warm bed to a cold room to warm clothes. Itard also used very hot baths in which Victor literally soaked for hours. Gradually the baths were made cooler and within three months Victor became aware of comfort as represented by hot and cold. The test of his progress in this kind of training was that Victor, who previously had never sneezed, finally caught a cold. Victor generalized his perception of hot and cold to touch, so that he could distinguish between hard and soft and rough and smooth, and also to the senses of smell and taste, but he made no generalization to sight and hearing. Itard finally concluded that hearing and sight were much more complex than the simple senses of feeling, touch, smell, and taste, so he abandoned his efforts to teach them directly and in a short time.

NEW IDEAS

The range of Victor's experience with the things and customs of the civilized world was so limited as to be almost nil. Itard, therefore, made a concerted effort to broaden that range by systematically introducing new things. He tried toys, but Victor did not know how to play. Instead he broke them or hid them. By this time Victor had established some definite food preferences so Itard used his favorites for playing little games. For example, he would hide a nut under one of several cups. When Victor found it he could eat it. This game was quickly learned, but Victor apparently never failed to enjoy playing it.

Itard also tried to introduce new foods in order to broaden this range of interests. Try as he might, Itard could not get Victor to like sweets, spices, or strong liquors. However, Victor became hooked on dining out. Whenever they were to go out for dinner, Itard would come home promptly at four o'clock and would allow Victor to observe his folded shirt and "dining out clothes" laid out. Victor soon associated these things with the event and would become very excited. On most of these occasions Madame Guerin, his governess, and her daughter Julie would join them. Since Victor was fond of both, dining out became one of his favorite pastimes.

SPEECH

Itard tried to teach Victor to speak by starting with nouns and using the imperious law of necessity. When Victor was thirsty, Itard would hold a glass of water just out of reach and say, *eau, eau*. Victor never did learn to say *eau*, so the attempt was abandoned. Later, when they were dining out, Itard tried again with milk saying, *lait*. To this Victor responded, but he said *lli*. Whether he actually was trying to say lait or whether he simply associated the sound with the name Julie, Itard could not tell. In either case, *lli* became his first word and was a major triumph. His second speech attempt was a two-syllable one. Mrs. Guerin frequently used the expression *Oh Dieu*. On occasions when Victor was happy he was soon saying *Oh Di*. Despite the distortion, the two syllables were distinct and clear. Subsequent attempts to extend the vocabulary resulted in some imitation, but no great progress, so Itard abandoned speech training and returned to sense training, in the area of hearing first because of the relationship between hearing and speech, and then vision.

Hearing training involved many strategies. With Victor blindfolded, Itard would make noises and have Victor locate them. Later he used different musical instruments which could be struck and had Victor identify them. Then Itard would strike different parts of a drum, and Victor would have to identify the part struck. In all these activities progress was always from gross to fine discrimination. Even when different instruments were used, such as various woodwinds, the progression was from gross to fine.

Eventually discrimination between vowels was taught. This was done by associating each of the vowels with a different finger and having Victor raise the appropriate finger when he heard the specific vowel. This worked quite well until Itard became impatient. Once, when Victor raised the wrong finger, Itard slapped his hand. This so startled Victor that he sat immobile for over a quarter of an hour. After that Victor was so fearful of making a mistake that he either did not respond or responded so slowly that Itard finally gave up completely.

VISION

After the traumatic experience trying to teach vowel discrimination, Itard switched to lessons on visual discrimination. Again he worked from gross to fine, but he did not again employ physical punishment. Instead he used patient correction and liberal praise.

Ordering was the first skill taught. This included such things as placing things in sequence, then mixing them up and having Victor put them in proper order again, as well as ordering by size and shape. Next, matching of objects, objects with pictures, and pictures with pictures was taught. Finally, discrimination of geometric shapes, colors, and even shades and tints was learned. Although Victor did extremely well in visual discrimination, a point was reached where Victor began to fail consistently. Once again Itard had to abandon the lessons because they were too difficult and became emotionally frustrating.

Since Victor had demonstrated some skill in matching, Itard introduced a formboard with letters of the alphabet. When Victor had mastered the letter formboard, Itard began spelling out words and associating the letters with objects. Milk became the first object. It did not take Victor long to learn to arrange LAIT when he wanted a drink of milk. Soon Itard used word cards which labeled nearly everything in sight. Once Victor had learned to match the cards and things, they were mixed up and used for games in which Victor fetched the object named on the word card.

MENTAL FUNCTIONS

As soon as Victor had learned to associate word cards as nouns with objects, Itard attempted to extend the lessons. For example, Victor learned to identify a knife so Itard got many different kinds of knives to teach Victor to generalize. The principle of instruction was from the specific to the general or more properly, from perceptions to concepts. Then Itard taught part–whole relationships, such as the separate parts of the book making up the whole book. When this concept had been grasped he introduced modifiers such as big and little, colors, and heavy and light all through the method of comparison. Verbs like *throw, touch, pick up,* and *bring,* were introduced next. Finally Victor was introduced to imitative copying of sentences and phrases using words already learned. Even though Victor had learned reading by a whole word method, the words had little other than specific meaning to him and any attempts to get him to speak the words resulted in failure.

At this point Itard gave up. He had devoted five years of concerted effort to the training of Victor but failed to teach him to read and write. The disappointment was not so much that he had failed to cure Victor as that the experiment neither confirmed nor condemned the philosophy of sensationalism. The results were simply inconclusive. As Victor went into adolescence he became so uncontrollable that it was necessary to place him in an institution. He remained there for some time but was finally paroled into the care of Mrs. Guerin with whom he lived until his death in 1828.

Although Itard had failed to cure Victor's idiocy, he had transformed him from "a degraded being, human only in shape" into "An almost normal child who could not speak but who lived like a human being." He also demonstrated the effectiveness of the pleasure-approach, pain-avoidance principle long before it was an established element of pedagogy. His method of reinforcement by using edibles, physical comfort, and praise are now accepted procedures in operant conditioning. His system of instruction—(1) behavior control, (2) sense training, (3) increasing the range of ideas, (4) speech, and (5) developing simple mental functions—has been modified in sequence, but the elements are still retained. But perhaps his most significant demonstration was that Victor showed near normal emotional reactions after only a few months of instruction. Itard demonstrated for all time to come that for the retarded, the area most susceptible to change was that of emotional behavior.

Edouard Onesimus Seguin: 1812–1880

Thirty-eight years his junior, Seguin was, in every sense of the word, a student of Itard. After studying at the College d'Auxerre and the Lycée St. Louis in Paris, Seguin joined the staff of the Hospice des

Incurables in 1837. He studied medicine and surgery under Itard, and apparently was a very able physician, having written a manual on Thermometry for mothers and also invented a Thermometer. At the Hospice des Incurables, he tutored a retarded boy for 18 months, teaching him to remember, compare, speak, write, and count. His success was so outstanding that he extended his work and in 1844 presented ten pupils to the Paris Academy of Sciences for examination. At that time Seguin described his work saying:

> Education is the ensemble of the means of developing harmoniously and effectively the moral, intellectual and physical functions.

His goal for education was to support the free will. The Academy was so impressed that they commissioned him to continue his work.

In 1848 the French Revolution caused him to leave France for the United States, settling first in Cleveland and Portsmouth, Ohio, and subsequently founding the Pennsylvania Training School in 1860. In 1870 he opened a private Physiological School for Weak Minded and Weak Bodied children in New York, which he ran until his death in 1880. Along the way, he helped found and became the first president of the Association of Medical Officers of American Institutions, the forerunner of the American Association on Mental Deficiency, and to write extensively on teaching the retarded. Most notable was his book *Idiocy: Its Treatment by the Physiological Method,* published in 1866.

Seguin became firmly convinced that the training of the senses separately as had been practiced by Itard was futile because he believed the human organism acted as an integrated whole and therefore should be instructed as a total unit. As he explained:

> Teaching a geometric point must not make us forgetful of the line to which this point belongs; the line of the body it limits; the body of its accessory properties; the properties of the possible associations . . . with its surroundings.

and again:

> An idea is not an isolated image of one thing, but the representation in a unit of all the facts related to the imagined object.

At the time of his work, neurologists had divided the nervous system into two major categories: the peripheral nervous system and the central nervous system. Using this theory as a base, Seguin believed that idiots failed to develop, not because they were not exposed to sensory stimulation from the environment, but because organic defects in the nervous system made it impossible for responses to stimuli to be learned or retained. He distinguished between two types of retardation: (1) superficial, in which the peripheral nervous system was blocked due to damaged or weakened receptor organs, and (2) profound, which resulted from central nervous system defects existing from birth. The educational methods for both kinds of retardation were, however, identical. His aim was:

> . . . to lead the child . . . from the education of the muscular system to that of the nervous system and the senses . . . (and) from the education of the senses to general notions, from general notions to abstract thought, from abstract thought to morality.

He proposed to do this through:

> . . . adoption of the principles of physiology, through the development of the dynamic, receptive, reflexive, and spontaneous functions of youth.

His program attempted to instruct (1) the muscle system, (2) touch, (3) the auditory sense, (4) speech, and (5) visual abilities.

MUSCLE TRAINING

Because Seguin believed that specific physical exercises would develop the receptor organs in superficial retardation and would also develop the nerve cells in the cortex in profound retardation, he used and extensive physical exercise program for all retarded youngsters. Since he felt that nothing should be taught indoors which could be taught outdoors, much use was made of playground games and equipment. In addition to natural playground equipment, he also used a table, a balancing pole, a ladder, and a springboard.

If a child could not move, Seguin moved him. If the legs could not bend, the child was put in a baby jumper. If the child could not walk, a springboard or a treadmill was used. In every case, new movements were encouraged using whatever means were necessary. Every activity was designed to provide opportunity for total, integrated movements. When a child lacked this kind of coordination, however, Seguin started first with getting movements in the feet, then the legs, body, shoulders, arms, wrists, hands, and finally the fingers. To achieve integrated motor movements he used children's games of running, jumping, dodging, changing direction, and catching. Throughout, all the children were encouraged to shout, yell, scream, and even sing, making vocalization an integral part of the games. His motor development program was basic to every other facet of his programs, so he devoted time and effort to making it successful and fun.

TOUCH TRAINING

Seguin apparently learned well from Itard the generalizability of the sense of touch, but he certainly added a dimension of his own making by declaring that touch was dependent upon well developed motor movements. His touch training program was little different from that used by Itard; using a blindfold, he taught his students to distinguish shape, size, texture, temperature, and weight. Once his pupils learned to distinguish objects by touch, Seguin then trained taste and smell, first because he believed they were related to touch and second because:

> . . . once disposed of we are at liberty to follow without interruption the education of the eye and ear as far as they will carry us into the intellectual training.

AUDITORY TRAINING

Although he taught his pupils to distinguish between and recognize general sounds, it was in the use of musical sounds and related vocal expression in which Seguin showed his greatest ingenuity. His reasons for using music were expressed as:

> Music pleases the child without hurting him; it gives rest from hard labor; it causes in the immovable child a tremulousness of all the fibers which is easily turned into incipiency of action; it prepares the nervous apparatus in a similar manner, awakens, quickens, and supports the thoughts wonderfully; it derives anger, weariness, melancholy, and disposes to gentle feelings; it is a moral sedative by excellence.

With such faith in the power of music, it is no wonder that he made music a constant in the learning environment. It was used to set the mood for activities: gay, bright music for morning studies; reflective music for afternoon activities; lively music during physical education; and prolonged, sustained tones for speech activities. Whenever possible the children could hum or sing with the music.

SPEECH

Seguin believed that speech was the most difficult skill to teach— probably because Itard had failed so dismally in his attempts to teach speech to Victor, and also because of his experience with deaf-mute children. This was reflected in his encouraging the children to vocalize during nearly every activity. When they played games they shouted and screamed; even when they studied they sang and hummed. Seguin encouraged the youngsters to sustain specific tones. For example if a child screamed as he jumped off a table, Sequin would try to get the child to use only an aah or oh for the scream. Then he would urge the child to vary the tones to get different scream effects. Soon he would get the child to convert the cries into purposeful sounds or singing or humming. Within a short time all the children had a variety of tones and sounds they could sustain or turn off at will. It was a small step to teaching articulation by imitative means. Music aided in this activity also, staccato sounds or sustained tones were imitated and used for games. Seguin even taught immobility using rests and pauses for emphasis. It is worth noting that "moral training" or free will or self-discipline was the ultimate objective of Seguin's program. Therefore teaching people not to move would be perfectly compatible with this purpose. Apparently, immobility was used between nearly every activity and was a very important part of his program.

ACADEMIC SKILLS

Once again apparently taking his cues from the failures of Itard, Seguin taught writing before he taught reading. The writing made use of the speech skills; as the children traced the words, they also said the sounds of the word. Thus visual, auditory, speech, and reading were effectively combined, but the purpose was to teach writing. If as a residual the youngster learned to read, that was fine, but it was not the chief purpose of the tracing of letters.

Reading was taught by saying the word, writing the word, and placing the object represented by the word in the child's hands. Seguin used pretty much the same sequence of words used by Itard; nouns, verbs, and then modifiers and many of the same exercises.

It is evident that Seguin learned from Itard's failures and drew heavily on Itard's successes. Yet he made contributions of his own which have stood the test of time. Whereas Itard tried to train each sense in isolation, Seguin insisted on an integrated or whole child approach. Such a principle is now one of the foundations upon which all education rests. He used both individual and group activities in all his work from sense training to academics, a practice which still persists. Perhaps most important, he validated a sequence of development from most basic to complex, placing great emphasis on motor activities and following with sense training of touch, taste, and smell, auditory and speech. Interestingly enough, although he did not neglect visual training, it was actually given a minor position in the training sequence in that it was taught in conjunction with other skills such as tracing words and was not formally introduced as were the other sense training activities. This is quite different from some of the learning procedures currently used which place great emphasis on visual–perceptual exercises.

One aspect of Seguin's program which has been overlooked but has become standard practice is that of cueing activities to the time of day and the weather. It is exemplified by his comment on reading:

> Individual reading may be more insisted upon in cool, mild weather, and in the morning when attention causes no effort, . . . on stormy days, and in the afternoon, dullness is prevented from settling down on the class by group teaching.

Dotloressa Maria Montessori: 1870–1952

The third of the great medical pioneers in the education of the mentally retarded was born in Chiaravalle in the province of Ancona, Italy. Although originally headed for a career in engineering, Montessori earned a degree in medicine from the University of Rome in 1894, becoming the first woman in Italy to earn such a degree.

Her first position as a staff member of the Psychiatric Clinic of the University of Rome took her into the wards of the mental hospitals to select patients for treatment. There she found many mentally retarded housed with the mentally ill. This so disturbed Montessori that she protested to her colleagues, contending that mental retardation was an educational problem while mental illness was a psychiatric one. Her argument was apparently eloquent because in 1898 she was appointed director of Scuola Ortofrenica, a school for defective children in Rome. There she developed her auto-teaching techniques. This highly individualized method of teaching was so effective with retarded children·that Montessori felt it would be even better for the average and gifted. Accordingly, she was able to open a school called the Casa dei Bambini or House of Children in 1907 specifically for average children from working class families.

The fame of the school was instantaneous, but it was not until the eminent American writer Dorothy Canfield Fisher described the work of Montessori in a book in 1913 that she became world famous. Schools organized in the style of the Casa dei Bambini were soon started all over the world and many contemporary private schools today designate themselves as Montessori schools.

Montessori leaned heavily on the earlier work of Itard and Seguin, but she added a number of elements which were strictly her own doing. She called her system the psychological method because it was based on three psychological principles: (1) children are all different from each other and hence must be treated individually; (2) children must wish to learn; and (3) children are so constituted that given proper conditions they prefer educating themselves to any other occupations. Her rules for the children were straightforward and uncomplicated: (1) an object used by a child must be returned to its original place, in its original order, after a child is finished with it; (2) any task, once begun, must be finished; (3) nobody else can use the object at the same time someone else is using it, and (4) no one can take any kind of materials to work with before the teacher has introduced it to him.

The entire Montessori system was aimed at providing children the materials they needed to develop their full potential as human beings, but her approach was based upon the belief that:

> . . . through . . . receiving sensations from his environment, he lays the foundation of his intelligence by a continual exercise of observations, comparison, and judgment.

Montessori believed that motor perceptions developed more rapidly in children than advanced intellectual skills so she developed materials which made use of materials which had to be manipulated to be used. From Itard she borrowed the notion that a relaxed environment with suitable stimuli was a potent factor in education and from Seguin she used the technique of presenting abstract notions in the concrete form of toys and toylike materials.

Contrary to the formal atmosphere of the schools then current in Italy, where the teachers determined what should be taught and conducted the classes in an autocratic climate, Montessori believed that each child was the best judge of his own level of ability and speed of learning. Her technique of instruction was to surround the child with materials and allow him to perform on those which were of interest to him. The reason for this was quite straightforward; children would demonstrate their own levels of development by the kinds and complexity of materials they selected. In this selection, they were actually better judges of their needs than were their teachers. Also Montessori felt that any time element which was imposed on children was arbitrary and did an injustice to individual differences. Since children had different abilities, there was no reason why they should learn to read at a certain age or learn to count at a certain age or graduate from school at a certain age. This was not realistic because each child was different. Each should learn at his own rate.

In the matter of what should be learned, Montessori was not flexible. She believed that the avenues for learning were the senses and that they emerged in a time sequence with touch first, then vision and hearing. These sensory skills were basic to the intellectual processes which also developed in a time sequence: first recognition, then recall, judgment, comparison, and interpretation. She developed materials which not only stimulated activity, but also controlled it, so that the child would be led through the sequence of sensory skills and through the sequence of intellectual processes, learning each in turn at his own speed. Reinforcement came only from the satisfaction the child received from successfully completing an exercise. The only real deviation from her rigid curriculum took place at the very beginning. In order for the child to profit from the exercises, he had to demonstrate self-care, self-control, and independence, so an environment was created which had many things of interest to children, like pets, play areas, and toys, plus some imposed routine of activities to allow him to learn to behave independently. Once the children showed the ability for the independent pursuit of the materials, they were instructed on the use of the materials and allowed to work on their own with no interference from anyone.

The exercises had specific, sequentially arranged purposes based on Montessori's conceptualization of the developmental stages with materials appropriate to each purpose. For example:

EXERCISE 1
 Purpose: To fix the child's attention on size and form.
 Apparatus: Solid geometric insets for a formboard.
EXERCISE 2
 Purpose: To coordinate movements of the fingers.
 Apparatus: Buttoning and dressing frames.
EXERCISE 7
 Purpose: To develop the sense of touch.
 Apparatus: Sandpaper boards.
EXERCISE 9
 Purpose: To develop the sense of touch (blindfolded).
 Apparatus: 1. Two pieces each of velvet, silk, wool, fine and coarse cotton, and fine and coarse linen.
   2. Other fabrics and materials found in the house.
   3. Solid wooden geometric forms—balls, cubes, etc.
   4. Miscellaneous objects around the house.
 Note: Child matches materials and objects by touch.
EXERCISE 10
 Purpose: To train the sense of hearing.
 Apparatus: Sound boxes filled with sand, gravel, stones, etc.
 Note: Supplementary exercises and games such as hide and seek and blindman's buff were used to determine the direction of sounds.
EXERCISES 11 AND 12
 Purpose: To prepare the child to learn to write (by learning forms and shapes).
 Apparatus: Plane geometric inserts.
EXERCISE 13
 Purpose: To use a pencil.
 Apparatus: Plane geometric inserts made of metal and paper plus a pencil.
 Note: Child traces around inserts.
EXERCISES 19 AND 20
 Purpose: To learn to write and read.
 Apparatus: Movable sandpaper letters.
EXERCISES 23 AND 24
 Purpose: To begin the first steps in arithmetic.
 Apparatus: Counting boxes and sandpaper numbers.

Once a child had completed the sense training exercises, he was introduced to the higher level academic skill exercises. In this progression, Montessori believed that writing was easier to learn than reading, so she developed a series of exercises which taught this skill. After the child had learned to hold a pencil and trace around geometric shapes and inside the inserts, he traced inside of boxes, circles, etc. which had two lines so he would learn to keep his pencil between the lines. Later he traced over the letters in words and then learned to copy words. Since each word had meaning to the child, this was not just a futile exercise. In addition the child said the sound of each letter as he copied the word. Because Italian is a phonetic alphabet, the child was actually learning phonics as he was copying the words. The child learned to read by a phonics method because he taught himself the phonetic elements by saying the word slowly as he copied it. Soon he could write and read simple phrases and sentences by the uncomplicated method of saying the word and writing the appropriate phonetic characters. Montessori's instruction in reading by no means stopped at this point, but the basic method of teaching reading was a phonics method.

Maria Montessori, although considerably influenced by the work of Itard and Seguin, was an educational innovator in her own right. In a time when teachers were autocrats and pupils were parrots, she recognized that you cannot teach anybody anything; you simply arrange the environment in such a way that a person learns by interacting with the materials. Thus the focus of her school was on the activity of the child—the teacher was only there as a guide. She also recognized that each child had his own speed of learning, which, if honored by the teacher, would maximize the results of his learning activity. Therefore the child, not the teacher, controlled the classroom. Perhaps most important, Montessori clearly identified exactly what it was the child was expected to learn and the performance of the child demonstrated when he had mastered the exercises. In her school there was no failure and no comparative grading. There was only one outcome possible—successful completion of an exercise. Thus there was no competition between students, since each child was his own control.

Montessori was not universally hailed as an educational Messiah. She first got into trouble with the Catholic church because she bore an illegitimate son and made no secret of her unmarried state. Soon the Jesuit order publicly criticized her educational program because it ignored the Catholic belief that man is by nature sinful and unclean. When the Italian dictator, Benito Mussolini, came to power, he forced her to leave Italy because her method of instruction did not stress allowing State authority to mold the personality of the students, but left them to develop in a climate of self-expression. And leave she did in 1934, going first to Spain and India, and finally settling in Holland after World War II.

Even in the United States, she was soundly criticized. The educational philosopher Kilpatrick pointed out that the method emphasizes individual rather than group activity, and that since a democratic society depends upon group cooperation for its survival, the method is not appropriate for a democracy. From a psychological point of view, the exercises have been criticized because they are specific and do not teach for transfer. In addition, the exercises are restrictive and do not teach for imaginative or creative thinking. Perhaps the most pervading resistance came from teachers themselves for her method required teachers to step down from an austere to a mingling relationship with the child and took the control of the child's activities from the teacher and gave it to the child. For many teachers such a reversal of role authority is unacceptable.

The effectiveness of the procedures of these three medical educators is undeniable, but it is obvious that their techniques were heavily influenced by the philosophy of medicine. Each concentrated on a cure technique by providing a systematic treatment of sensory learning avenues, but when a child had progressed to the point where further sharpening of sensory perceptions were futile, their programs had nowhere to go. Once the children had achieved the skills of reading and arithmetic fundamentals, the programs failed to provide for the use of those skills in higher level educational activities. The programs were excellent preparatory or preschool and primary programs, but contributed little to teaching the children to use their basic skills for vocational preparation, learning about their cultural heritage, or self-realization. As such they cannot be considered educational systems. They are preparatory techniques of great value, but they have limited usefulness in achieving the goals of education.

Ovide Decroly and Alice Descoeudres

Born in 1871 in Renaix, France, Decroly was the fourth of the medically trained educators of the retarded. After earning an M.D. degree at the University of Ghent, Decroly studied for a time in Berlin before accepting a post at the Polytechnic Hospital in Brussels, Belgium. His medical work with defective children convinced him, as it had Montessori, that mental retardation was fundamentally an educational problem so he established the Decroly School for defective and exceptional children in 1901 and directed the school until 1907. At that time Decroly established a school for normal children in the Rue de L'Ermitage based on the educational principles he had developed working with the retarded. In 1912 he started a training program for teachers of exceptional children but left that program in the hands of others to become head of the Child Psychology department at the University of Brussels in 1920 and subsequently head of the department of school hygiene in the Medical School of the University of Brussels in 1921.

Decroly was an educational innovator also, but he is not included in the trio with Itard, Seguin, and Montessori because his program was not a treatment oriented clinical-educational approach. Decroly went far beyond the sense training techniques of his predecessors by providing a total educational program which prepared his students for working and living in society.

The name Decroly gave his program was the Program of Associated Ideas. He was greatly influenced by the American philosopher John Dewey, organizing his school to "let the child prepare for life by living" and he arranged it to "organize the environment to afford adequate stimuli for the tendencies favorable to development."

At the Congress for the New Education held in Calais in 1921, Decroly outlined the essence of his program in a fifteen point statement:

1. The school should be located in natural surroundings so the environment will afford daily experience with the phenomena of nature and with manifestations of life led by living creatures in general and with man in particular.
2. Small numbers of children, from 10 to 15 of both sexes and ranging in age from 4 to 15 should be included in each class.

3. Equipment and furnishings should be a real departure from conventional classrooms. The room should resemble a laboratory or studio rather than an auditorium.
4. The staff must be intelligent and possessed of creative ability. They should be trained in methods of observing plant and animal life, and in making observations of children as well. They should be fond of children, and interested to acquire a knowledge of psychology and the allied sciences. They must be able to express themselves with facility, and to keep order and discipline with no special effort.
5. Groups within classes should be made up of children of approximately the same mental level and maturity.
6. Exceptional children should be placed in a special class with a teacher thoroughly trained in assisting and developing the retarded.
7. Reading, writing, spelling and number techniques should be taught in the early morning by lessons mostly in the form of games.
8. The remainder of the morning should be spent in such activities as observation, comparison and association using manual work, singing and active games which are related to the subject matter of the school.
9. Afternoons should be devoted to manual work and foreign languges.
10. Excursions should be arranged for mornings.
11. Thorough parent cooperation should be secured by informing the parents of the school's work and aims.
12. Disciplinary problems should be handled by trying to give the child an insight into his behavior so he will learn to exercise his own self control.
13. Class conferences should be used to develop initiative, self-confidence, and group spirit.
14. A constant variety of activities should be used to stimulate the interest of children. These may include such things as different arrangements of the classroom, collections, materials, pictures, books, and reference materials. The children should also be encouraged to make charts and boxes and envelopes for classifying materials and to care for aquaria and terraria. From these experiences the children get materials they can use to write original themes and stories. The children should be actively involved in the organization for classroom duties, for the group life of the class and the larger life of the school community.
15. All school activities should be organized around special groupings of subject matter of ideas which are associated in a realistic manner.

The aims of the Program of Associated Ideas were to give the child: first, a knowledge of himself, as a being, his needs, his desires, his purposes and ideals; and second, a knowledge of his environment.

These were accomplished, first, through activities that concern the individual, the study of individual functions, and second, through activities which concerned the species, the study of social functions.

In order to place this kind of study on the level of the child's thinking and within range of facts that he could observe for himself, Decroly identified core areas, the forerunner of units, for study. The days activities were divided much as Seguin had done with fairly formal academic work in the early morning followed by the core areas of more active participation and movement which emphasized social interaction in the late morning and afternoons.

The sense training activities which had been nearly the entire programs of Itard, Seguin, and Montessori were virtually ignored by Decroly. Not that he thought this training unimportant, but he believed in lessons which had relevance to the life of the child, so that sense training became incidental to purposeful activities. The teaching of reading is a good example of this. Decroly used what he called an "Idio-visual" method. Simple commands were given orally. Then they were written on placards. The placards were then used for acting out, reading aloud, speed recognition, and so on. After many placards with commands written on them had been prepared, the children looked for similar words which appeared on several placards. In essence, they did word comparison by visual configuration. Next, objects in the room were labeled including new things which were brought into the room. Eventually the children made lists of words which contained single vowels, consonants, and so on. This work was supplemented by playing syllabification games.

In his reading program Decroly started with phrases and short sentences which had meaning to the child. Then he worked for whole phrase or sentence recognition, then similar words, then similar sounds. He taught reading by a whole word method which was later supplemented by phonics and syllabification analysis.

The core studies of the Decroly schools centered on the needs of the children for food, shelter, and protection, defense against enemies and danger, and work, including the needs for activity, to work with others, the need for recreation, and for self-development. To learn effectively about associated ideas, the students used personal, direct observations; association, the indirect acquisition of facts; concrete expression, such as making models or drawing; and abstract expression, such as oral descriptions, writing, and reading.

Each year one of the child's fundamental needs was used as the center of interest or pivotal idea for the entire year's work. The method of study included observation, association, and expression dealing with various aspects of, for instance, food. The planting, growing, harvesting, processing, transporting, selling, buying, preparing, and eating would all be subtopics for study relating to the central care of and need for food. At higher levels of classes, various foods, digestion, health, and so on could be related or associated aspects of study. Although the basic needs identified by Decroly formed the core of the lessons, the interest and knowledge of the children were guiding features for determining what activities would actually be used. Pupil participation was integral to the program.

Alice Descoeudres was a student of Decroly's and received her training and interest in the retarded while working as his apprentice. However, unlike Decroly who switched his interest to normal children, Descoeudres continued to work with retarded children. Much of the program of Decroly, especially his emphasis on developing the higher thought processes, reflects what normal children can do and is quite unrealistic when it is applied to the retarded. Descoeudres, by contrast, developed a program which was practical, realistic, and eminently suited to the needs of retarded youngsters.

She accepted as a classification system that children fell into three groups, each with different educational needs. Normal children she felt should be educated in the main classes or Hauptklassen. She felt that a child was feebleminded if he could communicate orally with his peers but was educationally backward, two years below his chronological age if he were younger than nine years old, and three years behind in educational achievement if he were older than nine, provided his lack of educational achievement was not due to lack of educational opportunity. She advocated Forderklassen or advanced classes for children whose educational backwardness was due to lack of educational opportunity and Hilfklassen, literally help or special classes, for children whose backwardness was due to feeblemindedness. Descoeudres believed that seriously defective children should be placed in residential institutions. For the feebleminded (mildly and moderately retarded) she advocated special classes for average sized communities and independent special schools in big cities where large numbers of retarded children lived. Thus Descoeudres distinguished between educationally handicapped and mentally retarded children, with a remedial program for the educationally handicapped and a developmental program for the retarded.

Descoeudres organized the school day in much the same fashion as Decroly with fairly formal academic study in the early morning followed by core or unit activities in the late morning and afternoon. The timing of the academic work, however, was more like that of Seguin than Decroly. Rather than beginning with reading instruction, Descoeudres started with a thorough sense training program which was continued for one or two years before the child was introduced to reading. Because she believed the sense of touch to be the most basic sense, and because she found so many of the retarded children were physically as well as mentally backward, she made great use of the motor development and games program of Seguin. The other senses, vision, hearing, smell, and taste, were given similar careful attention. Here Descoeudres demonstrated her ingenuity by devising games which were specific to the sense being trained. Most of the games were some variation of lotto, the forerunner of modern bingo. Instead of using only numbers in the squares, she used pictures, shapes, colors, letters, words, and syllables in a variety of ways. For those senses which did not lend themselves to the lotto approach, she fell back on the techniques of Itard, Seguin, and Montessori.

To teach reading, she used both the syncretic or whole word technique of Decroly and an analytic approach which was phonics. From her experience with the retarded, she delayed the teaching of reading until the children were chronologically older than normal children. In effect this resulted in waiting until the retarded children had mental ages of very close to six (probably chronologically they would be about eight). Since she used the intervening years for motor development, sense training, and speech and language development, one can guess that her youngsters were as well prepared for reading as they could possibly be. This procedure is now common practice. In addition she was the first educator of the retarded to recognize individual differences in learning style. She identified children according to whether they were visual types or auditory types of learners and taught to their learning strength. The visual types were given mostly visual word presentation while the auditory types received teaching by phonics. Even though she had no formal diagnostic tests to assess learning style, she was practicing what has now come to be called prescriptive teaching.

When the youngsters had developed some skills in reading, writing, and arithmetic, Descoeudres provided opportunities to use those skills in meaningful activities related to the core areas Decroly had developed. At the lower age levels the core areas had to do mostly with bringing the children in contact with neighborhood places and things. However, when they reached high school age, employment opportunities and requirements became the core of study. Although there was no formal work preparatory program, employment was the desired end result. Thus Descoeudres should probably be credited with the first complete educational program specifically for the retarded.

Many of Descoeudres' innovations are identifiable in more recent approaches to teaching the retarded. One that is not, but seems eminently worth considering, was the Society for the Protection of Backward Children which she started. Made up of citizens who were concerned with the well-being of the retarded, the Society attended to the needs of the youngsters during their educational and also their post-school years. While the youngsters were in school the members were concerned with parent–teacher communication, providing money for their educational needs, and sending the children to the country during holidays. After the youngsters left school, the members of the Society scouted for suitable employment opportunities (mostly of a routine mechanical nature where the individual, by constant repetition, could learn to master the task as well as a normal person), provided job placement and supervision, bargained with employers for higher wages, and served as a protector for each person to report to on his progress, achievement, and welfare.

Decroly and Descoeudres provided the program framework which became the model for later programs. The identification of program goals of skills of independent work and self-management was a giant stride beyond the clinical tutoring of Itard, Seguin, and Montessori, because it recognized that retarded children grow up to become retarded adults and that with appropriate training they can become productive citizens. Given this goal, the program started with a sense training approach followed by academic instruction supplemented with core studies of things in the environment which were of interest to the children, and culminated in job placement with continuing post-school supervision. Her use of games to compensate for the inefficient learning of the retarded and her recognition that the retarded have individual differences in learning style were truly ingenious educational perceptions. Such an approach is quite clearly more complete than many present day offerings for the retarded.

Annie Dolman Inskeep

At about the same time that Descoeudres' work became known, Annie Inskeep described her work with retarded children in the United States. This was presented in a book titled *Teaching Dull and Retarded Children* published in 1926, two years before Descoeudres' book *The Education of Mentally Defective Children* was translated into English.

Quite independently of the European educators, Inskeep also believed that the retarded could and should be trained to be self-controlled and self-supporting citizens. Her approach to this goal was both similar to and different from the program of Descoeudres. Although Descoeudres grouped children according to mental level, Inskeep was much more precise because she used the mental age as a rough index of level. Her procedure is still in use. Briefly, the formula $\frac{CA \times IQ}{100} = MA$ was used and then translated into grade equivalent. For example, a child of six with an IQ of 70 would have an MA of a little more than four ($\frac{6 \times 70}{100} = 4.2$). Since an average child typically would not be introduced to beginning reading instruction until he was six years old with an MA of six ($\frac{6 \times 100}{100} = 6$), the child with the MA of four would really be equivalent to a preschooler in intellectual ability. Furthermore if the IQ of 70 is accurate and does not change, the child will have to be nearly nine years old before his MA is close enough to six to provide a reasonable chance for success in learning to read ($\frac{9 \times 70}{100} = 6.3$). The procedure of Inskeep was not only to delay reading instruction until the child was eight or nine years old, but also to use the years intervening between six and eight or nine for careful attention to sensory and readiness skills which would provide a good perceptual foundation for reading.

In the actual daily program, instead of using the morning for formal academics with units or projects in the afternoon, Inskeep used projects all day for as long as the interest of the children was sustained and then taught academics all day until interest waned again when another project was introduced. The projects dealt with health, social living, getting and holding a job, thrift and use of leisure time, problems which were believed by Inskeep to persist throughout the lifetime of the individual.

In the 1920s there were virtually no programs which trained teachers of mentally retarded children. Because of this it was common to find special classes taught by teachers trained in elementary education methods and who were sympathetic but not very knowledgeable about the learning characteristics of retarded children. Inskeep, therefore, tried to describe teaching methods which could be used by teachers trained in elementary education and which were not so different from what the teachers already knew that the teachers would be scared out of the classroom by techniques so new they bordered on the frightening. In essence she tried to encourage teachers to teach reading, writing, and arithmetic, but to individualize instruction by presenting books and materials which were consistent with the mental age of the child and were interesting and understandable to the child—not necessarily to the whole class. The projects were designed to involve the whole class in the study of areas which were realistic life problems. The fact that many teachers never got beyond the academic part of her program led to a labeling of a "watered down" curriculum. This does an injustice to Inskeep, who was the first educator to provide for individual differences using test information as a basis for curricular adjustment and therefore contributed a technique which is still used today. In addition she centered her projects on the forerunners of current "persistent life problems," areas of behavior such as health and thrift which needed to be dealt with by young as well as more mature persons in order to live satisfactorily in society. To be sure, her program did not include much of a vocational training nature and therefore was not complete; yet what was covered, was quite well done under the circumstances.

Christine P. Ingram

From her experience of more than 30 years as a teacher and supervisor of classes for retarded children in the public schools of

Rochester, New York, Ingram described her understanding of the learning needs and characteristics of retarded children in *The Education of Slow Learning Children*, first published in 1935. The book contained a very practical description of the behavior and learning characteristics of the children (some of which are listed in Chapter 4), a procedure for selecting the children for special classes, and a complete description of a program for the youngsters.

Ingram used a classification system by IQs which had previously not been used much in educational circles. In subsequent revisions of her book (1953 and 1960) she designated the "slow learners" as encompassing the range from 50 to 89 IQ. This range was further broken down so the mentally retarded or mentally handicapped (terms which she used synonymously) had IQs from 50 to 75, and the borderline or dull normals ranged from 75 to 89 in IQ. Although her program was designed to be equally appropriate for both groups of children, nearly all of the materials and suggestions came from actual experiences with the mentally retarded group because these were the children with whom she had worked.

The descriptions of the youngsters called attention to their below normal physical, mental, and social traits and the need for a program which would help them develop in each of these areas into self-sufficient, independent adults.

Ingram believed that the learning characteristics of the retarded were such that they required a program which grew out of needs of the children, which allowed the child to be conscious of success, by recognizing when he had made a right response, and which insured the meaningful recurrence of the activity. Her solution to these requirements was to divide the children into three levels for instruction: the Primary Unit for children aged seven or eight to eleven with MAs between four and eight; the Intermediate Unit for children aged eleven to thirteen or fourteen with MAs between six and nine; and the High School Unit for children aged thirteen or fourteen to sixteen or more with MAs from eight to eleven.

The subject matter areas were rejected for formal study because they were inappropriate to the learning characteristics of the children and also because they did not contribute to the goal of self-management. Instead Ingram used a modification of Descoeudres' persistent problems which included health (physical and mental), working knowledge of tool subjects (vocabulary, reading, number, writing), family and occupational life, community life, and use of leisure time. Expected outcomes of the instructional program were identified for each problem area at each level, so that the programs had a sequence which had been lacking heretofore. For example in the problem of family and occupational life at each level the child was expected to learn:

Primary Unit   Use of such mediums as paper, clay, wood and simple handskills in the use of tools and materials.

Intermediate Unit   Use of paper, clay, wood, cloth and other mediums such as cement or leather, to carry out activities and make useful products.

High School Unit   Elementary knowledge and understanding of labor and industry and the part they play in the daily life of the community; familiarity with the services and industries in the community; a knowledge of labor regulations and of suitable employment open to youth.

The clearly described behaviors expected as a result of the educational procedures at each level were pursued by a project method of instruction. These projects which were called units of instruction were quite similar to the core studies of Decroly except that they were better described by Ingram and restricted to the problem areas she felt were necessary to the full development of the retarded youngsters— health, tool subjects, family and occupational life, community life, and leisure time.

Much of her book is devoted to detailed descriptions of units which were successfully used in classes. An example is a unit on child care for a class of thirteen to sixteen year old girls which furthers the development of the desired outcomes indicated in the problem area of family living.

Interest in child care developed during a discussion in Home Economics which was continued in the special class. As a result of a discussion on babies' needs, two trips were taken: one to a model baby's room and one to a baby department in a department store. As an outcome of the trips, a model baby's room was made, complete with a layette. In order to carry out the project the students were involved in:

. . . finding information on child care from Health Bureau bulletins; putting the information found on cleanliness, rest, fresh air, time schedules, clinic service, and first-aid rules into simple statements for a child-care book; reading about child life of other times and in other countries; planning diets, clothes, and time schedules for babies and growing children in the girl's families; learning children's poems and lullabyes, enjoying pictures of children by Jessie Willcox Smith; bringing in a real baby to weigh, to bathe, and to dress; observing a two-year-old at play; planning a tea and inviting guests to see the results of their work.

Obviously, the unit on child care cut across virtually all of the subject matter fields to use reading, arithmetic, spelling, writing, and English and contributed to the personal and social development of the girls. It is small wonder that Ingram justifies the unit method of instruction on the grounds that:

1. It brings real purpose into much of the child's work and play.
2. It enables him to experience things first hand—to have sensory experiences, contacts with reality.
3. It gives meaning and interest to the commonplace in his environment.
4. It enables him to plan, execute, and judge in a simple way at the level of his stage of maturity.
5. It teaches him how to do things and how to conduct himself in actual situations so that behavior is integrated.

Although Ingram depended on units to carry her program, she cautioned teachers to set aside periods for teaching tool subject skills whenever necessary. Her program was characterized by flexible schedules much as Inskeep had, but she had a better organization of activities. However, while she described a High School Unit, actual work experience under the supervision of school personnel was given scant attention. Additionally, while Ingram did not emphasize the sense training activities of Itard, Seguin, and Montessori as Inskeep and Descoeudres had, from the standpoint of scope, sequence, and relevance, her program was remarkably good. Besides providing a form for developing units of instruction, she was the first person to describe the kinds of behaviors to be developed at each stage of the program. Thus she added a dimension to programs previously virtually ignored— sequence integrity. The impact of her work can be measured by the fact that her book was virtually unchallenged for more than 15 years and that even 35 years after the appearance of the book, the third edition still enjoys wide popularity.

John Duncan

One really new approach to the education of the retarded was offered with the publication of *Education of the Ordinary Child* by John Duncan in 1943. This book describes the work of Duncan while he was Headmaster of Lankhills School, a residential school for about 100 students located in Hampshire County, England.

The children were accepted into the school only after they had been certified as feebleminded by the Hampshire Local Education Authorities and various attempts for local community accommodation had been tried. His students, therefore, were not only feebleminded, but generally displayed various kinds of unacceptable social and personal behavior too. Thus the school was concerned not only with the academic programs, but also their personal habits, diet, rest, recreation, and social development.

Duncan was the first educator of the retarded to describe accurately the characteristics of his pupils, to design a program which was based on their characteristics, and to attempt to partially evaluate the results of the program. Even in regard to weight, for example, he states:

> The daily content per head of first class proteins (from animal sources) were 62 grammes. It was not a minimum diet, but one, we believe, approaching the optimum. The B.M.A. minimum diet for children of this average age gives only 37 grammes of first-class proteins per day.

He apparently based this belief of the optimum level of the diet, not only on the quantity of the food, but also on growth comparisons which showed that although Lankhill's eleven-year-olds were quite a bit shorter and lighter than average eleven-year-olds, the twelve-year-olds were only slightly below average. He attributes this to a growth spurt triggered by diet, rest, and exercise.

It was in the intellectual sphere that he was most notably accurate in planning a program based on data. Stanford–Binet test data indicated a range of IQs from 54 to 76 with a mean of 66. The IQs obtained from the Alexander Performance Tests yielded a range from 67 to 119 with a mean performance IQ of 96. Thus the average performance IQ of his students was very close to that of nonretarded children. Duncan was familiar with the intelligence theories of Spearman who had postulated that there was a general factor in intelligence made up of general verbal and abstract abilities (*gv*) and general concrete and practical abilities (*gF*) plus specific abilities (*s*) which accounted for such things as special talents in art, music, social sensitivity, and the like. Duncan believed that his students were, as a group, inferior in *gv* or abstract ability because that was what was measured by the Binet. But he believed the students were essentially normal in *gF* or practical intelligence as measured by the Alexander tests, so he developed a program of instruction which called for practical intelligence rather than verbal abstractions. It was a "do" program rather than a talk program. His reasoning was:

> General ability (or *g*) may be said to be the ability to educe new relationships and correlates.
>
> (i) If words are used in measuring ability, the test is one of the relationship of words and abstract concepts (*g* + *v*). In other terms, a verbal test (the Stanford–Binet Test is chiefly verbal) measures the flow of intelligence through verbal channels. The results are an indication of ability to acquire academic learning and to benefit from verbal methods. In this respect, these defective children are markedly inferior to children of middle ability (cf. Mean IQs 66 and 100).
>
> (ii) In Alexander's tests, things that can be seen and handled are used, and the tests measure the ability to educe relationships and correlates in visual and concrete situations (*g* + *F*). In other words, the test measures the flow of intelligence through practical channels. In this respect these defective children are approximately equal to children of middle ability (cf. Mean PQs 96 to 100).

The art of teaching, as practiced by Duncan, involved preparing lessons which provided the opportunity for pupil activity and then stimulating the interest of the pupils in the lessons. Learning was believed by Duncan to involve observing, comparing, and contrasting, applying relationships to obtain new knowledge, applying and planning, and thinking in series and sequences. After a careful tryout of various methods of teaching, Duncan rejected the unit method of Ingram in favor of his subject system. He felt that the project method had two weaknesses:

> (i) It offers great difficulties in the planning of exercises that will enable all children in a class to work at their highest possible intellectual

levels. Much of the work is apt to be repetitive and much may be merely of manipulative type calling for little or no intellectual effort. If the exercises for children are planned to suit their abilities, they have often an artificial and unreal connection with the project. Projects thus tend to impose limitations.

(ii) Education in the form of a series of Projects tends to lack continuity. There is for the child no steady progress.

In order to assure that steady progress in educing relationships and correlates would occur for the child, Duncan identified 13 subject areas for study. These were: paper and cardboard work, woodwork, needlework, art, domestic subjects (cookery, housewifery, laundry work), physical training, country dancing, gardening, rural science; and for the more advanced classes, English, numbers, history, and geography. Each area was attacked in a series of stages. Stage 1 introduced elements of simple measurement such as marking off the paper in whole inches or even fractions to make a pattern. Stage 2 introduced simple scales from conventional measuring instruments like a ruler so the youngsters would learn the concepts of continuity and relationships. Stage 3 involved the actual making of models, first from rough sketches and then by measuring the object and reducing it to scale for execution. Stage 4 was the actual making of the model from a three-dimensional drawing. This was more abstract than Stage 3 because the object was not present. Stage 5 was making the model from a verbal or written description and Stage 6 was the making of unknown models from description.

When it is remembered that nearly all of the Lankhill's children were at least eleven years old and most were much older, it is understandable that the construction sequence of stages was applicable and practical in teaching the youngsters to use higher level intellectual skills in a practical, concrete manner.

Duncan was the first educator of the retarded to base his program on the intellectual strengths of the youngsters and to design studies which taught thought processes from a simple to a very complex level. As a dividend, the subjects studied were those which were selected from the living styles of the children; they were the kinds of activities common in lower class English homes and jobs. Thus although Duncan did not have a systematic vocational preparation program, the children learned domestic, mechanical, and carpentry skills which were immediately salable in the community. At the lower age levels, he did not have a well developed sense training program because his children were too old to need one. Perhaps because Duncan did not have a complete program, or because he ran a residential school, or because his subjects and stages were considered artificial or perhaps for all of these reasons, Duncan's system never became popular in the United States, yet elements of his program are included in many contemporary programs—especially the use of concrete projects to teach intellectual skills.

Richard Hungerford

As the director of the Bureau for Children with Retarded Mental Development in New York City, Hungerford felt that regardless of what kind of educational program was offered, each was a dead-end program if it did not culminate in vocational training, placement, and supervision. He was the first educator of the retarded to use a method of job analysis to provide guidance for curriculum. His procedure was to observe carefully and describe the skills and knowledges required for the successful performance of specific jobs which could be done by the retarded, and then to teach those skills in the classes in the schools so the youngsters would be employable. The descriptions of the jobs and the accompanying lessons in job preparation were published in a series of booklets (actually a kind of magazine) called Occupational Education. The first of the series appeared about 1941 and they continued to be published until 1944.

The excellently prepared pamphlets were specific to jobs in such areas as the needle trades, service occupations, light industry, and unskilled and semiskilled work. Thus although Hungerford made no specific attempt to train the intelligence of his students, concentrating instead on teaching skills which would make them employable, he used the same kind (but a better developed) system of community job analysis on which to develop a program as had Duncan.

Hungerford's system of occupational information, vocational guidance, vocational training, vocational placement, social placement, and vocational and social supervision never became popular. Perhaps many teachers felt the Occupational Education magazines were applicable only to New York or the East and therefore not relevant to other parts of the country, or perhaps some teachers found it difficult to adapt their own methods to an occupational training program, but another explanation could also be considered. Hungerford's program was publicized just as World War II started. The subsequent mobilization of nearly all resources in the country for the support of the war effort meant that nearly everyone who was not in military service was employed, regardless of what kinds of abilities he might have. Consequently the retarded had jobs available to them and therefore had no need for training, so that teachers were not faced with a requirement for vocational programs for their students. Furthermore, the military services relaxed their acceptance requirements so that people with very limited ability became members of the armed forces. Whatever the factors operating, high school level programs for the retarded were not seen as crucial to the welfare of the students during the early 1940s and Hungerford's system was not universally adopted. His sequence was, however, and after 1945 many school systems became concerned with providing occupational information, guidance, training, placement, and supervision to bridge the gap between school and community living. Hungerford was the first educator of the retarded to make the sequence explicit.

Samuel A. Kirk and G. Orville Johnson

Kirk brought to his position as Director of the Institute for Research on Exceptional Children at the University of Illinois training in experimental psychology and remedial reading and experience as a counselor and teacher of the mentally retarded. Together with his student, Johnson, who had also been a teacher of the retarded, he sifted practices and ideas from prior programs for appropriateness for a total program of education for the retarded. The Kirk and Johnson program was presented in *Educating the Retarded Child*, published in 1951. The book draws heavily on the writings of other professionals in the field, but Kirk and Johnson were the first writers to gear their program to changing developmental needs of the children.

The authors believed that various tests should be given to the children which yield information on the intellectual, social, and academic skills of the child. This data should then be combined with medical, educational, and developmental histories of the child in a case conference to determine the placement of the child and what kind of educational treatment is apt to be most successful. This procedure was based upon the fact that mentally retarded children are alike in that they are intellectually less able than average children, but they differ widely among each other in social, physical, emotional, and even intellectual styles. This recognition of individual differences in educational needs had first been pointed out by Descoeudres, but its validity had not been accepted until Kirk and Johnson included it in their program. In their thinking, this need for individual diagnosis was not a one-time thing, but should be integral at each program level: preschool, primary, intermediate, high school, and post-school.

At the preschool level the program was designed to follow:

> . . . three major principles: (1) educating the children according to good child development principles and good nursery school educational techniques; (2) using special clinical educational procedures with some of the children that show special disabilities over and above their lower mental abilities; and (3) supplying additional provisions which must be adapted to the lower cultural and mental abilities of most of these children.

The preschool program was aimed at fostering emotional health through security, belongingness, and accomplishment and developing physical health, self-help, imagination, and social, motor, and intellectual skills. Throughout, parent education and special clinical education for special disabilities of individual children were given particularly careful attention.

At the primary level, the program was for children between six and ten years old but whose verbal mental ages were below six and so were not generally ready to learn the academic skills of reading, writing, and arithmetic. In addition the children were presumed to come from subcultural homes, to have experienced a considerable amount of failure, generally to dislike school, and to suffer rejection and isolation from the other children. Physically they may resemble second and third grade children, but mentally they are more like kindergarteners. In addition to fostering the same goals as the preschool program (mental health, physical health, parent education, social development, motor abilities) at the primary level language, quantitative thinking, visual discrimination and memory, auditory discrimination and memory, speech, and higher mental processes came in for special attention. It should be noted that the primary program stresses what are usually recognized as academic readiness skills similar to those sensory skills which made up the bulk of the programs of Itard, Seguin, and Montessori.

The intermediate level program was for children who were between ten and thirteen years old and who had mental ages of from six and a half to eight. With such mental age development all the children would be ready to learn to read, write, spell, and perform some arithmetical functions. The curriculum was designed to (1) teach the tool subjects and (2) provide experiences in the areas of living. The tool subjects (reading, writing, spelling, arithmetic) were taught in fairly formal classes in the morning. The experience in areas of living (adjustment to the physical, social, and personal environments) was taught through units as Descoeudres and Ingram had done. In all units provisions to integrate the formal areas of instruction were provided whenever possible.

The secondary school level was designed for youngsters thirteen to eighteen years old whose verbal mental ages ranged from eight to twelve. They would be expected to be at least three years retarded academically below average thirteen-year-olds but would show enough maturity to adjust to the requirements of the usual secondary school routine. The curriculum aimed at areas of experience and personal guidance. To achieve these ends, Kirk and Johnson recommend instruction in home-building, occupational education, social relationship, and physical and mental health. The personal guidance assumes some integration in regular classes so individual tutoring in tool subjects would be provided specifically to aid them in coping with the requirements of the regular classes. In addition, personal, social, and occupational guidance would be provided through study, role playing, and conferences.

A post-school program is proposed because:

> It is unrealistic to presuppose that because a child has been a member of a special class for eight or ten years, this special program has corrected his basic difficulty—the inability to learn as much in a specified period of time as the average person.

The authors therefore propose that adult education programs, vocational schools and vocational rehabilitation programs be used to bridge the gap between school and community living and working. They do not propose an explicit mechanism for this, but do propose that the post-school program should include:

> . . . (1) a school–work–experience program, (2) a job placement program, (3) a further training program, and (4) a follow-up program.

It is worthy of note that the Kirk and Johnson program is not a description of some program actually run by these authors. Because it is not, it does not suffer from the restriction of including only what they did. Instead, Kirk and Johnson borrowed heavily from preceding descriptions of practices provided by Itard, Seguin, Decroly, Descoeudres, Ingram, and Duncan and filled in the program gaps of those writers who described what they did in specific settings with specific children in specific practices. It is small wonder that the Kirk and Johnson program has emerged as the most complete program of all those reviewed. It is a tribute to their ingenuity and a commentary on their skill that the book, *Educating the Retarded Child*, has continued to be a best seller in the field for nearly twenty years.

Alfred A. Strauss and Laura E. Lehtinen

From the Cove School in Racine, Wisconsin, Strauss and Lehtinen published an account in 1947 of their work with children they called brain-injured. This book, *Psychopathology and Education of the Brain-Injured Child*, appeared four years before Kirk and Johnson's but is not a part of the linear development of educational provisions for the retarded. It started a completely different line of treatment for retarded children in whom the retardation is considered curable rather than chronic.

Brain-injured children, according to Strauss and Lehtinen, are youngsters who are intellectually intact at conception but who suffer some injury to the brain before birth, at the time of birth or at an early age which seriously disrupts neurological functions. More specifically, the cortical areas of the brain are believed to exert a control on the subcortical areas. Injury or destruction of areas of the cortex destroys the control activity so the child behaves in an uncontrolled manner. This lack of control is shown in disorders of perception, thinking, and behavior.

The degree of disorder may range from very little to quite severe; intelligence test performance is not a good indicator of the problems of the child because test scores may run from mental retardation to above average yet be essentially unrelated to lack of self control. That is, it is as likely that brain-injured children will show average or above IQ test scores as below average; yet they will have in common the inability to inhibit their reactions in perception, thinking, and behavior. It is this lack of control which is the critical factor.

Strauss and Lehtinen identify the exogenous child as one who meets the following criteria:

1. A history shows incidence of injury to the brain by trauma or inflammatory processes before, during, or shortly after birth.
2. Slight neurological signs are present which indicate a brain lesion.
3. When the psychological disturbance is of such severity that a measurable retardation of intellectual growth can be observed, the immediate family history indicates that the child comes from normal family stock and that he is, in general, the only one of the sibship so afflicted.
4. When no mental retardation exists, the presence of psychological disturbances can be discovered by the use of some of our qualitative tests for perceptual and conceptual disturbances.

They describe perception as an activity of the mind which is intermediate between sensation and thought. That is, perception gives meaning to sensation, so it acts as a preliminary to thinking. One of the characteristics of perception is its wholeness, that it has a total and integrated meaning uniquely its own. A second characteristic is that perceptions are generally seen as a foreground figure against a background and that we give greater selective value to the foreground while the background sensations are considered relatively unimportant.

To test for intact perceptions, Strauss and Lehtinen devised a marble board test. The board was grey and had darker grey indentations to hold the marbles spaced one inch apart. In all, the board had 100 indentations (10 $\times$ 10) but only about 50 black marbles and 30 red ones were used in the designs. The procedure for the test was to have the examiner construct a design with the marbles which the child was asked to reproduce on another board. It was the contention of the authors that the qualitative analysis of the procedure used by the child was critical to revealing brain injury. Young normal children and familial mentally retarded children generally use an orderly and sequentially continuous procedure. The brain-injured child uses a procedure characterized by discontinuity and incoherence. A third type of procedure, the constructive approach, involved a higher level of thought—essentially a demonstration that the child was not just copying the pattern but rather that he understood all components and their relationships. The basic requirement of the marble board test was that the child was expected to use discrete elements to form a continuous whole,

> . . . achieving as an end result a figure whose unity and organization depended not upon the objective fact of continuity but upon subjective perceptual experience.

A second type of marble board test was used to discover if the brain-injured children could distinguish between figure and background. This board was similar to the plain grey board of the first test except that patterns were painted on the board and then the marbles were superimposed over the painted patterns in a different arrangement. Experiments demonstrated that the brain-injured children had difficulty distinguishing between figure and background. Other studies demonstrated that this difficulty was also evident when only tactual cues were presented so it was not just a phenomenon of visual perception—it was a generalized perceptual disturbance. In addition the children demonstrated a tendency to perseverate, that is, to repeat previous responses to new and unrelated stimulus cues.

Brain-injured children also demonstrated an inability to use proper mental images. They used bizarre methods for classifying or grouping common objects and therefore had great problems in forming concepts. They associated ideas in far-fetched, often incomprehensible ways and often followed minor aspects of a discussion as though they were the main concerns.

In addition to perceptual disorganization and peculiar concept formation and thought processes, brain-injured children, whether retarded or not, showed a wide range of behavior deviations. Among the many descriptions of behavior emerge words like clumsy, erratic, impulsive, childish, explosive, excessive, flighty, annoying, distractable, and many others. Interestingly, the children do not seem to show behavior generally associated with fear. Instead of being afraid of such things as high buildings, the dark, and automobiles, they appear to be fearless and lack prudence.

The educational program devised by Strauss and Lehtenin was based on the assumption that:

> We may deduce from the researches with brain-injured adults and the recognized benefits of physiotherapy for cerebral palsied children that the undamaged portions of the brain hold resources from which the organism may substitute, compensate for, or restitute the disabilities resulting from the injury. It is this intact reserve which we attempt to reach in education.

Since the characteristics of the children were principally disorders of perception, thinking, and behavior, the entire program was geared to:

> . . . manipulating and controlling the external, overstimulating environment and in educating the child to the exercise of voluntary control.

The physical arrangement of the room, the materials used, and the techniques employed were the products of the ingenuity of these educators, developed on the basis of the characteristics of the children. The room was large enough to provide plenty of space between each child and his neighbor. The small class of no more than twelve children was shielded from overstimulation in every manner possible. At first the room had no pictures, murals, or bulletin boards on its drab walls, but as the children learned to inhibit impulsive reactions to stimuli, decorations relative to the interests of the children were gradually introduced. Windows were screened with opaque materials which would let in light, but blocked out the outside view. Even the dress of the teacher was drab; running to mauve and grey with an absence of jewelry, make-up, and decorations. Isolation screens were used to provide private cubicles for each child and the materials used were devoid of all except the essentials for instruction.

Since the children had difficulty with figure–background perceptions, the integration of visual form and space, auditory perceptions and general integration, materials were semi-auto-teaching devices specific to overcoming each dysfunction. Concrete materials which involved the child in motor manipulation and color cues to lend visual vividness were frequently used. For example, writing with red pencil on paper with blue lines or using block letters in which all *o*s are red, *i*s are blue, etc. Individual words were often blocked out by colored dividers and phrases and sentences were put on individual pieces of tagboard in order to avoid visual perceptual confusion.

The objective of the entire program was remedial. That is, each child was taught in a manner and with materials that would correct his dysfunction and allow him to learn to control his attention and behavior so he could return to a regular classroom setting as a participating class member rather than a disruptor. Because of this goal, Strauss and Lehtinen did not have a complete program in the sense of that of Ingram or Kirk and Johnson. They contributed a method of teaching based upon the learning characteristics of the children as revealed by diagnostic tests and which assumed that the learning dysfunctions were curable, but they did not attempt to train for employment.

Newell C. Kephart

In 1955, Kephart, a Professor of Psychology at Purdue University, co-authored with Strauss Volume II of the *Psychopathology and Education of the Brain-Injured Child*. This book, which describes progress in theory and clinic, uses the functions of the brain to show how psychopathology of perception, language, concept formation, and behavior can occur.

They explain that physiologically, the neural cells of the brain respond to two kinds of stimulation. In the one case, a chain of neurons may excite each other in a reverberating circuit so that parts of the brain are in a continual state of activity. This activity is rhythmical, occurring at the rate of about ten per second, and accounts for the alpha waves evident in encephalographic tracings. It is this constant, rhythmical activity of the brain which means that every sensory impulse from outside the organism enters an electrochemical field and adds its coding to that activity already in progress. The second kind of activity comes from sensory stimulation transmitted by neurons activated by environmental stimulation. Each neuron transmits its own energy to the connection with the next neuron where it releases its energy into the gap or synapse to activate the connecting nerve endings. The sense impulses may intrude into a closed chain of synaptic knobs thus influencing ongoing activity or they may be released into a synapse where multiple connections activate many different areas of the brain. That is, the neural impulse may influence local activity and/or may serve to initiate activity in other more remote areas of the brain.

Strauss and Kephart point out that the brain functions in three fundamental ways: (1) a feedback control loop, and (2) rhythmical sensory scanning, both of which are necessary for the maintenance of (3) homeostasis.

A feedback loop is similar to a self-correction servomechanism in that sensory information is transmitted to areas of the brain which are directing activity to indicate whether the activity in progress is actually achieving its desired result. If it is not, a correction is signaled and again checked for its result. This is apparently identical with the TOTE unit described by Miller, Galanter, and Pribram. Scanning apparently is both general and specific. It is suggested that the alpha wave may be a reflection of the rate at which the organism carries on a regular test of the environment (about ten waves per second) to determine the state of the world, and that this is automatic and continuous. At the same time, scanning occurs within the brain itself; sensory impulses through synapse connections with multiple chains are sent to many different areas of the brain to sort over memory information. Any information which is pertinent to the ongoing activity is fed back into consciousness so that its importance can be evaluated. Thus both scanning and feedback correction are necessary to maintaining the organism in harmony with the world, that is, achieving homeostasis. In one respect, the concept of homeostasis is not quite identical to Miller, Galanter, and Pribram's notion of congruence. In Strauss and Kephart's description, no mention is made of how it is that one individual's condition of homeostasis may differ from that of another. In subjective behaviorism, the standards for congruity or harmony with the world are established by plans which are made by each person for his own behavior goals. Thus each person determines what his desired behavior will be and the scanning and feedback functions of the brain assist in mediating his progress toward those goals. This difference does not appear to be inconsistent with the homeostasis concept of Strauss and Kephart. Rather, it explains how homeostasis can be a dynamic rather than static condition and how it can differ from person to person. Obviously, any dysfunction of neural functions results in disorganization of behavior.

Although the basic development of perception, language, concept formation, and behavior control are discussed in the book, Kephart has elaborated these in subsequent writings. Kephart together with Marylou and James B. Ebersole in 1968 described six developmental stages of learning which occur in sequential order as (1) gross motor, (2) motor–perceptual, (3) perceptual–motor, (4) perceptual, (5) perceptual–conceptual, and (6) conceptual. (They did not mention conceptual–perceptual.)

Gross motor development is the attempt of a child to organize information about his environment by movement, touch, and feeling. Just movement by itself does little to supply the child with this information. Movement may reflect only motor skills, but this stage of development can provide the child with well developed motor patterns which allow the child to generalize his behavior so he can use a combination of motor patterns to serve his purposes. This stage of development is essential to later perceptual and conceptual organization. It is made up of locomotion patterns which move the body through space, balance and posture maintenance patterns, contact such as reaching, grasping, and releasing, and receipt and propulsion as in pushing and pulling.

The motor–perceptual stage differs from the gross motor stage in the efficiency with which motor exploring is used. The chief characteristic is that motor exploration is now directed by a fairly well organized body of perceptions, so that the child does not need to be a victim of random motor activity.

Perceptual–motor development is characterized by the child's ability to control his motor maneuvering in order to stabilize accurate impressions. This is accomplished by what Kephart calls a perceptual–motor match.

> Visual information is controlled by the direction in which the eyes are pointed . . . The pointing of the eyes is controlled by extraocular muscles. The child must learn to explore an object with his eyes in the

same way in which he previously explored it with his hands. It is important, however, that the exploration with the eyes duplicate the exploration with the hands, so that the resulting information *matches* when it is compared.

In the perceptual stage the child manipulates one perception against another but without intervening motor manipulation except as an occasional method of validating the perceptual information. In this stage the child learns and practices auditory discrimination, memory, and sequencing, and visual discrimination, memory, and sequencing. He can at this stage, for example, sort geometric shapes by simply looking at them.

The perceptual–conceptual stage is demonstrated when the child can deal with perceptual similarities by combining them into a higher level of organization. The child knows, for instance, that a square and triangle differ because the square has four sides and the triangle three.

The conceptual stage is characterized by the generalizing of perceptual information. He not only knows the essential elements of squareness, but he can use the characteristics of squares (equal and parallel sides) for useful purposes. The conceptual stage requires a symbol system which can be manipulated in the form of abstract ideas without the presence of the objects represented by the symbols.

Roach and Kephart in 1966 presented the Purdue Perceptual–Motor Survey consisting of twenty-two tests which allow an assessment of the perceptual–motor abilities of a child. Kephart contends that a child without basic motor patterns will have difficulty generalizing learning experiences. He bases his assessment program on developmental principles discovered by other investigators. The 1929 work of Coghill demonstrated that motor movements of salamanders were mass movements. Later, as maturation and learning interact, the movements become differentiated and restricted to just those movement elements needed for efficient behavior. Still later, the salamanders learn to integrate the behavior patterns for highly purposeful activities. The mass–differentiated–integrated theory of Coghill is believed by Kephart to be applicable to the motor development of humans. Mass motor movements are the general norm for infants. When a baby cries, for instance, he cries all over—even his toes are involved. With maturation, the infant learns to become more specific and inhibit movement which is unnecessary to achieving particular goals. This differentiation of movement develops according to two principles: (1) the cephalo-caudal in which differentiation develops from the head end of the organism to the feet (literally the tail), and (2) the proximo-distal in which differentiation proceeds from the midline axis of the body outward toward the periphery. It is this differentiation that makes independent control of body parts become possible and which ultimately results in motor response systems. Kephart draws a clear distinction between motor skills and motor patterns:

> Motor skill implies the development of high degrees of precision in specific activities . . . It permits the child to do one thing extremely well. The motor pattern, on the other hand, stresses the purpose of the act and, thus, the outcome of the movement. The motor pattern allows the child to do many things acceptably.

Since the motor pattern is believed to be the foundation for more complex learning because it is fundamental to orientation, the generalization of motor behavior is seen as a critical aspect of learning. In addition, laterality (the ability to distinguish between left and right), the perceptual–motor match, and directionality (right–left, up–down and before–behind distinctions) are deemed crucial to abstract conceptual thinking.

It is the contention of Kephart that learning difficulties are traceable to inadequate development at some stage in the gross motor, motor–perceptual, perceptual–motor, perceptual, perceptual–conceptual, conceptual sequence. The Purdue Perceptual Motor Survey was designed as a diagnostic tool for pinpointing the source of the developmental problem. The authors stress that the Survey does not diagnose the problem, but only identifies the stage at which the problem appears. Thus the score earned by a child does not give much useful information. Rather it is the clinical evaluation of failure to perform the tasks that provides information useful for planning a remedial program.

To provide this clinical information the following tasks are used.
Walking Board. This is a section of two by four boards from eight to twelve feet long placed on brackets so it is about six inches off the ground. The four-inch side of the board is used. The child walks on

the board forward, backward, and sidewise. Observation of his performance is used to indicate the degree of general balance skill displayed.

Jumping. The child is asked to jump one step forward with both feet, the right foot and then the left foot. He is then asked to skip and hop in different patterns: for instance, hop twice on one foot and once on the other. The tasks reveal information on laterality, body image, rhythm, and neuromuscular control.

Identifying Body Parts. The child is instructed to touch his shoulders, hips, head, ankles, ears, feet, eyes, elbows, and mouth. The performance of the child reveals his ability in space localization.

Imitation of Movements. The child is asked to imitate 17 arm positions similar to semaphore signals performed by the examiner. The test provides observation of neuromuscular control and the ability to translate visual cues into motor movement. Within the semaphore signals are unilateral, bilateral, and contralateral movements.

Obstacle Course. A stick is held parallel to the floor with one end against the wall. The child is instructed to step over the stick when it is held at knee height, duck under the stick when it is held at eye height, and slide between the stick and the wall when it is pulled away from the wall just a little more than body width. The test is used to assess the ability to react spatially to objects in his environment.

Kraus-Weber. Lying on his stomach with a small pillow under his hips the child clasps his hands behind his head then raises his head, shoulders, and chest off the floor. He must maintain this position for ten seconds. Next the child puts his hands under his face and raises his legs off the floor without bending his knees. This position is to be maintained for ten seconds also. Performance on these tests has been found to be related to academic achievement among elementary school children, but the reason for the relationship is not explainable at present.

Angels-in-the-Snow. Lying on his back with legs together and arms at his side, the child is instructed to move specific limbs away from his body and then back. In succession he is instructed to move one arm, one leg, both arms, both legs, an arm and leg on one side of the body, and finally opposite arms and legs. The tasks provide information on the child's ability to identify the limbs to be moved, the actual ability to move the limbs, and the ability to inhibit overflow from the movements to other limbs. The tasks provide information on neuromuscular differentiation and left-right sidedness.

Chalkboard. The child is instructed to draw a circle in front of him so he must cross the body midline. With two pieces of chalk he then draws two large circles simultaneously with both hands. Two *x*s about 2 feet apart are then to be connected by a straight line horizontally and finally vertically. The tasks provide observation on the ability to match motor and perceptual data on a continuing basis.

Rhythmic Writing. Copying eight different writing patterns from simple (⌒⌐⌒) to complex (ϸℓϸℓ) provides observation of the ability for visual–motor translation in continuous activity.

Ocular Pursuits. The child is required to follow the path of the tip of a pencil or pen as it is moved horizontally, vertically, and diagonally with either eye and both eyes. The ability to maintain eye contact with a moving target is observed.

Visual Achievement. Seven geometric shapes are copied using pencil and paper. They are: circle, cross, square, triangle, horizontal diamond, vertical diamond, and divided rectangle. The test provides information on form perception and organizing ability.

Scoring is done on a four-point scale: $4 =$ smooth performance, $3 =$ minor problems, $2 =$ great difficulty, and $1 =$ virtually unable to perform. This provides a profile of levels of abilities in each of the five areas of balance and posture, body image and differentiation, perceptual–motor match, ocular control, and form perception. This information is then evaluated clinically to identify the stage of development at which a child fails to demonstrate integrated behavior.

The remedial program is designed to help the child learn integrated behavior patterns at whatever developmental level he shows disorganization. This is done through what Kephart calls redundancy —the repetition of skill training using a large number and variety of exercises and materials. The final test of the effectiveness of the treatment is demonstrated when the child can generalize his behavior. Once this ability to generalize is shown at one level, the child is ready to develop those skills at the next higher level.

Ever since Descoeudres called attention to the fact that all retarded children do not learn in the same manner, reference to specific learning problems has been included in the writings of professional educators in the field. Strauss paid particular attention to problems of lack of inhibition of response to stimuli, disorganized behavior control, and perceptual problems of figure–ground, perseveration, and the realistic mediation of sense impressions into related wholes. Kephart, however, has pointed out that the stage at which disorganized behavior is observed is a necessary consideration if remediation is to be effective. If the child is unable to demonstrate integrated behavior of locomotion, space, body image, and differentiation, his gross motor behavior needs to be specifically aided. If he is unable to demonstrate perceptual–motor matching, a different kind of treatment is indicated. Thus the remedial program of Strauss and Lehtinen was conceived as a general approach to disorganized behavior for children of any age while Kephart's program of correction takes into account the stage of motor–perceptual–conceptual development of the child. Both approaches have in common the goal of curing or eliminating inappropriate intellectual processes so in this way they are similar in intent. However, if the methods do not eliminate the retardation, neither program provides for training the youngsters to learn those skills necessary for working and living independently in society. They are corrective programs which treat retardation as curable, rather than long-range developmental programs which regard the condition of retardation as chronic. Nevertheless, the educational treatments are based upon careful, individual diagnostic study which is interpreted by the clinician to determine the kind and source of the disorganized behavior so treatment can be tailored to the cause of the learning problem rather than the symptoms. To the degree that the theory of causes is valid, so then will the treatment be effective. To the degree that retardation is a condition which is associated with brain pathology, so will it respond or improve under clinical–educational treatment. However, the validation of the theory has so far not been demonstrated, and retardation does not always stem from any single cause where a previously intact brain has been subjected to injury from some outside source. Thus the clinical–educational approach can scarcely be considered a total program suitable for all retarded children.

References

Coghill, G. C., *Anatomy and the Problems of Behavior*. New York: The Macmillan Company, 1929.

Descoeudres, Alice, *The Education of Mentally Defective Children*, trans. by Ernest F. Row. Boston: D. C. Heath and Company, 1928.

Duncan, John, *The Education of the Ordinary Child*. New York: The Ronald Press Company, 1943.

Ebersole, Marilou, Newell C. Kephart, and James B. Ebersole, *Steps to Achievement for the Slow Learner*. Columbus, Ohio: Charles E. Merrill Books, Inc., 1968.

Fisher, Dorothy Canfield, *The Montessori Manual*. Chicago: W. E. Richardson Company, 1913.

Hamaide, Amelie, *The Decroly Class*. New York: E. P. Dutton and Company, Inc., 1924.

Hungerford, Richard, *Occupational Education*. Association for New York City Teachers of Special Education, 1943 *ff.*

Ingram, Christine P., *The Education of Slow Learning Children*, 2d ed. New York: The Ronald Press Company, 1953.

Inskeep, Annie, *Teaching Dull and Retarded Children*. New York: The Macmillan Company, 1926.

Itard, Jean Marc Gaspard, *The Wild Boy of Averyron*, trans. by George and Muriel Humphreys. New York: Appleton-Century-Crofts, 1962.

Kephart, Newell C., *The Slow Learner in the Classroom*. Columbus, Ohio: Charles E. Merrill Books, Inc., 1960.

Kirk, Samuel A. and G. Orville Johnson, *Educating the Retarded Child*. Boston: Houghton Mifflin Company, 1951.

Roach, Eugene G. and Newell C. Kephart, *The Purdue Perceptual-Motor Survey*. Columbus, Ohio: Charles E. Merrill Books, Inc., 1966.

Seguin, Edouard, *Idiocy and Its Treatment by the Physiological Method*, 1866. New York: Teachers College, Columbia University, 1907.

Strauss, Alfred A. and Newell C. Kephart, *Psychopathology and Education of the Brain-Injured Child: Volume II, Progress in Theory and Clinic*. New York: Grune & Stratton, Inc., 1955.

Strauss, Alfred A. and Laura E. Lehtinen, *Psychopathology and Education of the Brain-Injured Child*. New York: Grune & Stratton, Inc., 1947.

CHAPTER 6

Educational Planning

The kind of treatment given the mentally retarded has often depended upon how societies have believed the retarded would affect their functioning. In western civilizations this has been influenced by many concerns, political, religious, philosophical, economic, and moral. Farber (1968) has called attention to the fact that prior to the early 1950s the major provisions for the retarded were based on a belief that retardation represented a condition of deviance which was a threat to society.

The actual reasons for believing that the retarded were dangerous to have around probably had their roots in the idea that retardation was inherited and passed from one generation to the next through recessive genes. This notion may also have been given some support from the observation that social ne'er-do-wells were essentially undesirable people and that their children generally did not do much better than their parents. There probably was also some conviction that those people who were shiftless could do better if they really tried, so that their condition in life was probably their own fault. It would follow that any provisions for the retarded would be concerned with the effect on society first and the effect on the retarded second—if at all. The sterilization laws were aimed at protecting society against being overrun with children of retarded parents who would in turn be retarded and who would produce retarded offspring. In the absence of universal sterilization, placing the retarded in institutions would have the same effect, because society would not have to accept the retarded in the mainstream of life and the segregated living conditions in the institutions would effectively minimize any possibilities of procreation. Even if, by some accident of fate, children were conceived in the institution, they could be born and remain segregated from the rest of society. Those persons who were neither sterilized nor institutionalized could be permitted to live their marginal lives on the fringes of society so long as they were relatively docile and untroublesome. Should they demonstrate a threat, this could be dealt with by institutional commitment and society would once again be safe.

Since World War II a quiet revolution has taken place in the field of mental retardation. The intuitive stereotype of the retarded as dull, unaware, clumsy, crude, socially deviant misfits has gradually been dissipated. Studies of the adult retarded who participated either in the war economy work force or as members of the armed forces revealed a surprising record of significant service. Additional research such as the Baller (1936), Charles (1953), and the Kennedy (1962) studies which spanned as much as forty years in the life of the retarded found them to be productive and responsible citizens distinguished from the general population only by somewhat less social participation, a lower and less serious incidence of crime, and greater job stability, less absenteeism, and less mobility. Furthermore, the follow up studies demonstrated that the retarded were promoted in their jobs and managed their own financial and living affairs much like any other segments of society. Research in genetics demonstrated that mental retardation was not transmitted as a recessive gene. Indeed, retardation has been found to stem from at least 200 different causes and the influence of environment is believed to be substantial.

As a consequence of these findings, mental retardation has come to be considered essentially a condition of intellectual incompetence in which social deviance is not a necessary corollary. Since the social and behavior skills are the result of training, the majority of the retarded are beginning to be considered as a natural resource with every human right to be given the training which will allow them to take a useful place in society as self-managing, responsible citizens. The right to work, to serve, to participate, subject only to individual capability and motivation, is being extended to the retarded in new Federal civil service regulations, in Federal vocational education laws, and in a rapidly expanding labor market. And the right to an education consistent with their abilities and needs is being recognized by special education laws in every section of the country.

As the mentally retarded have begun to be recognized as potentially capable of making a significant contribution to society, the recognition has also included the chronicity of the condition. That is, since retardation may need to be considered relative to the life span of an individual, it has an impact on virtually every agency concerned with human welfare. If there were no such condition as retardation, many services and institutions would not need to exist. Since retardation does exist, provisions for minimizing its limiting influences on the individual, his family, and society may be needed in varying amounts and at various times throughout his lifetime. In order to maximize the effectiveness of the services an orderly plan for services needs to be provided. In many places a large number of services are already available, but they often lack cohesiveness and sequential integrity. They are piecemeal rather than coordinated, so that vital services may be unavailable at a time when they are critically needed.

Fundamental to providing services for the retarded is the fact that retardation is basically a family problem. Farber (1968) has suggested that the greater the burden of restriction felt by the family, the greater the disruptive influence of the presence of the child. The obvious implication of this finding is that if appropriate services can be made available to the child and his family at the proper time, despair may be replaced by hope and family disintegration need not occur. Everyone benefits: the child, his family, and society.

Services Needed

While it may be impossible to prevent retardation in all instances in the first place, it is not outside the realm of possibility to minimize the incompetence which is the core of the condition. This simply means that the major goals for professionals in the field are to prevent retardation from occurring if possible, and if not, to maximize the opportunities for the retarded to learn to manage their own lives in as competent a fashion as possible.

Efforts to prevent retardation really should start long before children are born. At the present time nearly all states require blood tests for couples who wish to be married. Unfortunately these tests are usually confined only to the detection of social diseases such as syphilis and the like. This requirement and the treatments available to cope with the disease have been extraordinarily effective in virtually eliminating mental retardation caused by syphilis, yet there are many other conditions which could be checked for if premarital laboratory tests were made more extensive. Rh incompatibility, for instance, can become a cause of retardation if it is not identified and treated, yet the typical premarital blood tests usually do not check for this condition. It would cost very little in either time or money to include such tests as routine laboratory work. Similarly, cytological studies where the cells of the couple to be married are examined for chromosome and genetic abnormalities are now generally possible and not very expensive in nearly every public health laboratory. Surely the requirement of these tests as a precondition of marriage would pay for the modest costs of tests many fold in helping prevent retardation. This should not be interpreted to mean that couples whose marriage may herald a high probability of producing retarded children should be prevented from marrying. What it does suggest is that the information from blood tests and cytological studies will help the couple be aware of the preventive measures they may need to take. It will also help them identify options so they can prepare themselves to cope with whatever eventualities occur. At the same time as the blood tests are taken there seems no valid reason why the immunization history of the prospective parents should not be taken. Recent advances in the control of infectious diseases such as measles which may cause retardation call attention to the salutary effects which may be expected when prospective mothers are properly immunized. Since immunizations are required of all persons who apply for travel passports, it would seem reasonable to extend a similar requirement to those who apply for marriage licenses.

During every pregnancy, there are many precautions which could reduce the particular vulnerability of the fetus to damage. The entire field of maternal care has come in for extensive study in the past twenty years, but all the accumulated knowledge goes for naught if the mother never visits a physician during her pregnancy period. Even though free prenatal care is available in many parts of the country, an alarming number of women do not visit the clinics. While the percent is higher among the poor and the culturally disadvantaged, the number of women who need but do not seek prenatal care extends to every strata of society. The causative factor appears to be ignorance and apathy. Perhaps extensive educational programs starting in junior and senior high schools and including all the communications media could be effective. When the prospective mothers do visit the clinics, blood tests, cytological studies, immunization programs, and diet control should be mandatory.

Once a child has been born, public health nurses should be notified so they may offer their services to the family. A home visit by the county nurse soon after the mother and child come home and periodically thereafter at least during the first year of the child's life should be so commonplace as to be taken for granted. Socioeconomic status should not even be a consideration; the service should be given to all newborn children and their mothers. Part of the duties of the nurses would be to institute screening procedures for detecting unusual conditions such as metabolic problems like phenylketonuria (PKU), galactosemia, and maple sugar syndrome. Another duty would be to supervise any corrective or developmental diet prescribed. But one of the chief contributions would be advice and help in child management for parents who have difficulty learning to live at ease with their new family addition.

During the preschool years those factors which seem to be most important to a child are diet, emotional health, language development, sensory perceptual training, and the physical conditions of rest, exercise, and protection. While programs such as Head Start, preschools, and kindergartens make a concerted effort to provide for these factors, children are typically not eligible for the programs until they are four or five years old. It now appears that the years between birth and four or five are the years in which either great progress or irreparable restriction of development takes place. Particularly during this period, diagnostic evaluation, child development, and parent counseling services from a clinical staff of professionals should be within a reasonable geographical distance for every family. In this connection, the labeling of a child as mentally retarded while he is still young because of his score on a test which yields an IQ is a questionable practice. Even more important are the words of the President's Panel on Mental Retardation:

. . . it is possible that to have one's intelligence measured and found wanting may in and of itself be a tremendous handicap to further intellectual and social development as a result of the attitudes of one's guardians . . . or the result of well-meaning but improper prescriptions by professionals. If such a possibility is taken seriously, it cautions great care in the management of the individual whose intellectual deficit is determined early in life.

On the other hand, since the early years of a child's life are so important, early detection and treatment can pay greater dividends than if treatment is delayed. The solution to this apparent dilemma is to recognize that the low IQ is not an identification of mental retardation. It is, however, a sure indication of a learning difficulty which needs to be treated if correction is to be hoped for. It is a signal for intervention but not a certain diagnosis of retardation because mental retardation is only revealed (at the present time) by the observation of an arrest of thought processes below the level of formal or hypothetical thought. To detect this arrest, observation must be made after the child is chronologically mature. Thus the clinical services should be used to search for the reasons why the child has failed to develop properly and then institute a program of remediation. In this way, early identification does not include labeling; the purpose is evaluation and remedial programming, so that precious time for learning will not be lost.

In the event that the child does not show much progress even from a well conceived remedial program, in order for the child to develop his full potential, he will need a total educational program suited to his abilities and needs. Foremost in the requirements is some system for finding children who need help before they suffer the trauma of being exposed to educational requirements which will be so difficult and inappropriate that failure is virtually guaranteed. Every school system should have a method for finding these youngsters of high educational risk either before or when they enter school so that they may be given immediate help with their learning problems. Teacher observation and child study teams are minimum provisions, but even more satisfactory are school clinical services that concentrate on preventing minor problems from becoming serious.

While some provisions may be short term, it is still the better part of prudence to plan long term developmental programs so those youngsters who learn slowly will not be constantly harassed by the arbitrary expectation of learning a certain amount in a certain period of time. There is nothing scientifically justifiable about expecting a child to learn to read in one or two years. Some children learn quickly and some slowly. The important consideration is that they be given an environment which protects them against the unrealistic demands of time. They can learn to read, but they must be allowed to learn on their own highly individual time schedules. The important thing is that they learn; when they learn is not very crucial.

Many good school systems offer a special program which encompasses five instructional levels—preprimary, primary, intermediate, prevocational, and vocational—while other systems use more conventional levels. Regardless of what kind of instructional division is used, the program should provide a basis for academic work, instruction in academic skills, instruction in the use of the skills, occupational information, occupational training, and placement. Permeating this training is attention to social and behavioral skills necessary for independent living and working.

Services for the adult retarded need not be constant. Instead the services may be needed at certain critical times. Such events as the loss of a job, a marriage, a change of residence, or difficulty with an employer may call for the exercise of a level of judgment of which the retarded person may not be capable. The need for help from some person or agency could arise at any time, but the help would probably be short term rather than continuing. However, there is no way of knowing in advance just when the services may be needed, so the services need to be available at a moment's notice.

Services Delivery

Unlike the mentally ill, most retarded individuals do not call attention to themselves by behaving in a bizarre manner. They do not think or learn as well as other people, but they ordinarily behave in an acceptable fashion; therefore society does not ordinarily thrust services upon them. Even though the retarded may need services for their optimum development, they can scarcely be expected to know what services they need or seek those services themselves. They need someone or some agency to help identify their needs and see that the necessary services are matched to those needs.

One method of assuring the right services in the right place at the right time is through the use of a mental retardation representative (MRR). Such a system is being considered in the states of Oregon and North Dakota. In North Dakota, the state is divided into eight geographical areas, each of which houses an Area Social Services Center staffed by the State Board of Public Welfare. Although some direct services are given by the Center staff, unlike the county welfare offices, the ASSC does not usually provide direct support to persons in need of welfare help. More often the Center staff seeks to determine what help is needed by their clients and then they solicit that help from other agencies. This is consistent with the role envisioned for the mental retardation representative. That is, the MRR would be chiefly responsible for securing services from other agencies rather than providing services directly. The reason for this is that because the needs of the retarded are so complex and because they vary so much from person to person and family to family, no one agency could possibly provide for all the needs. It is, therefore, more effective to have one agency responsible for coordinating the many services for the retarded than to try to be all things to all people.

Conceptually, the mental retardation representative would have three major responsibilities: (1) to be a fixed point of referral for the retarded and their families, (2) to establish a services plan for each client, and (3) to maintain a tracking system for all the retarded in his area.

The need for a fixed point of referral is tragically documented by reports of parents who have gone from agency to agency and clinic to clinic trying to secure services for their retarded children. In nearly all reports the parents have received a courteous hearing, but the agencies are limited in what they are able to do. This kind of frustrating experience is apparently one of the major forces in the founding of the National Association for Retarded Children. Even though that organization has made enormous gains in securing legislation, services, and understanding for the retarded, there remains a need for an individual or agency who can coordinate the services to fit the needs. Furthermore, service agencies themselves are often beset by requests from many quarters for help they are neither authorized nor equipped to give. The MRR could channel requests to the proper agencies, thus preserving the functional integrity of the agencies themselves. Most important, however, the MRR would be clearly identified as the person who is responsible. There would be no ambiguity about whom to see for help.

One of the major frustrations faced by the retarded and their families is that while there may be many bits and pieces of services available which are often of excellent quality, there is no continuum of services which spans the life of the individual. The provisions are fragmented rather than cohesive, so that there is an absence of a program of integrated help. If the Mental Retardation Representative was required to develop a services plan for each client, he would necessarily have to identify what services are needed immediately as well as the approximate time in the future when other specific services will need to be secured. This has the effect, first, of letting the parents know what they and their child can look forward to at each developmental stage so they can plan for the next element of the program, and, second, it provides a method of identifying the strategy which will be used to cope with the condition. In essence, an integrated plan for services will be written which can be a road map for the optimum development of each child's potential.

Since one copy of the services plan would be retained in the area office, one would be given to the parents, and one would be sent to a central State registry, it would be possible to establish a tracking system. One of the concerns expressed by many critics of government is the difficulty of establishing agency accountability—finding a way to determine whether agency services are effectively achieving their goals. By periodically reviewing the services plans it would be abundantly clear whether the plans were being followed. Furthermore, if they were not, it would be apparent just which services were not being offered or which ones were ineffective. This information could be brought to the attention of the agencies responsible as well as to legislative funding bodies and the general public so corrective measures could be initiated. In addition, review of the services plans could be used to guide officials in future priorities planning. For example if five retarded children aged three or so were found to be living in a particular community, it would be evident that within three more years a preprimary class would need to be available in the local school system. Another benefit which could come from the tracking system could be the reduction of agency hopping, the commonly observed practice of parents going from agency to agency for essentially the same kind of services. In some places this practice can result in a substantial waste of taxpayers' money because of the duplication and overlap of services from rather expensive and scarce professional personnel. If the MRR checks the applications for services against central registry records, unnecessary duplication can be avoided. For example, it is a common practice for many agencies to require a psychological assessment of every new client. It is not unusual, therefore, for children to have been tested by several clinics, the public schools, private schools, welfare departments, the courts, and perhaps other concerned persons all within a few months or years of each other and often with the same tests. At from $25 to $100 per assessment, it does not take long to run up a sizable bill which buys virtually no new information, besides subjecting the child to identical anxiety producing demands for performance for no good reason. A well monitored tracking system could eliminate this practice with obvious benefit to all concerned.

There are many other functions which could be performed by the MRR. One of these would be that of advocate or spokesman for the retarded. From the vantage point of being the person ultimately responsible for services, the MRR is in a perfect position to report accurately on the effectiveness of services, areas in which new or modified provisions are needed and to assess when some previously offered services are no longer needed. The MRR could also be expected to have current, up-to-date statistics on all aspects of the area and to share those data with the general public. Additionally, the MRR could function as a "friend of the court" in those instances where the retarded might be involved in legal matters. Finally, any retarded person paroled from an institution would have an available mentor, counselor, and sponsor to support his efforts of adjusting to community living. There probably are many other ways in which the MRR could help the retarded, but they would probably vary from place to place and arise in response to local needs. It would be a dynamic, changing position, not a static one.

The placement of the MRR in the social services branch of the Department of Welfare is by no means the only option. In Oregon, where the idea was originated by Jerry McGee, the MRR is attached to the Department of Health at the State level and the representatives are housed in mental health clinics in geographically strategic locations. Furthermore, any of the MRRs are authorized to start and operate services needed in their particular regions if services are needed and not available. Thus the MRRs not only solicit services from other agencies, but also are authorized to provide services. There are no doubt advantages to either arrangement and there may be even greater advantages to some other possible arrangements. Regardless of the organization used, the need for some central responsibility of the type suggested is evident, immediate, and widespread.

Educational Provisions

The role that education can play in helping the retarded develop their potentialities to the maximum has been recognized by legislative support for special educational programs only since about the middle 1940s. To be sure, progressive states and local school systems did provide special help prior to that time, but the practice did not become general until after World War II. In the next two decades, nearly every state in the Union recognized the wisdom of training the retarded to become self-managing adults and supported the efforts of public schools to provide an appropriate program by passing laws which supplemented local financial efforts with State funds for educating the retarded. The underlying principles which sustained this effort were that education for all children regardless of ability to learn was a democratic right, and that an investment in an educational program for the retarded would be more economical and safer than risking the probability that the untrained retarded would need to be supported by society through institutional or welfare agencies. The extra financial costs were justified on humanitarian grounds but also on the premise that appropriate training would make retarded adults who would be taxpayers rather than tax eaters.

Even though many school systems have developed extensive programs for the retarded, much controversy exists regarding both the best strategy (over-all plan) of the program and the best tactics (ways of achieving the goals of the plan) to be employed. Part of the disagreement may stem from confusion about what education is, part from the lack of certainty about what kind of program organization will net the greatest return, and part from what mental retardation is believed to be.

In 1968 Gray suggested that schooling and education are not the same thing. Schooling is part of the process of securing an education because it usually takes place in a fairly formal setting and involves the systematic exposure of a person to instruction. Education, however, is a qualitative concept characterized by four levels of development which enables a person to act wisely. At the lowest level one may simply accumulate information. The next level of education is demonstrated when a person relates the information he has learned to form knowledge. Knowledge is then associated or synthesized with related areas of information to demonstrate an understanding of interrelationships. Finally, the true test of an educated person is that he is able to use the information, knowledge, and understanding to act wisely. Ultimately, the educational level of any person is judged not by the academic degrees he may have earned but rather by whether he demonstrates that he has a fund of information, that he knows all about something, that he understands the relationships between things, or that he acts with wisdom.

Certain tools and skills are necessary to achieve each of Gray's levels of education, most of which are intellectual, but some of which are not. Foremost of the requirements is the existence of a symbol system. Not only must the language enable an individual to use convenient symbol substitutes for real things, but it must be flexible enough to allow one to manipulate time so that past, present, and future can provide some perspectives for evaluating events. It must also allow for some method of information reduction so that thousands upon thousands of sense stimuli can be synthesized into manageable units for grouping, classifying, sequencing, and associating. Finally it must be conventional so that the symbols will have the same meanings to others that they have to oneself; it must allow for communication.

Gray's conceptualization of education also assumes that learning is a universal attribute. Learning, the ability to accept, store, manipulate, and use information to change behavior, is presumed to be ongoing and to persist throughout one's lifetime. It is constant in the sense that the behavior of people continually changes.

Given a conventional language system and the constancy of learning which are common to both Gray and Piaget, the levels of education described by Gray are strikingly similar to the levels of intellectual development described by Piaget. Accumulating information would appear to be similar to the stage of perceptual organization described by Piaget. To be sure, while this is a rather low level of thinking, it is, nevertheless, essential for subsequent higher levels of thinking and it is a never ending process. Knowledge would seem to require that perceptions be related and organized into concepts. This seems to occur as a consequence of experiences of living, first in a primitive fashion as concepts represent only a salient characteristic or are based on coincidence, and later as the concept is a meticulous cataloging of reality into classes, orders, and transformations. Knowledge would seem to require the exercise of the thought processes at Piaget's level of concrete–operational thinking.

Both understanding and wisdom would seem to require the exercise of formal or hypothetical thought. To relate the information and knowledge in order to understand interrelationships so one may choose wisely from among alternatives would require thought processes of a very high order: the ability to use a symbol system to reason about nonpresent things, the ability to check one's own logic for reasonableness, the ability to combine mental operations for the solution to problems, and the ability to select from among alternatives the best solution to fit specific circumstances.

Gray's levels of education would seem to depend not only on the constancy of learning and the existence of a usable symbol system, but also on the emergence of increasingly complex modes of thinking or information processing. The mentally retarded are at a distinct disadvantage if they are expected to fit into this framework. Vast tracts of literature document the inefficiency with which the retarded learn and the poverty in their use of language. Additionally it now seems apparent that even the most able of the retarded do not demonstrate much skill in hypothetical thought, and the more limited retarded may not progress beyond intuitive thought. The level of education which might be expected of the retarded would be that of being able to secure information and demonstrate some knowledge of an area but to have virtually no understanding of interrelationships and be unable to demonstrate wisdom. An appropriate educational program would need to recognize these limitations and concentrate on attempting to capitalize on the strengths of the retarded.

The overall strategy of programs for the retarded has generated continuing concern for many decades. One of the first comprehensive criticisms of special programs was voiced by Johnson in 1962. After reviewing research on the effectiveness of special classes, Johnson concludes:

> It is indeed paradoxical that mentally handicapped children having teachers especially trained, having more money (per capita) spent on their education, and being enrolled in classes with fewer children and a program designed to provide for their unique needs, should be accomplishing the objectives of their education at the same or at a lower level than similar mentally handicapped children who have not had these advantages and have been forced to remain in the regular grades.

Two aspects of Johnson's conclusions are particularly important. The first is his contention that the retarded youngsters who were studied from special classes and in regular classes were actually similar, and the second is that those children in regular grades were forced to remain there. In the first two studies reviewed by Johnson (Bennett 1932 and Pertsch 1936) the children apparently came from the same school systems. If the usual practice of referral was followed, the retarded children assigned to the special classes would have been referred by their teachers for a special program while those retarded who remained in the regular grades were not referred. Thus it would be expected that the children in the special classes would be the ones who were "forced," not the youngsters in the regular classes. Furthermore, the teachers typically nominate their troublesome pupils for child study and testing, not the well behaved and well motivated ones. This factor of how the children were selected strongly suggests that the troublesome youngsters are assigned to the special classes while the well behaved are not. It would be most doubtful that under such conditions of selection the children in the special and regular classes could be considered similar.

Johnson also cites the studies by Baller (1936), Charles (1953), and Kennedy (1962) as evidence that the amount of time spent by the retarded in special classes was not related to their adult employment status. Essentially, Johnson contends that the development of those skills and attitudes needed for successful employment were no better learned in special classes than in regular classes.

The charge that special classes have failed to fulfill their educational goals really rests on the believability of the research. In this area, Johnson's references are all older than 1961 and the follow-up studies of adults were all done before 1953. Fortunately research from the 1960s has corrected many of the errors of the earlier studies and probably is more believable than the previous studies.

Goldstein, Jordan, and Moss, for example, in 1965 assured that the children they studied would be similar by randomly assigning the youngsters to special and regular classes. In addition they assured that none would have been exposed to school failure by selecting only youngsters who were entering school for the first time. All of the entering first grade students in three school systems in Illinois were given the Thurstone Test of Primary Mental Abilities (PMA). Those children who earned IQs below 85 were then given individually administered Binet tests. Then those children who earned IQs below 85 were assigned by chance to regular or special classes. This procedure assured each child an equal chance of being in either program. After four years of instruction the children were compared on IQ, achievement, and social knowledge. The findings are interesting:

1. The mean IQs of both groups rose from about 75 to about 82.
2. Neither group was superior to the other in academic achievements.
3. Neither group was superior in a test of social knowledge.

From this study where the children were indeed "similar" and both groups were "forced" into their respective placements, Johnson's contention that the special classes were no better than the regular classes was confirmed. However, looked at from a different point of view, the special classes did not penalize the children intellectually nor academically. Special class placement was no better than regular class placement, but it was no worse.

The intellectual or academic improvement, however, is not a true test of the effectiveness of a program which is really aimed at preparing individuals for working and living independently in society. Here the research on the effects of special class programs on the adult success of the retarded which has been done since 1953 is very clear. Perhaps the 1967 study by Chaffin is the best designed and therefore most believable. Youngsters from two different kinds of secondary school programs were carefully equated to assure they were similar and then compared for employment success after they left school. In one program the youngsters were provided no work training while in the other program the students had a program of work experience with related study and eventually help and supervision in finding a job. Although 65 percent of the youngsters in the nonwork–study program were able to secure employment, 91 percent or an increase of nearly 50 percent more from the work training program were employed. Thus in the work–study treatment, for nine out of ten, the goals of the program were achieved whereas only about six in ten were successful from the nonspecial program. Far from being isolated instances, these percentages of success from good work–study programs have been duplicated in Michigan, Missouri, and California. In the area of employment preparation there appears to exist not one shred of evidence to suggest that regular class placement produces a better or more successful worker than those who have had work–study programs. On the contrary, all the evidence suggests that the products from the regular classes are inferior.

Johnson's conclusion that the special classes do not live up to their claim of being special appears to be correct when academic achievement factors are the basis for evaluating the effectiveness of the offerings. However, those elements which are critical to independent living and successful employment are nonintellectual and nonacademic factors such as motivation, persistence, initiative, and motor and social skills. In these areas, the special class programs particularly at the secondary level have been and are clearly superior.

Despite this evidence, Dunn (1968) has added his voice to the chorus of criticism questioning whether much of special education is justifiable. He expresses his concern saying:

> . . . I have loyally supported and promoted special classes for the educable mentally retarded for most of the last 20 years, but with growing disaffection. In my view, much of our past and present practices are morally and educationally wrong. We have been living at the mercy of general educators who have referred their problem children to us. And we have been generally ill prepared and ineffective in educating these children. Let us stop being pressured into continuing and expanding a special education program that we know now to be undesirable for many of the children we are dedicated to serve.

Although Dunn thus questions nearly all of the practices, he actually limits his criticism to only certain children included in the educable or mildly retarded category.

> A better education than special class placement is needed for socio-culturally deprived children with mild learning problems who have been labeled educable mentally retarded. Over the years, the status of these pupils who come from poverty, broken and inadequate homes, and low status ethnic groups has been a checkered one.

Dunn then presents much the same evidence as did Johnson (including the quote from Johnson presented above) to document his charges of the ineffectiveness of special classes in teaching academic skills. He adduces the legal argument against establishing separate lower tracks in the Washington D.C. school system, given by Judge J. Skelly Wright, that the track system was in violation of the Fifth Amendment of the Constitution. However, Dunn then points out that when the children and their teachers were returned to the regular classrooms:

> Complaints followed from the regular teachers that these children were taking an inordinate amount of their time. A few parents observed that their slow learning children were frustrated by the more academic program and were rejected by the other students. Thus, there are efforts afoot to develop a special education program in D.C. which cannot be labeled a track.

Evidently neither the teachers nor the parents were very happy when the special classes which Dunn suggests should be abolished actually were. Even those youngsters who were no doubt at the upper level of educability apparently found the regular academic programs unsuitable.

In the remainder of his article, Dunn suggests an early educational intervention program of a remedial nature for the socioculturally deprived youngsters with the clear implication that this kind of intervention will remove the learning disabilities and with that any further need for special classes for the educable mentally retarded, yet he presents no evidence to indicate that such an approach has actually achieved the results he projects.

It is probably well to recall that clinical-tutoring programs which have aimed at curing retardation have, even from the earliest records of Itard, essentially been failures. Even after five years of intensive and total intervention, Victor remained a savage. Likewise, even though Seguin's pupils made substantial progress, he makes no claims that his treatment did more than effect improvement. More recently Jensen (1969) has noted that even the well conceived and funded efforts represented by Head Start and the Durham and Appalachia programs have been significantly ineffective.

If special educators abandon the current special class arrangement in favor of a remedial program several unfortunate consequences could result. First, it is probable that fostering the notion of the curability of retardation will raise expectations for a measure of improvement that professional educators will be unable to fulfill. Second, emphasizing the academic achievement of the youngsters may result in a substantial decrease in efforts to develop those attitudinal, social, and motor skills which have been the focus of past special class efforts and in which the major achievements of the programs have been manifested. Third, confining all the special programs to the early developmental years will result in a neglect of the later work preparatory programs which have shown such marked success. Fourth, if the tutoring efforts are not as successful as we may wish them to be, there may be a tendency to write off responsibility to the youngsters by blaming our failures on emotional causes, family interference, or ineffective methods. Fifth, since we can now promise with considerable certainty that employability can be a reality for from 85 to 95 percent of our students, this would seem to be much too high a probability level to summarily discard.

It would appear that the present criticisms aimed at special classes for the retarded are probably not really criticism so much of the classes themselves as they are of certain aspects of the total program. Dunn, for instance, seems to be concerned that a particular subgroup of the retarded, namely, children from socioculturally deprived and unstable homes who come from racial or ethnic minorities, need a program different from special class placement. There is also an implication that once the children have been assigned to the special classes, the assignment is apt to be permanent with no hope of escape or parole and that the program is a dead end which leads to no socially useful goals. If these criticisms are valid, it is the fault of the administration of the programs: the use of IQ tests to define retardation, the emphasis on academic achievement within narrowly conceived time limits, a failure to regularly re-evaluate the effectiveness of the program for individual children, and the absence of a work preparatory sequence which bridges the gap from school to community living, not the classes themselves.

Even though special classes differ quite widely in their organization and operation, they generally have some common approaches. First, they are tuned to individual differences and they typically do not present impossible tasks to the children. For example, reading is not expected of children until their mental ages are sufficiently high to assure a high probability of success—usually about a mental age of six regardless of chronological age. Thus the classes provide expectations of achievement consistent with the abilities of the children. Second, the teachers use concrete materials for instruction. This allows the children to participate actively in learning rather than be passive recipients and it does not require them to deal with abstractions which they are ill equipped to understand. Third, they make use of the everyday experiences of the children for the content of the lessons, thus insuring that the learning will be relevant. Fourth, they try to capitalize on the failures which the youngsters encounter. By turning these disappointments into successes they preserve the personal integrity of each child by making him feel successful and worthwhile. Fifth, they not only teach the fundamentals of academic, personal, social, and motor skills, but they try to provide realistic settings in which the use of the skills in productive and realistic work can be learned. Thus they emphasize both learning and application. Sixth, many schools now recognize that education is a lifetime enterprise, so they maintain an "open campus" plan that allows the youngsters to return to school for retraining, counseling, or upgrading their skills as their adult status demands change. In a nutshell, special classes generally try to gear the program to fit the abilities and needs of the children rather than to make the children fit the program.

Educational Offerings

Regardless of what organization of services is used, it must be consistent with the characteristics of the retarded if it is to be effective. Jordan (1965) presents a conceptualization of the condition which describes these characteristics:

The afflicted person at maturity has an ability to attain concepts most comparable to that found in children, qualitatively and quantitatively.

There exists a ceiling to development which is variable both from individual to individual as a matter of degree of retardation and within any given individual as an expression of individual differences.

While a ceiling exists to the possible degree of maturity in the individual, it affects some, but not necessarily all, traits. Thus height and weight may reach normality, as may personality variables such as achievement motivation, but other factors such as abstraction ability and syllogistic reasoning may be inherently limited.

Jordan further suggests that a given individual may have characteristics which are ontological (limited by the tissue restrictions which cause the condition), functional (limited by the restricted experiences of the individual), and ecological (shaped by the values, attitudes, and expectations of those authority figures encountered in his daily life).

In intellectual skills, it appears that the trainable retarded are quite capable of learning sensory–motor perceptions in both language and number which can be used to order the world according to coincidence, contiguity, and one or two salient characteristics. The educable youngsters can learn to categorize and order in at least two dimensions, understand and accept the physical constancy of substances even when their shapes change, recognize the concept of class inclusion, and quite comfortably handle the complexities of reversibility. Essentially, however, the retarded are restricted to the world as it is; they do not seem capable of dealing very effectively with the hypothetical world of what might be.

The learning characteristics of the retarded as identified in Chapter 4 are as follows:

1. Learning for the retarded is mental age specific.
2. Initial learning is haphazard but once the retarded understand what is to be done, they learn at the same rate as normal children of similar mental age. Whether the initial errors are due to psychological (attention) or physiological (stimulus trace) deficiencies is not yet established.
3. The learning style of the retarded is concrete. Information gathering and information reduction for storage purposes is apt to be based on obvious relations such as contrast and coordination rather than the more abstract systems like action, using synonyms and superordinate sets.

4. The retarded are just as susceptible to learning interferences from the presentation of similar materials, interpolated information, competing stimuli, and lack of practice as are other children.
5. They transfer by identical elements rather than principle.
6. They learn incidentally as well as normal children of equal MA, but their cultural backgrounds tend to make them appear to be deficient in behavior amenities and this has contributed to the belief that they are deficient in incidental learning.
7. They pattern their behavior on the pleasure–pain principle up to about a mental age of about seven, but adopt the success-striving versus failure-avoiding strategy beyond that MA level. However, there seem to be few success-strivers compared with failure-avoiders.
8. Social inadequacy is a pervading corollary of retardation.

In order to establish a procedure which is consistent with the characteristics of the retarded, a theory of learning needs to be selected. The theory which seems to be most compatible with the characteristics is the subjective behaviorism of Miller, Galanter, and Pribram because it:

1. Replaces the reflex-arc behavior control unit with a feedback loop servosystem which can allow for self-initiated behavior.
2. Is a dynamic explanation of behavior because it recognizes that each person has a unique perception of the world which is a product of the development and experience of that person.
3. Recognizes the principle of reinforcement as fundamental to behavior control.

When mentally retarded individuals are recognized as being able to learn to become employable, self-managing adults, it becomes crucial that every aspect of the educational program be as well conceived and effective as possible. Because the learning of the retarded is so mental age specific, the program should be tuned to that key with chronological age becoming a relatively minor or at best a secondary concern. In this way, the developmental sequences of Piaget can be used to guide the program offerings for sequence. That is, instead of tying the program to chronological age as Piaget has done, mental ages can be substituted.

At the beginning level, the sensory–motor–language development of the child becomes the core of the program up to a mental age of about six. Since the IQ is (at present) used to identify mental age, this would mean that the chronological ages of the youngsters would be eight at a minimum and more likely higher. In most instances it is quite unlikely that the children will be identified before the chronological age of four, or more often the age of six (when they first come to school). Thus the schools should be prepared to offer a sensory–motor–language program which lasts for from two to five years.

For the content of the program we can look to the practices of many of those educators who have worked with retarded children in clinical educational settings. If Kephart is correct in his contention that efficient motor behavior is basic to future intellectual skills, and Seguin is correct in his declaration that the sense of touch is basic to all future sensory skills, the place to start is with motor–kinesthetic training. If a child cannot physically move he should be moved. Baby jumpers, springboards, and trampolines can be used to help a child to learn to bend his legs and to walk. Climbing ladders, a balance beam, open culverts, wagons, tricycles, scooters, bellyboards, and jungle gyms can be used to develop movement of the feet, legs, body, shoulders, arms, wrists, and fingers. Skills of locomotion, balance, posture control, reaching, grasping, releasing, pushing, and pulling can be learned through children's games that involve running, jumping, dodging, changing directions, throwing, and catching. These should be well planned and directed (not haphazard) programs which are presented in related sequences. Perhaps the worst thing which can be done to the children is to insist on regimentation within specified time limits. The goal is the development of motor skills—how long it takes is of no real consequence.

Touch training which will teach the child to identify, without using his sight, shape, size, texture, temperature, and weight and to relate these to taste and smell can help the child transduce (translate sensory stimuli from one sense channel to other senses) sensory information and effect accurate perceptual–motor matches. Throughout the programs of motor–kinesthetic training, the children should be encouraged to yell, scream, shout encouragement and directions to others, and generally learn to correlate speech with the ongoing activities. This is particularly important because language used in this manner is employed to communicate at a cognitive rather than a purely affective level. It is used to talk about things and events which are exciting and meaningful so it can be spontaneous, shared, and free rather than personal and inhibited.

The visual and auditory skills should be given special attention.

Here the sensory skills probed by the Illinois Test of Psycholinguistic Abilities provide the clues for what the program should include. Visual memory, visual discrimination, visual sequencing, and visual closure should be systematically developed. In like manner auditory memory, auditory discrimination, auditory sequencing, auditory closure, and sound blending should also be systematically taught.

Throughout the entire program language should be used to explain, direct, discuss, debate, and describe. Particular attention should be paid to having the children learn to use exclusive words like "or" and "not," inclusive words like "and" and "with," plus prepositions, particularly those dealing with directionality such as "in," "on," "front," "behind," and so on. In addition, polar opposites such as up–down and high–low, and simple if–then statements should be practiced (if I go, then I will not be here). In all language activities correct usage and pronunciation should be practiced and to the greatest extent possible the children should learn to use language in a cognitive manner.

Since the self-concept of each child will ultimately determine whether he will become essentially a failure-avoider or a success-striver, the development of the ability to handle failure experiences without becoming devastated looms as a major goal. Unearned success experiences seem to be as ineffective as continual failure in helping the child. What seems to be called for is not the avoidance of failure, but rather the opportunity to turn failure into success by the application of effort.

Every child's thought processes should be re-evaluated after he has had an opportunity to participate in the foregoing program for a year or two and certainly before he is promoted to the next phase of the program, the academic phase. Should he demonstrate the ability to think and learn like his chronological peers, access to regular class instruction should be made available, at least on a part-time basis. Those children whose thinking and learning skills seem to be mental age oriented should continue to have the adjusted program of a special class offered to them. Since most will have mental ages of about six, even though they will be chronologically eight years or older, they can be started on an academic program with every confidence that they will have the intellectual and readiness skills to allow success.

For the content of the program, we get our clues principally from those educators who have run developmental programs. Generally speaking, the children need not only to learn academic skills, but to learn to use the skills in meaningful activities. The mornings can be used for more formal instruction with the afternoons devoted to core or unit work of an integrated nature. While this arrangement would appear to be a satisfactory one, every education program reviewed has stressed the need for flexibility in scheduling. Rigidity in either demands, organization, or schedules may well defeat all the efforts.

It is not completely demonstrated that any one tactic of teaching retarded children to read is clearly superior to any other. Yet whether tracing of words is presented first or whether labeling of things is used, the teaching of a whole word sight vocabulary is a first step. After the youngsters have learned to recognize instantly a large number of whole words and phrases, methods of word analysis are taught. These include phonics, syllabication, the use of context clues, and the use of dictionaries. Finally the youngsters must be given a great deal of practice in using reading for particular purposes: to find information, search for central ideas, make comparisons, and for pleasure or entertainment. They first learn the mechanics of reading, then they read to learn. Throughout this phase of the program, the academic skills should be put to use during that part of the day devoted to unit instruction.

Other elements of the language arts program dealing with writing, spelling, and grammar need the same formal developmental attention, and then the youngsters need the opportunity to use their writing, spelling, and grammar skills in unit work. In this way redundancy or the repeating of the things learned in a variety of situations not only provides for overlearning, but also assists the development of skills which will generalize to new situations.

Arithmetic facts and processes, measurement, time, and money not only need specific instruction, but they also need to be practiced and used. Again the meaningful use of skills in the units of instruction must be provided. Parenthetically, formal instruction can become terribly boring and even self-defeating unless variety is provided. Descoeudres' use of games for drill appears to be a useful practice to emulate.

Units of instruction have the advantages of bringing real purpose to the children's work; they allow the children to experience things first hand; they require them to plan, execute, and evaluate a course of action, and they allow them to integrate many skills and bits of knowledge for a specific purpose. These purposeful activities are not usually a part of formal periods of instruction but are a necessary and invaluable element of the program. For these reasons, it seems essential to include time and opportunity for unit work in the program. In order to assure that the academic skills will be used in the units, however, experience charts should become the medium for carrying the unit. An experience chart is simply a written record of the progress of the work. The charts are usually dictated or written by the students on a blackboard or on chart paper. Then they are used by the teacher for word study, reading, spelling, and writing in seatwork form. They are immensely versatile because they may range from only a few sentences of a very few words to rather lengthy and quite complex dissertations. Since the children participate in their preparation, however, there is every assurance that they will be within their level of understanding and they will be relevant to the subject being studied. In the beginning the units should deal with the home and neighborhood. As the children mature they may study the region, state, nation, and world. The possibilities are limited only by the maturity and interests of the youngsters.

The last phase of the school program should be devoted to preparing and assisting the youngsters to become employable, self-managing adults. Chronologically the youngsters would be about fourteen years old when they begin this part of the program and would range from eighteen to over twenty-one at the time of completion. Their mental ages would be between nine and about eleven. Typically the program would be centered in a junior high school building for the first part of the program and in a senior high school building during the final part. To be effective, the program should combine work experience with related study in an orderly sequence. In the beginning, the youngsters should study the occupational opportunities and requirements in the surrounding area. At the same time they may be introduced to work experiences, perhaps for a period or two each day in such settings as the school cafeteria, garage, buildings and grounds maintenance, administrative offices, or as teachers' aides in art, music, library, audio-visual, and physical education. Later they should be provided opportunities for work experiences in a variety of businesses and industries in the community for up to half a day every day. Usually the youngsters should be treated as trainees rather than employees and should be provided with at least four and preferably more different work settings before permanent work placement is sought. Supplemental study should deal with finding jobs, applying for jobs, grooming on the job, getting along with employers and employees, and figuring pay. In addition units on the requirements of independent living should deal with such things as budgeting and buying, maintaining property and clothes, meal planning and preparation, child care and family living, dependability and responsibility, and the management of time both for working and leisure.

In the final part of the program the youngster should be working full time but still with supervision by a school work counselor. Weekly seminars with required attendance should be devoted to solving problems which are job and living related or should provide the opportunity to learn specific skills necessary for promotion or a new job. Graduation from the program should be a reality, but if a youngster needs to return to the school for further help in his work or living, the school should be open to him on an unprejudiced basis. There is no rational reason why continuing education should not be as certain a right for the retarded as for the nonretarded.

A Final Thought

In the past few decades it has become increasingly clear that society cannot afford to neglect or despoil its natural resources without serious consequences to all of life. People who are mentally retarded are now being recognized as possessing the potential for leading useful, satisfying lives and contributing to the welfare of society. All that is needed to realize that potential is an intelligent program of services and training of the right kind in the right place at the right time. The universal establishment of these services is a considerable challenge, but, as has been the case in other fields of conservation, the returns on such investments are not only very high, but also have a permanent effect of lifting life to a higher plane of enjoyment. From such efforts, all of us profit.

References

Atlas of Mental Retardation Syndromes. U. S. Department of Health, Education and Welfare, Social and Rehabilitation Service, Rehabilitation Services Administration, Division of Mental Retardation, Washington, D.C., July 1968.

Baller, Warren R., "A Study of the Present Social Status of a Group of Adults Who, When They Were in Elementary School, Were Classified as Mentally Deficient." *Genetic Psychological Monographs,* III, June 1936.

Bennett, Annette, *A Comparative Study of Subnormal Children in the Elementary Grades.* New York: Bureau of Publications, Teachers College, Columbia University, 1932.

Chaffin, Jerry D., "Production Rate as a Variable in the Job Success of Failure of Educable Mentally Retarded Adolescents." Unpublished doctoral dissertation, University of Kansas, 1967.

Charles, D. C., "Ability and Accomplishment of Persons Earlier Judged Mentally Deficient." *Genetic Psychological Monographs,* XLVII, February, 1953.

Dunn, Lloyd M., "Special Education for the Mildly Retarded—Is Much of it Justifiable?" *Exceptional Children,* Vol. 35, No. 1, September 1968, pp. 5–22.

Farber, Bernard, *Mental Retardation: Its Social Context and Social Consequences.* Boston: Houghton Mifflin Company, 1968.

Goldstein, Herbert, Laura Jordan, and James Moss, "The Efficacy of Special Class Training on the Development of Mentally Retarded Children." U. S. Cooperative Research Project No. 619, University of Illinois, 1965.

Gray, Jesse Glen B., *The Promise of Wisdom: An Introduction to Philosophy of Education.* Philadelphia: J. B. Lippincott Company, 1968.

Jensen, Arthur R., "How Much Can We Boost I.Q. and Scholastic Achievement?" *Harvard Educational Review,* Vol. 39, No. 1, Winter 1969, pp. 1–123.

Johnson, G. Orville, "Special Education for the Mentally Handicapped—A Paradox." *Exceptional Children,* Vol. 29, No. 2, October 1962, pp. 62–69.

Jordan, Thomas E., *Perspectives in Mental Retardation.* Carbondale, Illinois: Southern Illinois University Press, 1965.

Kennedy, Ruby Jo Reeves, *A Connecticut Community Revisited: A Study of the Social Adjustment of a Group of Mentally Deficient Adults in 1948 and 1960.* U. S. Office of Vocational Rehabilitation, 1962.

Kirk, Samuel A., *Teaching Reading to Slow Learning Children.* Boston: ʼǍoughton Mifflin Company, 1941.

Kolstoe, Oliver P., Bill R. Gearheart, and Steven Hoffelt, *A Report to the North Dakota Legislative Council on a Survey of Services for the Mentally Retarded in North Dakota.* Bismarck, North Dakota, September 15, 1970.

Pertsch, C. F., "A Comparative Study of the Progress of Subnormal Pupils in the Grades and in Special Classes." Unpublished doctoral dissertation, Teachers College, Columbia University, 1936.

President's Panel on Mental Retardation, *Report of the Task Force on Prevention, Clinical Services and Residential Care*, 1962.

Winchester, A. M., *Concepts of Zoology*. Princeton, New Jersey: D. Van Nostrand Company, Inc., 1970.

INDEX